The Housing Service of the Future

Other titles in this series

Longman/Institute of Housing

The Housing Practice Series

The Housing Service of the Future

Longman

INSTITUTE OF
HOUSING

Edited by David Donnison and Duncan Maclennan

Published by the Institute of Housing (Services) Ltd, Units 15 and 16, Mercia Business Village, Westwood Business Park, TorwoodClose, Coventry CV4 8HX and Longman Group UK Ltd, 6th Floor, Westgate House, The High, Harlow, Essex, CM20 1YR

Telephone (0279) 442601; Fax (0279) 444501

Published in the IoH/Longman Housing Practice Series under the General Editorship of Peter Williams

A catalogue record for this book is available from the British Library

ISBN 0-582-07923 3

Typeset by Expo Holdings, Malaysia Sdn Bhd.
Printed and bound in Great Britain by
Biddles Ltd, Guildford and King's Lynn

Contents

Part I
The context

Chapter 1
Housing problems

Introduction

This book is written for everyone who is interested in Britain's public housing service — for the people who work in those services, decide their policies or live in their houses, for the people responsible for housing associations and co-operatives, and for students and teachers interested in this field. Although we have some things to say about national policies, these have not been our main concern in this book. Our aim is to help people who are trying to cope at a local level with whatever policies central governments may hand down to them.

This chapter briefly introduces the main questions which a book designed for these purposes must explore, with pointers to later chapters in which they are discussed. It is followed by the chapter by Adrian Kearns and Duncan Maclennan which explains the changing financial and administrative framework of Britain's housing services. They set the stage for the rest of the book. After that comes the main body of our work: eight chapters dealing with more specific aspects of local housing services. We conclude with four more which look to the future — the last of them dealing with the broad priorities suggested by arguments presented throughout the book.

The project for writing this book originated in Glasgow University's Centre for Housing Research, and nine of its seventeen authors started on it while working at the Centre. Two others were working for Glasgow's Housing Department, and six more, producing three chapters between them, joined in from elsewhere. The Centre's team have done a lot of work in Glasgow and in Northern Ireland so the book draws frequently on the experience of these places — not only because we know them well. They also happen to have two of the most innovative housing authorities in the United Kingdom. We have quoted examples of good practice: not the errors and unresolved problems which are to be found here, as elsewhere. Our aim is not to evaluate their performance but to share good ideas which may be useful to others.

We have not attempted to present unanimous views or to shape this book into a continuous and consistent argument. Each chapter is capable of standing on its own. But in their different ways they deal with the same fundamental themes. How can we best enlarge choices and advance standards in the housing field — particularly for those who most need help in achieving these things? These are the fundamental questions that concern us.

This has been a difficult but an interesting time at which to write such a book. Never, since 1919, has British housing policy been changing so profoundly. This brief introductory chapter begins with a reminder of some of these changes, starting with the economy at large, then turning to the role of the state, and finally to the housing market which is emerging from these developments. That sets the scene for an attempt to pose the questions which the housing service of the future will have to answer.

A changing world

First the good news. Incomes, for most people in Britain with secure jobs, have been rising a lot faster than prices. Thanks to the growth of jobs for women — mainly part-time jobs — more and more households have two or more earners in them. Tax rates have been sharply reduced at the upper end of the income range, where earnings have risen most rapidly. The abolition of local rates and their replacement by a new tax will give another boost to disposable incomes at the upper end of the range. It was by no accident that Britain overtook the United States to become, in 1985, the world's principal importer of champagne.

Meanwhile, property ownership has spread through the middle income groups. Thanks largely to the sale of council housing and of nationalised industries, more and more people own their own homes and some shares. Later on, more and more of them will inherit a home when older members of their families die. Already, many own second homes or a time share in one.

But there is bad news for those at the bottom of the income range. Technological changes leading to widespread restructuring of industry may have reversed the long run tendency of advanced capitalist economies to create a more equal distribution of earnings. It is too early to be sure. What cannot be disputed is that in Britain over the past fifteen years the numbers of unemployed people have risen — by far more than the repeatedly doctored figures reveal. Within these figures, the numbers out of work for a year or more have risen still more dramatically. Unemployment tends to be concentrated in the same families and neighbourhoods, so the numbers of households with no earners and the numbers of streets with few earners in them have also risen. The new part-time jobs for women are mainly taken by people who already have a full-time earner in their household. Thus the families that benefit from them are rarely the poorest.

Housing opportunities depend on the resources of the household, however, not just the individual's. There are far more one-person households than ever before and more adults living on their own with young children. These include some of the poorest households of all. There are also more physically and mentally handicapped people living in the community — partly because there are more very old people, partly because we have grown more skilled at saving the lives of people injured in accidents or by diseases, and partly because we have closed many of the long-stay wards and hospitals in which such people used to live.

Most of these trends towards increasing inequality among households would have occurred under any government. They are to be seen throughout the world's more affluent economies. But in Britain the state has reinforced them. The distribution of tax reductions to people in the upper reaches of the income range has been combined at the lower end with tax and benefit changes which have reduced the disposable incomes of many people and increased the severity of poverty traps. The new family credit scheme may do something to change this, but not much. Despite heavy advertising, it fails to reach about half of those entitled to it.

Meanwhile, it has become clear to most people that the complacent expectation that 'a rising tide lifts all boats' — eliminating poverty painlessly through economic progress — is illusory. The tide of economic revival which rises in the leafier suburbs of southern England, where the tax cuts exert their biggest impact, soon generates inflation and trade deficits that compel the Chancellor to choke if off before it flows strongly enough into the poorer quarters of Liverpool, Glasgow and Belfast to lift their people back into decent jobs.

There is also a more fundamental reason why prosperity, in profoundly unequal societies, does not eliminate poverty. In such a world, each generation invents new kinds of poverty by transforming some of the luxuries of its predecessors into necessities. There are rural communities in Britain where cars are becoming a necessity because services such as the grocer's shop and the doctor's surgery have been centralised into larger units which stand in small towns, and public transport to these centres is increasingly expensive and infrequent. Likewise there are housing estates on the fringes of our cities where central heating is becoming a necessity because open fires and corner shops selling bags of coal have disappeared. Here too, the cheapest way to get to a good shop and the only way to get to a hospital in an emergency is by car or taxi. Then people living in centrally heated flats with no shops nearby find that they need refrigerators to store their food. All this is very satisfactory for those who can afford these new necessities. This is what the 'rising tide' *means*. But social security benefits and low wages were never intended to pay for cars or taxis, the more expensive forms of central heating or refrigerators. So people in such neighbourhoods half starve themselves to keep their cars on the road, to pay their fuel bills and to keep up the payments on a fridge, and they borrow money at cruel rates of interest from illicit lenders who bring in their 'heavies' to exact repayments. The results of this increasingly unequal society often emerge as housing problems — in rent arrears, vandalism, and neglected and violent neighbourhoods where no-one with any choice in the matter would choose to live and maintenance staff are reluctant to work.

The role of government

The financial crises produced in the advanced capitalist economies by the 'oil shocks' of the seventies and the restructuring of manufacturing industries which shed huge numbers of workers in the eighties brought to an end a period of fairly continuous growth in the share of their national incomes devoted to public services in general and to their 'welfare states' in particular. They also hastened the end of a love affair with the state, the public service professions, and centralised, bureaucratic forms of authority — a whole political and administrative culture which had served these nations pretty well during the years of war and post-war reconstruction but which was less successful in coping with the problems characteristic of the new age. In many countries people have turned back to older mistresses: to markets and to 'community'. (Duncan Maclennan has a good deal to say about the disciplines of the market in Chapters 11 and 12. Tim Mason, Robina Goodlad, and Ian Cole and his colleagues have more to say about community in Chapters 7, 8 and 10.)

Within the apparatus of the state, priorities have been changing, partly as a result of the successes achieved in previous years. In Britain, as in other European countries, housing was for a long time after the war one of the most salient political issues. During the years of desperate shortage, ministers made their names by getting more houses built than their predecessors. Others were damaged by housing scandals. Housing and rehousing huge numbers of ordinary families in decent homes became a nation-wide campaign: how to tackle it was a fiercely debated question, but the importance of the cause was never in doubt. However, as the numbers of people with serious housing difficulties dwindled and came increasingly to consist of scattered, marginal groups, not readily mobilised as a political force, housing slipped further and further down the lists of politically significant topics identified in opinion polls.

Developments of this kind, which occurred in many countries at this time, would have taken place under any British Government. But the Conservative administration elected in 1979 imposed its own imprint on the trends. For five years it scarcely had a housing policy. Instead, it pursued policies for reducing public expenditure and cutting income tax, for transferring public property and public services to private hands, and for bringing what it saw as spendthrift local authorities under control. Public housing was the victim of all three. Cuts in capital expenditure on housing were the quickest way to reduce local government's spending. Selling council houses at heavy discounts to their tenants was the most dramatic, and one of the most popular, forms of privatisation.

Regional policies were abandoned too. Programmes which previous governments of both parties had developed with some success to counterbalance disparities in the job opportunities, the incomes and the infrastructure of different regions were cut back. Meanwhile, rate support grant and housing subsidies were withdrawn on a massive scale from the old industrial cities which had benefited most from previous policies. Bigger public spending on defence and aerospace and on the motorways of the south east became, in effect, the new 'Regional' policy, powerfully reinforcing disparities between north and south, and between inner cities and suburbs.

What had appeared to be a settlement of the forty-year-long controversy about the acquisition for the community of a share in the enhanced land values brought about by urban development — a settlement achieved through the taxation of developers' profits rather than the taxation of land — was also abandoned.

Meanwhile, private building as well as public building fell for a while to historically low levels and are now on the way down again, owing partly to the mechanisms used by the Government to regulate a failing economy. But what would have been a political disaster in previous years made scarcely a dent in the Government's reputation.

Recently, however, the Government has begun to formulate more positive policies for rented housing and for the regeneration of the 'inner cities' and the big council estates. These developments are intended to revive private investment in rented housing, to diversify the ownership of 'social rented housing', to give tenants a wider choice of landlords, and to bring market disciplines into this field. They are traced in greater detail by Adrian Kearns and Duncan Maclennan in the next chapter. Such a strategy, as Peter Kemp shows in Chapter 5, depends heavily for its success upon a more efficient system of housing benefits, which the Government has tried to create. It is too soon to predict what the new policies will achieve.

The housing market

The market, public and private, which emerges from these developments reflects the society which created it. Owner occupation has spread and the price of houses, particularly in the south of England, has risen dramatically, partly as a result of Government policies for taxation and tax relief — now reinforced by the poll tax. Existing owners in general, and the richer ones particularly, benefit from these trends and have borrowed more and more money on the strength of their housing assets to spend on other things. But marginal buyers and renters are struggling for survival. Mortgage arrears and repossession of defaulters' homes, though still on a very small scale, have sharply increased. The numbers of homeless people have grown even more dramatically. In the Capital and other big cities, more and more sleep in cardboard boxes and on railway stations. In many places private landlords' houses, grotty though they often were, used to provide a safety net for those in trouble and a 'waiting room' (to use Peter Kemp's phrase) for those on the waiting lists. These houses have almost disappeared. Regional differences in living and housing standards, which had for many years been narrowing, have begun to grow larger. In short, an increasingly unequal society is creating growing stresses for those at the bottom of the housing market.

Meanwhile, within the public sector there is also a growing diversity of standards. That is due partly to the greater variety of housing (measured by age, type and construction materials) belonging to local authorities, partly to loss of subsidies and to restrictions on their expenditure, partly to the growth of poverty among tenants, partly to incompetent and short-sighted policies for repairs and modernisation, and partly to allocation procedures which concentrate the poorest and the most vulnerable in the least attractive neighbourhoods. (Clapham, Kintrea and McNaughton throw light on various aspects of these patterns in Chapters 4 and 6; so do Allan and Evaskitas in Chapter 9.) Whatever the reasons for it, the growth of neighbourhoods of squalor and disorder has gone far to discredit local government and to alienate people from public housing and the political movement which created and administered so much of it.

Unresolved questions

This, very briefly sketched, is the evolving situation we face, and these are the main questions it poses for anyone concerned about the housing service of the future.

There are more, not fewer, vulnerable people — people who cannot be decently housed without the help of their fellow citizens — in all sectors of the housing market and in all parts of the country. Who will house or subsidise them, and who will take responsibility for ensuring that they do not become homeless or end up living in squalor? Where does the buck stop? The present local housing authorities will not necessarily provide the answer to that question. There are countries which have solved the problem pretty effectively without having municipal housing departments, as Maclennan reminds us in Chapter 12. But if some other organisation is to take over this responsibility we must know which it is to be and what resources it will be given for the job. We must know, too, what support the responsible body will be given by social security, health, social work and other agencies — as Allan and Evaskitas show in Chapter 9.

The agencies housing the more vulnerable people must not create stigmatised ghettos which serve to exclude their residents from mainstream society which serve to exclude their residents from mainstream society even more completely than before. Thus they must operate on quite a large scale, housing many people who have willingly chosen to be where they are. What forms of property ownership will these agencies rely on? Such agencies, be they local authorities, housing associations or co-operatives, or some combination of all three, must have some kind of secure, collective ownership of their property. That gives them some equity in the housing market, the holding gains conferred by inflation on property owners, and elbow room for pooling and redeploying rents and subsidies amongst houses built or acquired at different times and at different prices. Individual ownership, governed only by market motives and pressures, has never been able to do this job.

If people are to be given any choice about their homes and living conditions, they must be able to pay for it. So how do we ensure that poor people can pay the rent? The flows of funds transferred through subsidies and tax reliefs linked to housing are easily capable of solving this problem. To put it another way: the problem is political, not economic. Whether it will be solved is a different matter, depending heavily on policies of the central government, but also partly on the character and quality of local housing services — as all our authors make clear.

Can we regenerate decaying, economically stricken cities, and help their unemployed people back into the economy? If we only tidy up houses and the surrounding landscape, leaving the people as poor as ever, decay will eventually re-emerge wherever they come to rest. Neither the private nor the public sector are prepared to invest consistently in neighbourhoods where only the poor live. What part can housing investment play in bringing about an expansion of economic opportunities? What part can it play in arresting the flight of those who gain these economic opportunities from the neglected neighbourhoods in which they lived? Cole and his colleagues, Clapham, Kintrea and Maclennan all have something to say about these issues.

How do we make the managers of social rented housing of all kinds more accountable to their customers? To make these bodies more efficient and more humane we shall have to break the power of monopolies which always tends to lead ultimately to abuses. The 1988 Housing Act will help to bring that about. But that will not be enough: the customers will have to take action too. McNaughton, Mason, Goodlad and Cole explore various aspects of this problem.

The answers to these questions will make heavy demands on the profession principally responsible for managing local housing services — people who are likely, in future, to work in various kinds of agency, public, voluntary and commercial, in the course of their careers. How they will cope with those demands and what training they will need for the purpose is discussed by Bert Provan and Peter Williams in Chapter 13.

The difficult task a local authority will have in monitoring developments in the local housing market and its links with other sectors of the economy, and in planning a strategy to make effective use of the various investors operating there — whether, indeed, there will *be* democratically elected local housing authorities in future — these are further questions to which much better answers are needed, as Maclennan shows in Chapter 12.

We conclude our book with a brief discussion of the common themes and concerns emerging from its authors' attempts to explore these and other questions about the housing service of the future.

Chapter 2
Public finance for housing in Britain

Introduction

There have been profound changes in the British economy, society and polity in the last decade. The housing sector, one of the key areas of the postwar 'Welfare State', has more directly reflected the 'Thatcher Experiment' than most other areas of public policy.

The main task of this chapter is to review major changes in government expenditure on housing in England, Scotland and Wales over the last decade. This review is intended to bring together in a concise and comprehensive fashion much of the available evidence about public expenditure on the various components of housing policy in Britain. The main trends are described, as well as shifts between programmes and sectors. Some estimates are also made of the approximate regional incidences of these expenditures.

The context

In the three post war decades from 1945 to 1975, increased investment in municipal housing in Great Britain was not only the backbone of shelter provision within the expanding welfare state but for more than half that period exceeded private residential output. As recently as 1976, for instance, there were 145,000 public sector and 16,000 housing association units built in a single year. An expansion in the share of housing policy spending in government expenditure reflected central government's willingness to allow local authorities to borrow for the construction of municipal housing. Rents set well below market levels, with subsidies tied to dwellings rather than household circumstances, were the key incentives for households to enter the sector. Subsidies were paid for by both central and local government.

Throughout these decades the share of public spending, within a growing real total, devoted to housing expenditure rose from 3 per cent to just under 10 per cent. Now, a little more than a decade later, housing spending has fallen to under 3 per cent of total public expenditure and, in addition, local authorities have been rejected by central government as the 'motor' for future change.

Housing capital expenditure is a programme which can be curtailed relatively quickly although the consequences of cutback tend to be subtle and long term, often impacting on the poorest people. It was not surprising therefore that, as in so many other European countries after 1975, housing capital expenditure in Great Britain was reduced as a result of policies to curtail the Public Sector Borrowing Requirement. Initial cutbacks were legitimated by the then emerging belief, as was stated in the 1977 Green Paper, that there was a growing surplus of housing units over household numbers. Cutbacks since then cannot be attributed to such favourable indicators of housing sector change, as the doubling of homelessness and sharp increases in the ratio of housing payments to income both suggest housing shortage. They reflect a radical shift of perspective by central government on the appropriate housing policies for Britain.

Current account subsidies, to support household expenditures on housing and housing management services, have been a less pronounced area of cutback. In the 1970s, high national inflation rates implied increased costs of providing and managing housing at the same time as unemployment and 'dependence' were growing. In this area of policy, from 1975 to the present, restructuring rather than real reduction of subsidies has prevailed with a switch from 'tied' to income related subsidies (housing benefit payments) occurring.

Cutbacks in government expenditure on housing investment and subsidies may present no problem if incomes are growing and the market sector is expanding.[1] However, by historic standards, the 1980s has not been a decade of intense private housing investment in Britain. The economic policies pursued by the government for the economy as a whole, certainly from 1979 to 1983, undoubtedly inhibited investment in home ownership over these years. And since 1988 high interest rates have been associated with a slump in new private starts and land prices which is currently unparalleled in the rest of Europe.

Economic policies in the same period markedly increased the real user cost of capital for the housing sector. Throughout the 1970s real income growth and negative real mortgage interest rates, which were generally more negative the higher the inflation rate, encouraged people to borrow money and buy homes, as did the prevailing system of tax reliefs on mortgage interest payments. In the early 1980s, the shift in emphasis in monetary policy, international economic influences and capital market deregulation were all associated with positive real mortgage rates of 5 to 7.5 per cent. Income and employment uncertainties curtailed expansion and private housing output fell sharply to 1981 and only recovered to its 1975 level in 1985. After 1986 reductions in higher marginal tax rates have also increased the user cost of capital as have post 1987 interest rate increases. However, as a counter argument, there is little doubt that over the decade macroeconomic policies facilitated a sustained period of high real income growth (for those in employment) from 1983 to 1989 which undoubtedly increased housing demand after 1984. This effect should not be underemphasised in any discussion of the 'Thatcher Years'. The years 1979 to 1984 perhaps represent the 'short run' of policy change with considerable structural disorder. From 1984 to 1988 the medium term benefits of policy become more apparent. In that period, if the government increased the user cost of housing capital they also increased the real incomes used by households to purchase that housing capital, with income effects apparently outweighing price effects. However, from 1988 onwards rapidly increased real interest rates, explicitly directed at reducing consumer demand by raising mortgage loan payments, have created major difficulties for new and moving owners who purchased properties in the house price boom of 1985–87.

Private building of rented houses has made little contribution to output over the decade. The private rented sector in Britain has collapsed over the past 70 years under pressures of subsidised competition from other sectors and rent controls. In consequence marginal changes in the user cost of rental sector capital have generally had no impact on housing provision. Post-1988 rent deregulation and, more obviously, tax incentives under the Business Expansion Scheme have reversed this trend, but only marginally and not in all regions.

Against, this background, social sector housing output (local councils plus housing associations) has declined continually since 1976 and is now only one sixth of its total in that year (26,000 units compared with 161,000). In broad terms, the public sector produced half of Britain's new housing in 1975 but only one fifth in 1989. Moreover, the output from all sectors fell by 40 per cent over the same period. The considerable growth in home ownership which took place in the 1980s has been led by council house sales, which accounted for two thirds of the 10 per cent rise in owner occupation in recent years. These sales commonly occur at a discount of 50 per cent or more of their imputed market value.

It would not be unfair to suggest that 'tenure choice', rather than economic stability, efficient production or equitable subsidies, was the dominant concern of British housing policy from 1979 until the present. This preoccupation helped to bring about a contraction of public expenditure on housing and a consequent tightening of the housing system. Compared to 1979, people are now paying more for their housing. The ratio of rent to income has risen in all sectors but this increase occured prior to 1985. Mean municipal rents to income ratios have risen from 6 (1979), through 8 (1985) to 8 (1989) per cent; and the equivalent figures for association tenants are 9, 10 and 10 per cent. The price-to-income ratio for new and second time buyers is now historically high. With a base of 1970 = 100, the real house price index was 135 in 1979, 137 in 1985 and 230 in 1989. This is a dramatic change. Waiting lists for council housing have grown by one third; homelessness has doubled to more than 150,000 persons per year in Great Britain. At the same time it must be recognised that there are fewer houses without amenities, more households are in their preferred tenures and housing 'satisfaction' scores are certainly no less, on average, than a decade ago. However, as in relation to income and employment, the apparent widening gap between mean housing conditions and the circumstances of the poorest 10 per cent of households is a source of concern.

Looking back over the years, it is clear that the Government's 1977 housing review under-estimated, or did not anticipate, several important changes; the growing number of British households (which housing plans have always tended to under-estimate); the spread of unemployment and benefit dependence; the implications of an ageing population in council housing; and the qualitative decline of council housing, even of some recently built. Similarly, the 1985 Inquiry Report by the Duke of Edinburgh's committee did not foresee how boom and bust cycles in the national economy and housing market would so imperil the growing number of UK home-owners.

It took from 1977 until 1985 for governments to recognise that a more purposeful housing policy was required to cope with these problems and thereafter to sketch out a vision of what this policy might be. Important clues with regard to intent and feasibility are given by a look at the government's record on public expenditure on housing through the 1980s.

Patterns of gross and net capital expenditure on housing

Changes in real terms in gross capital expenditure on housing during the 1980s in England, Scotland and Wales are shown in Tables 2.1, 2.2 and 2.3 respectively.[2] The tables make a number of points. First, on a year by year basis, the decade has not seen continuing cuts. The reduction from 1979 to 1982 was sharp and sudden, as it was in 1985/86. Since 1985/86 there has been a period of stability, arguably at an inadequate resource level, in real expenditures. Second, there have been marked regional shifts. Over the whole period, gross capital expenditure has fallen by over one third in real terms in England and by 5 per cent in Scotland, but has risen by 60 per cent in Wales following large increases in 1982/83 and 1983/84.

Third, the tables also show the changing balance in expenditure between local authorities and the voluntary housing sector (housing associations). In Scotland, the Housing Corporation increased its share of gross capital expenditure by 3 per cent between 1981/82 and 1988/89 and the local authorities' share rose by 4 per cent, both at

Table 2.1 Gross capital expenditure on housing in England

	Total Expenditure 1988 Price (£billion)	Index in Real Terms	Local Authorities (%)	Housing Corporation (%)
1979/80	6.0	100	82	13
1980/81	4.7	79	77	17
1981/82	3.7	62	75	20
1982/83	4.4	73	75	23
1983/84	5.1	85	79	18
1984/85	4.8	80	80	18
1985/86	3.9	65	78	21
1986/87	3.8	63	75	24
1987/88	3.9	65	76	23
1988/89	3.8	64	77	22
1989/90(P)	3.9	63	74	23
1990/91(E)	3.9	63	72	25

(P) Provisional
(E) Planned

Table 2.2 Gross capital expenditure on housing in Scotland

	1988 prices (£'000)	Index in Real Terms	Local Authorities (%)	Housing Corporation (%)	SSHA (%)
1981/82	545	100	62	22	16
1982/83	532	97	58	26	14
1983/84	613	112	73	20	7
1984/85	482	88	65	23	12
1985/86	458	84	64	24	12
1986/87	517	95	66	22	12
1987/88	607	111	71	21	8
1988/89	519	95	66	25	9

the expense of the Scottish Special Housing Association. In Wales over the same period the share of gross capital expenditure channelled through the Housing Corporation fell by 11 per cent, but a rise in 1988/89 suggests that this decline may soon be reversed. In any case, the Housing Corporation's programme in Wales has proportionately far more significant, at 41 per cent of total expenditure, than it was in England or Scotland.

As well as changes in the sectoral division of housing capital expenditure, there have also been variations in the composition of activities supported by such expenditure and in the balance between new net

Table 2.3 Gross capital expenditure on housing in Wales

	1988 Prices (£'000	Index in Real Terms	Local Authorities (%)	Housing Corporation (%)
1981/82	91	100	48	52
1982/83	132	145	55	45
1983/84	226	249	77	23
1984/85	155	170	64	36
1985/86	122	134	63	37
1986/87	163	180	70	30
1987/88	168	185	65	35
1988/89	148	162	59	41

Sources for Tables 2.1, 2.2, and 2.3: Government expenditure plans, cmnds 784, 9428, 56 and 288

Table 2.4 Composition of local authority gross capital expenditure on housing in England

	New Build For rent (%)	Support to Private Sector (%)	Renovation of Council stock (%)	Capital Receipts (%)
1978/79	55	24	21	22
1979/80	45	27	28	17
1980/81	45	25	30	25
1981/82	39	28	33	51
1982/83	31	28	41	74
1983/84	24	38	38	58
1984/85	26	32	42	53
1985/86	26	25	49	60
1986/87	24	23	53	74
1987/88	21	22	57	83
1988/89	19	21	60	64
1989/90(P)	16	22	62	69
1990/91(E)	13	23	64	71

Sources: Government expenditure plans, cmnds 288, 56, 9702, 9428 and 9143

expenditure and funding from capital receipts. Table 2.4 shows that these changes over the period 1979/80 to 1990/91 in the case of local authority capital expenditure on housing in England (the proportion in Scotland being much lower at around 20 per cent).

The share of local authority capital expenditure on housing which is funded from capital receipts from the sale of council houses has risen from 25 per cent or less at the start of the 1980s to 70–80 per cent in the late 1980s and early 1990s. In real terms, net central government funding of local authority capital expenditure on housing has fallen by 72 per cent between 1978–79 and 1988–89.

The distinction in the source of funding is important. Expenditure financed by government borrowing naturally increases the Public Sector Borrowing Requirement and this will, *ceteris paribus*, put upward pressure on interest rates and inflation. Sales receipts do not add to the PSBR. They do, however, add to private mortgage borrowing and the sheer volume of council sales may have contributed to higher mortgage interest payments. These magnitudes have not been assessed in the UK although the Government has argued that the reduced PSBR effects were positive for the economy.

Funding for the construction of new council housing has also fallen dramatically, and particularly since 1985. In 1978–79, over half local authority capital expenditure was devoted to new provision of housing for rent, whereas for 1990–91 this proportion will be just 13 per cent. The majority of local authority capital expenditure in 1990–91 will be on the renovation of existing council stock; in 1978–79 only a fifth of total capital expenditure was for this purpose. In a sense, it could be argued that new provision of council housing has been sacrificed in order to give priority to the repair and improvement of that which already exists, but the drop in central government's contribution belies this interpretation, and we must conclude that the expenditure patterns reflect the government's view that the share of local authority housing in the national housing system should continue to fall. Moreover, the present level of gross expenditure on renovation and modernisation of council housing mean that it will take 20 years to deal with the repairs bill estimated at £30 bn for England in 1985.

Not all the trends identified above will continue in the same form into the future. The Government will give greater emphasis to the use of accumulated receipts (some £6–7 bn) for the clearance of outstanding debts rather than for new investment (see DoE 1988a), and in the future local authorities will be permitted to use 25 per cent of recurrent council house sales receipts for new investment. Although the Government still predicts a continuing growth in sales receipts for local authorities each year, many commentators predict that this will soon tail off for two reasons. First, it is argued, that there is a diminishing proportion of council tenants able to purchase, even with a discount. Second, discounts have been increased in order to encourage the purchase of less attractive properties. In England and Wales the average discount in 1980–81 was £6000 or 39 per cent of the average market price; in 1987–88 it was £14,000 or 48 per cent of the market price (Hansard 7 November 1988 col. 83–84)

Thus, not only is the level of sales declining, but the capital receipt from each sale is being squeezed as the discount increases. Our view is that the decline in sales receipts is, in the next decade, more likely to be attributable to the latter rather than the former consideration. First, a recent sample survey (1985/86) of council tenants in England indicates that around 40 per cent of existing tenants are delaying purchase until their household circumstances are appropriate. Second, whilst 'dependency' rates in the council sector are high, at least one third of households have incomes which will grow. Sales receipts, from individual purchases may then be more stable than commentators expect and, of course, in time they may be boosted by receipts from sales under the new schemes giving tenants a 'right to transfer' to new landlords or, if introduced, 'rent-to-mortgage' plans.

Whether or not capital receipts in due course fall below the level the government would like in order to assist with the funding of the new capital programme, ministers may decide to encourage sales further by earmarking part of the tenants' rental payments as a contribution towards a deposit for future purchase. Despite any such move, the most significant additional capital receipts to local authorities in the future will come not from council house sales but from sales of land holdings to developers in order to bolster regional economies by attracting new housing, retailing and high technology projects. It is unlikely that authorities will be permitted to use these receipts to fund new housing investment, other than as a replacement for central government funds.

For individual local authorities in England and Wales the government, using 1989 legislation, will issue credit approvals (limits on the commitments an authority may enter into for housing capital expenditure in any one year) in the light of the authority's potential spending power from receipts. This new system of financing capital expenditure has some distinct advantages over the present mechanisms. First, under the system which has existed since 1980, the government has not taken any account of the ability of individual authorities to use receipts when making capital allocations, thus producing mismatches between the perceived pattern of need and the resulting pattern of new expenditure. Second, credit approvals will be given over a three-year period, and not on a year-by-year basis as at present, thus introducing some certainty against which councils can plan expenditure programmes.

There are, however, some uncertainties over the new system of finance for capital expenditure. It is unclear exactly how the system will operate if the government is not to take a view on the rate at which the proportion of receipts theoretically available to an authority for capital investment should be spent. There will also be concern among local authorities about the time limits to be placed on the repayment from the Housing Revenue Account of any principal sums borrowed, thus the consequent rental implications of borrowing may deter new investment.

Housing subsidy and the housing revenue account

After 1980–82 the Government sharply reduced its expenditure on revenue subsidies to local authority housing revenue accounts. Previously, this subsidy (called housing subsidy in England and Wales and called housing support grant in Scotland) had been the main instru-

Table 2.5 Housing subsidy and housing support grant in real terms 1979–80 to 1988–89 (1979–80 = 100)

	England and Wales	Scotland
1979–80	100	100
1980–81	95	90
1981–82	54	58
1982–83	29	35
1983–84	15	23
1984–85	17	21
1985–86	19	19
1986–87	24	13
1987–88	20	11
1988–89	19	14

Sources: Government expenditure plans, cmnds. 9143 and 288, and Hansard 15 July 1988. cols 399–400

ment for reducing housing costs faced by council tenants. Table 2.5 shows the movements over the decade 1979–80 to 1988–89 in central government expenditure on housing subsidy and housing support grant in real terms. The biggest reduction was in 1981–82, but the downward trend has continued since then, so that in 1988–89 these subsidies will be less than one fifth of their value in 1979–80 in real terms. In addition, there has been a contraction in the number of local authorities receiving subsidy. In 1986–87, only 24 per cent of local authorities in England and Wales received housing subsidy, compared to 95 per cent in 1981–82.

The result of these changes in expenditure on subsidies has been a shift in the regional impact of housing subsidy and housing support grant as shown in Table 2.6. Between 1981–82 and 1987–88, there has been a large increase in the proportion of total grant going to the London boroughs, from 41 per cent to 70 per cent. The only other region to maintain something close to its earlier share was the North West. Scotland's share of the total subsidy has halved from 15 per cent to 8 per cent.

Another consequence of the reductions in subsidies has been the restructuring of the housing revenue accounts, as shown in Table 2.7. Housing subsidy in England and Wales covered just 8 per cent of housing revenue account expenditure in 1987–88 compared to almost one third in 1980–81. Faced with falling subsidies and rising costs, local authorities could either increase rents or increase the level of contributions made from the general rate fund to the housing revenue account. Since the Government was anxious to restrict the growth of overall local authority spending, penalties and restrictions have curtailed the use of rate fund contribution (RFCs), so that they covered only 9 per cent of HRA expenditure in Great Britain in 1987–88 compared to 15 per cent in 1980–81.

Table 2.6 Regional distribution of housing subsidy and housing support grant

	1981–82 (%)	1987–88 (%)
Northern	4.4	2.3
Yorkshire and Humberside	4.6	0.1
East Midlands	3.6	2.1
Eastern	4.7	2.0
London	41.3	69.6
South Eastern	6.7	4.7
South West	2.3	0.6
West Midlands	6.2	1.9
North West	7.8	6.5
Wales	3.3	2.0
Scotland	15.1	8.1
	100.0	100.0

Sources: CIPFA housing revenue account statistics and Hansard, 15 July 1988, cols 399–400

Table 2.7 Structure of the housing revenue account in England and Wales

	1980–81 (%)	1987–88 (%)
Revenue		
Rents	48	68
Rate fund contribution	10	8
Exchequer subsidy	32	8
Interest on unspent		
Capital receipt	5	11
Other income	5	6
	100	100
Expenditure		
Loan interest and repayment	66	51
Repair and maintenance	20	27
Supervision and management	12	19
Other expenditure	2	2
Transfer to rate fund	0	1
	100	100

The majority of HRA expenditure is now met by rental income, almost two thirds for Great Britain as a whole. Table 2.8 gives relevant indices of local authority rents, average incomes and inflation separately for England and Wales and for Scotland from 1977 to 1986.

Table 2.8 Nominal indices for council rents, average earnings and inflation, 1977 to 1986

	Unrebated LA rents		Average Gross Weekly earnings		Rent as a per cent of income		RPI
	Scotland	England and Wales	Scotland	England and Wales	Scotland	England and Wales	
1977	100	100	100	100	6.1	8.3	100
1978	111	106	114	114	5.9	7.7	108
1979	122	116	129	133	5.7	7.3	126
1980	146	147	153	155	5.8	7.9	146
1981	191	205	173	172	6.7	9.9	163
1982	224	242	188	188	7.3	10.7	174
1983	245	252	203	206	7.3	10.2	183
1984	260	264	217	220	7.3	10.0	192
1985	287	280	235	238	7.4	9.8	202
1986	323	294	251	253	7.8	9.7	208

Source: *Housing Bulletin*, Scottish office

The process of removing housing support grant and restricting rate fund contributions from the housing revenue account is continuing apace in Scotland, where the rent-to-income ratio is still below that for England and Wales despite the fact that the average local authority rent has proportionately increased more in Scotland than elsewhere over this period. (Ring fencing legislation has not been introduced in Scotland.) In both cases, though, rent increases in the local authority sector have been higher than general inflation rates. For England and Wales, taking 1976–77 as a base of 100, real council rents had an index of 139 in 1984–85 and 146 in 1987–88.

As a result of the curtailment of local authority investment in new council housing over the past decade, the proportion of housing revenue account receipts devoted to repayments of capital and interest on loans is falling. In 1980–81, two thirds of expenditure on the housing revenue account was devoted to this purpose, whereas in 1987–88 it was down to one half. The gain has been in the amounts of income spent on management and maintenance, 19 per cent and 27 per cent respectively in England and Wales in 1987–88. Between 1980 and 1985 the real expenditure per dwelling on management and maintenance rose by 50 per cent and 35 per cent respectively, and this trend has grown since 1985. There is the prospect that in the future, with rising council rents and diminishing levels of new building there may be further reductions in subsidy to the housing revenue account and perhaps also improvements in the quality of housing management services facilitated by higher levels of spending, unless on the other hand capital spending on, for example, modernisation, is increasingly funded from revenue income.

Past restrictions by the government on the proportion of receipts from council house sales which may be reinvested in housing has meant that by 1989 around £8 bn has been locked into enforced savings with the annual interest therefrom covering over 10 per cent of HRA expenditure and indirectly reducing the government's expenditure on housing benefit subsidy to council tenants. This imposed saving during the 1980s, which took some time to be significant in scale, has to be contrasted with the poor state of the council housing stock and the levels of unemployment in the building industry. Our view is that increased short run investment would have done more good than long term savings in revenue expenditure.

From April 1990, the basis of the housing revenue account was altered in order that the Government may target subsidy to authorities most 'needing' it and to provide incentives for efficient housing management (see DoE 1988b). This was achieved by a tighter definition of the housing revenue account (what has become known as 'ring fencing') which will limit transfers in either direction between the HRA and other accounts of the general rate fund, and by the introduction of housing revenue account subsidy to replace the range of current subsidies into the HRA, namely housing subsidy, rate fund contributions supported by rate support grant and the rent rebate element of housing benefit subsidy. Further, rents on council properties are to be brought into line with rates of return to be earned on the average value of an authority's sales receipts.

There have been a number of immediate effects of these changes to the housing revenue account. First, council housing will have to 'stand on its own feet' much more than at pre-1990, and in particular will have to lay no burden on the community charge. Although rate fund contributions (RFCs) made up only 8 per cent of the total income to the HRA in England and Wales in 1987–88, in some authorities the discretionary RFC has been very significant in covering HRA expenditure. Of all local authorities in England and Wales, 194 made contributions from the general rate fund to the HRA in 1987–88, and 126 authorities made transfers from the HRA to the general rate fund. In the case of 32 of the 194 authorities the discretionary RFC covered 10 per cent or more of the expenditure on the HRA. The new 'sales value' basis for estimating reckonable income has implied sharply increased rents in southern areas with relatively high property values, but smaller increases are likely in many northern areas.

A further effect of the HRA changes was that councils will no longer be automatically entitled to funds from central government through housing benefit subsidy to help poorer tenants meet their housing costs. The local HRA will in effect only receive rent rebate subsidies to the extent that the HRA as a whole cannot provide this. Rent rebates to council tenants will in actual fact be expenditure from the HRA, but the Government's consultation paper does not identify them as such (see DoE 1988 p.6). In the past authorities could choose to have high rents and low expenditures, thus generating local surpluses. However, central government, through housing benefit, paid at least 50 per cent of these increases. The new system precludes this 'rentmanship' and, in this respect, proposes a more efficient subsidy system. One net effect of this will be to encourage any tenants who can afford to do so, to move out of the council sector either by purchasing their home under the right-to-buy scheme or by moving, since otherwise the richer tenants will be forced to subsidise the poorer tenants. Ring fencing has also encouraged some authorities to transfer stock to alternative landlords, usually housing associations.

In calculating the HRA subsidy each year the Government will in effect be heavily influencing, if not determining, actual decisions local authorities will take on rents, maintenance and efficiency standards since assumptions will be made about each of these items in order to work out the notional deficit to be met by the subsidy. The patchy and often poor management performance of councils, including many who spend too little on management, as illustrated in the Maclennan Report[3], may well justify this new central approach. However, a great deal of information will be required by government if it is to carry out this exercise accurately and fairly. The use of management and maintenance allowances for councils in a similar way to those already applied to housing associations could do much to improve standards.

Housing benefit subsidy and rent rebates

Personal subsidies, through housing benefit, have become the main source of assistance with housing costs during the 1980s. Whilst housing subsidy and housing support grant was over £500 mn in 1988–89, central government expenditure on rent rebates (that part of the housing benefit system applicable to council tenants) totalled £2700 mn. Indeed, the cost of administering the housing benefit system, at £208 mn in 1988–89, was approximately half the amount of housing subsidy. Table 2.9 shows actual and planned central government expenditure on rent rebates from 1983–84 when the housing benefit system was fully operational.

In real terms, total spending on rent rebates to council tenants has been rising so that in 1987–88 around 54 per cent of council tenants in Great Britain received an average rebate of £790 per year. If it is assumed that the average housing benefit recipient pays the average council rent, then rent rebates cover 60 per cent of the costs of providing housing services to those council tenants in receipt of this benefit, who numbered 3.37 mn tenants in 1988–89

Table 2.9 Central government expenditure on rent rebates to council tenants

	Cash (£000)	Index in Real terms (1988 prices)
1983–84	1980	100
1984–85	2145	103
1985–86	2294	104
1986–87	2421	106
1987–88	2563	108
1988–89	2720	108
1989–90(P)	2800	111
1990–91(E)	3000	119

Source: Government supply estimates

One consequence of the shift from 'bricks and mortar' subsidies to personal subsidies is that government has less control over, and less knowledge of, the links between charges, payments and subsidies. Not only at an aggregate level, but also in the case of regions and individual local authorities, central government, and particularly the housing ministry, is unaware of how charges are paid through a mixture of housing benefit subsidies from central government, housing benefit payments made by local authorities after receipt of subsidy, and rent payments from the tenants' own incomes. Furthermore, the consequences of authorities' charging policies for this complex of funding sources is little understood (see Maclennan, Gibb and More, 1991).

Table 2.10 shows the regional distribution of housing benefit subsidy paid into housing revenue accounts in 1987–88 and compares this to the regional distribution of local authority dwellings in the same year. The two distributions are remarkably similar apart from the fact that the South East and the West Midlands regions have much higher shares of the rent rebate subsidy then their shares of the total number of local authority dwellings. In particular, the West Midlands region had 8 per cent of council housing but received 12 per cent of the housing benefit subsidy. Assuming that council tenants in the West Midlands are not that much poorer than council tenants elsewhere, this situation must be considered an anomaly permissible under the current system of housing finance. This situation may arise either because tenants in some areas are paying for the recent construction of their homes and hence face higher interest charges, or because some councils choose to charge higher rents in order to provide a better service or to avoid the consequences of monopolistic inefficiencies which have grown up in other places.

Table 2.10 Regional distribution of rent rebate subsidy 1987–88

	(£mn)	(%)	LA dwellings (%)
Northern	178.6	8.3	7.6
Yorkshire and Humberside	237.2	11.1	12.6
East Midlands	144.3	6.7	7.8
Eastern	155.5	7.3	9.6
London	330.9	15.4	17.1
South East	252.4	11.8	9.9
South West	147.1	6.9	7.1
West Midlands	262.8	12.3	7.8
North West	313.7	14.7	15.3
Wales	117.6	5.5	5.2
	2140.1	100.0	100.0

Source: CIPFA housing revenue account statistics

The Government's published plans for future expenditure on rent rebate subsidy at best could maintain their value in real terms but do not allow any expansion of this area of expenditure. However, it will be more difficult to make a judgement on them in the future if they are subsumed within the proposed housing revenue account subsidy for expenditure planning purposes.

Financial assistance to owner occupiers

To put the trends and prospects for expenditure on housing in proper context, it is worthwhile looking at financial support to the owner occupied sector. The public expenditure costs over the period 1978–79 to 1988–89 of tax allowances and reliefs to owner occupiers in the United Kingdom are shown in Table 2.11; these are the principal forms of financial assistance to owner occupiers.

Table 2.11 The cost of direct tax allowances and reliefs to owner occupiers

	Mortgage Interest tax relief (£mn) Index in real terms (1988 prices)		Exemption from capital gains tax (£mn) Index in real terms (1988 prices)	
1978–79	1100	100	1500	100
1979–80	1450	115	2000	118
1980–81	1960	132	2400	120
1981–82	2050	123	2800	125
1982–83	2150	119	3000	123
1983–84	2780	147	2500	98
1984–85	3580	181	2500	93
1985–86	4750	226	2500	88
1986–87	4750	219	3000	102
1987–88	4850	214	3500	114
1988 –89	4250	177	n/a	n/a

Sources: Government expenditure plans and Hansard, 10 June 1988, cols 702–704

In real terms the cost of tax relief on mortgage interest payments more than doubled between 1978–79 and 1987–88, and the total is expected to exceed £7 bn in 1991 even with the 1988–89 restriction of relief to loans of £30,000 per property rather than per borrower as previously, to the lowering of tax rates and the abolition of higher rate tax relief in the 1991 budget. This mortgage interest tax relief goes to almost 9 mn tax payers with the wealthiest third receiving two-thirds of the assistance. In addition, 334,000 owner occupiers received assistance with their mortgage interest payments through supplementary benefit in 1987, costing £335 mn, a doubling in real terms since 1981. The full cost in expenditure and foregone income of support to owner occupation is currently, therefore, around £10 bn per year. The average value of mortgage interest tax relief to each mortgagor was £570 per year in 1990. The regressive nature of the relief is such that those on annual incomes of £25,000 receive twice the value of mortgage interest tax relief as do those on incomes of £5000. Those on incomes of £40,000 receive relief equivalent to three times that received by the poorest owner occupiers. Furthermore, fewer owner occupiers in the lower income bands actually receive mortgage interest tax relief. Of those owner occupiers on incomes below £5000, 38 per cent do not receive tax relief on mortgage interest payments and of those on incomes between £5,000 and £10,000, 42 per cent do not receive such relief. Some of these people may not have a mortgage any longer, but others will not be tax payers and therefore would not qualify for the relief (see Maclennen, Gibb and More, 1991).

The regional incidence of mortgage interest tax relief for all mortgagors in 1979–80 and for new borrowers in 1987 is shown in Table 2.12a. This can only serve as a rough estimate because the introduction of mortgage interest tax relief at source (MIRAS) has meant that the Inland Revenue are no longer able to provide a complete picture of the situation, no longer being responsible for the administration of MIRAS to standard rate taxpayers. The 1987 estimate is therefore based upon the relative values of tax relief for mortgagors in different income bands; the income distribution of new mortgagors (first time buyers and former owner occupiers) is known for each standard region. This method may lead to an underestimation of the share of tax relief going to London and the South East where the incidence of multiple borrowers per loan may be more common and where insufficient detail is known about the earnings of higher income borrowers. However, it is clear that London and the South East are the only regions to receive disproportionate share of the total value of mortgage interest tax relief, but that situation is changing as levels of owner occupation and of house prices rise in other regions in England.

We can add to this picture by looking at Table 2.12b, which is based on a written answer given in the House of Commons by the Treasury Minister, Norman Lamont, on the 13 February 1989. He indicated the regional distribution of the total cost of mortgage interest tax relief, based on the Inland Revenue's survey of personal incomes for the years 1979–80 to 1982–83, and based on the family expenditure survey (FES) for the years 1984–86. It must be recognised that we no longer have a reliable source for this information and the FES cannot suffice.

Nonetheless, the figures confirm a steady decline in London's share of mortgage interest tax relief. Several other regions have experienced fluctuating fortunes, with their share rising and falling at various intervals, notably in the case of the North West, West Midlands, South East (which reached a peak of 30 per cent in the mid-1980s) and the South West.

Comparing the regional distribution of all mortgage interest tax relief in 1984–86 (Table 2.12b), and our estimate of the regional distribution of mortgage interest tax relief on new mortgages in 1987, there would appear to be four regions in particular whose total share of all mortgage interest tax relief is set to increase: Northern, Yorkshire and Humberside, East Midlands and South West. With the restriction of mortgage interest tax relief to a maximum loan of £30,000 *per property,* in time the distribution of tax relief will move closer to the distribution of new purchase transactions. Two factors could inhibit this. First, if any region has a disproportionate number of higher rate tax payers engaged in house-buying, which could perpetuate London and the South East's slightly disproportionate shares of tax relief. However, with the property-specific nature of tax relief, some of these buyers can be expected in future to look to cheaper regions. Second, if any region has a disproportionate share of properties with market values below the £30,000 limit. Over time, this situation will become less prevalent. On the assumption that the number of transactions becomes the crucial factor, then we may see Scotland's share of mortgage interest tax relief increasing once again (as it did in the early to mid-1980s) as the level of home ownership in Scotland, which currently lags behind that of other regions, rises in response to government policy and to increased demand from young households.

Table 2.12a Regional distribution of mortgage interest tax relief—inland revenue data and authors' estimates

	Total value of tax relief on All mortgages 1979–80(%)	Tax relief on new mortgages 1987		
		Number (%)	Total value (%)	Per capital cost(UK=100)
Northern	4.1	6.7	6.3	91
Yorkshire and Humberside	7.9	10.6	9.9	90
East Midlands	5.9	8.3	7.9	93
Eastern	3.3	4.1	4.1	96
London	42.3	7.6	8.5	109
South East		22.4	24.2	105
South West	7.5	9.3	9.3	97
West Midlands	10.1	9.3	8.9	93
North West	9.5	11.1	10.6	92
Wales	3.2	4.2	4.0	92
Scotland	6.2	6.4	6.3	96
	100.0	100.0	100.0	

Sources: Inland revenue survey of personal incomes 1979–80; BSA Bulletin no. 54, April 1988; DoE/BSA 5 per cent sample survey of new mortgages 1987; Hansard, 14 July 1988, cols 323–324

Table 2.12b Regional distribution of mortgage interest tax relief (ministerial answer, February 1989)

	1979–80 (%)	1980–81 (%)	1981–82 (%)	1982–83 (%)	1984–85 (%)
Northern	4.2	4.1	3.5	4.5	3.8
Yorkshire and Humberside	7.7	8.0	7.4	7.5	7.3
East Midlands	5.9	6.0	5.4	6.1	6.4
Eastern	3.1	2.6	3.0	3.5	3.5
London	16.4	14.5	14.3	12.3	14.3
South East	26.2	28.8	29.7	30.7	26.9
South West	7.7	7.3	8.4	6.6	8.6
West Midlands	10.1	8.3	9.4	8.0	7.9
North West	9.4	10.4	8.9	10.1	9.4
Wales	3.1	3.4	4.0	3.8	4.2
Scotland	5.9	6.5	5.9	6.6	7.5
	100.0	100.0	100.0	100.0	100.0

The other major area of public expenditure related to owner occupation is the improvement grant programme. Levels of expenditure have fluctuated during the 1980s, reflecting shifting views on the effectiveness of the grants and the fact that they have been used as a means of expanding or contracting expenditure to meet departmental cash limits. Table 2.13 shows the patterns of expenditure on improvement grants and the numbers of dwellings improved in England since 1978–79. In real terms, expenditure on improvement grants has more than doubled, though by 1978 activity had already declined from the peak of 260,000 dwellings improved in Great Britain in 1973. Since 1984–85 the number of dwellings assisted has fallen, but the share of total capital expenditure on housing in England devoted to improvement grants has risen nearly five-fold, from 3 per cent in 1978–79 to 14 per cent in 1988–89

Table 2.13 Capital expenditure on improvement grants to owner occupiers in England

	Cash (£mn)	Index in real terms (1988 prices)	Number of dwellings
1978–79	98	100	57,600
1979–80	134	121	65,400
1980–81	144	110	74,500
1981–82	197	134	72,300
1982–83	425	267	131,600
1983–84	911	547	250,600
1984–85	735	420	195,200
1985–86	444	239	124,400
1986–87	440	229	112,800
1987–88	n/a	n/a	120,000
1989–90	534	252	n/a

Sources: Government expenditure plans, cmnds 8789 and 56

Being faced with a continually deteriorating private sector housing stock, the government has introduced a means-tested improvement grants system in England and Wales (see DoE 1988c) so that we may not see any further increase in the levels of public expenditure in this area. Rather than administering a widely available range of grants for the improvement of private housing, local authorities will be more involved in the promotion of good practice among home owners and mortgage lenders, with a variety of savings schemes being devised to assist with planning maintenance expenditure.

Finance for housing associations

As noted earlier, housing associations, especially in England, have been receiving a growing share of the available gross capital expenditure for housing. The ratio of investment in new homes between local authorities and housing associations in England has shifted from 3:1 in 1979–80 in favour of local authorities to 1.5:1 in favour of housing associations in 1988–89 and this ratio is likely to shift to 5:1 in the early 1990s. The growth of government funding of housing associations, a real increase across Britain of 13 per cent between 1981–82 and 1988–89, is set to expand markedly in the decade ahead.

Prior to 1989, central government was closely involved in setting all the relevant financial measures for housing associations, so that their financial behaviour was much more controlled by central government than was that of local authorities. Housing associations capital spending is mainly financed by loans drawn from the national loans fund and channelled through the housing corporation; very few operated directly in the capital market as did local authorities. Since 1974, rents for housing association dwellings have been set by rent officers under the fair rent system. The capital grant to fund new construction was determined by the size of 'residual loan' which could be serviced from rental income after deductions of standard amounts for the management and maintenance of the dwellings; these amounts are set by government and are known as allowances. The housing association grant has typically met over 90 per cent of capital costs of new dwellings in the sector, and has rarely fallen below 80 per cent. The only control exercised over the size of the grant is through the scrutiny of scheme proposals and costs.

Housing associations were also entitled to revenue grants to meet deficits incurred in their business, providing the deficits are not due to unreasonable landlord behaviour. This form of support was declining and the annual expenditure on revenue deficit grant (RDG) and hostel deficit grant (HDG) was only £24 mn in 1987–88 with the number of associations receiving RDG falling over five years from 500 to 130. Where the opposite occurs, as rental income rises above costs (remembering that fair rents are on average one fifth above council rents) housing associations were required to repay portions of the initial capital grant in the form of grant redemption funds. The net effect, as Hills (1987) shows, can be that in the long term HAG acts as a form of index linked loan rather than as a grant *per se*.

Since the majority of associations' capital debt is wiped out by HAG (at least in the first place) it is unsurprising that real management and maintenance spending by associations runs at double the council average, outside London. As a result of generous capital grants and favourable guaranteed levels of current expenditure, housing associations have been promoted to the moral high ground in debates about good housing management practice and the future of social housing. The Government wishes to see housing associations play a much more significant role in the future provision and management of social rented housing. In tandem with this objective it has implemented since 1989, a number of changes to the financial structure supporting the voluntary housing sector.

The changes are designed to remove any barriers to the efficient running of housing associations resulting from the existing system of capital and revenue grants and allowances, and to enable the government's public expenditure for the provision of new homes by housing associations to be 'stretched' further (for a fuller review of the reasons for the changes see Kearns 1988). The main alterations were: the phasing out of fair rents and their replacement by higher, 'affordable rents'; an increasing share of the development programme for new dwellings was to be funded by a mixture of public and private funding; and, for these mixed funded schemes, associations are to bear a greater element of the risks involved with additional capital grants to cover unforeseen or additional costs paid out in limited cases, and the withdrawal of any future recourse to revenue deficit grants if, for example, repayment costs on private loans rise due to interest rate movements.

There are a number of aspects of these changes which need to be considered. In the initial consultation period it was maintained by the Treasury that only where the private component of funding on a project constituted 50 per cent or more of the total funding could the private component be classed as private expenditure and not public, since in these cases the project would have market approval based on risk assessment, and public guarantees would not be underpinning the private investment. In other cases, where private funding made up less than half the costs of a housing project, even the private finance would have to be considered as public expenditure. Against this approach, an obvious inconsistency is the situation where a private landlord's investment is classed entirely as private even though it might be made feasible by housing benefit subsidy to the tenants and improvement grant subsidy to the landlord or developer. In strict economic terms, the 'public' component of private expenditure is the value of the risk premium required to offset the danger of project default, which is charged by the lender and met by subsidy. Since 1988, however, the Treasury has, importantly, conceded that only the HAG proportion of expenditure should count as 'public' if the residual loan is privately funded.

In March 1988 the Housing Minister announced grant rates of between 50 per cent and 70 per cent for a mixed funded programme in England. In fact the mixed funded programme was placed alongside the traditionally funded programme as a separate part of the housing corporation's approved development programme, which caused difficulties. There was no necessity for this separation and for the over-ambitious HAG targets set for the new mixed funded development programme, other than the Treasury's aversion to HAG rates above 50 per cent. For if HAG levels were reduced slightly on all new schemes, with a higher national HAG target for one development programme in which all schemes for rented housing were included, the net effect would be the same as running what some see as a glamorous, separate mixed funded programme aiming at HAG levels of 50 to 75 per cent and in which only a limited number of associations can participate. In 1989, an overall average HAG target of 75 per cent replaced these procedures, and for 1990/91 the HAG rate allowed will be higher.

The present system places responsibilities on housing associations which should properly rest with government. Government should decide what 'affordability' means and issue detailed guidance not only on this but also on rent-setting procedures and the most sensible provisions to make for the depreciation of properties. The issue of affordability is the proper concern of housing Ministers and and those in government responsible for income support systems. Otherwise, there is a danger that the Housing Corporation in England, Homes for Wales and Scottish Homes will adopt too crude a definition of affordability which will not reflect the reality of households' circumstances. The other danger is that those responsible for housing benefit may not work to the same definition of affordability as those calculating capital grants for housing, and as a result the tenant is left stranded somewhere in the middle.

Since 1985, the idea of 'affordable rents' has become a major policy thrust which is not clearly based upon economic principles. Affordable rents is an odd pricing scheme for a sector which the Government wishes to behave in a more efficient manner. With such rents there is unlikely to be any clear relationship between quality and price and such a relationship is essential to a well designed rental sector.

No private sector operator would price a good almost entirely on the basis of what he thought the customer could pay with no regard to the cost characteristics of the good itself or his desired rate of return. Here, Capital Value Rents, or Target Rents (see Hills 1988) or even the weaker rent/quality schemes examined in Maclennan (1986) have something useful to offer. Although the affordability assumptions contained in the concept of target rents would not be essential if the income support mechanisms relating to housing costs were sensibly and sensitively constructed. One must, however, recall that it would not be easy to determine capital values in the social housing sector and that the specification of rates of return on capital values is difficult in an imperfect market. We believe that the pricing reforms of the 1988 Act have, in the short term, fudged the pricing issue. The relationships between rent levels, income support and producer subsidies constitute even more of a morass than in 1985 and they merited the attention of the reconvened Duke of Edinburgh Inquiry (Inquiry Report, 1991).

The basic principles which should be adhered to in seeking a new financing system for the housing associations sector are essentially two-fold. First, the pricing policy should come before the subsidy system rather than being determined by it and this policy should maintain a relationship between price and quality and indeed be equalised across all of the rental sectors. Second, the finance system should be broadly applicable to all housing associations. Third, the range of subsidy systems relevant to the sector needs to be examined together with a dialogue between those responsible for income subsidies relating to housing costs and those responsible for the capital subsidy system. The 'Thatcher years' have seen numerous reforms based on economic realities and an honest assessment in many fields of negative as well as positive policy outcomes. Why is rented housing still an exception? Market or capital value rents based on a judgement of rent/income ratio limits, good information about tenants' incomes and an honest assessment of the housing benefit implications would have provided a better basis for the 1990s.

Towards 2000: grand ideas and poor finances

Great Britain has, for at least 25 years, required a radical reform of its public and private rented housing systems. The Government's stated commitment in the late 1980s to remake the structure of rented housing with an expansion of supply, greater choice for the consumer and efficient, responsive and responsible landlords, is to be welcomed. Optimism does not automatically follow assent, though, since the changes passed through Parliament in 1988 will only succeed if the financial arrangements are satisfactory.

Although the Government has pledged itself to stimulating a growth in the rented housing market, the arrangements to achieve this are insufficient and *ad hoc*. Gross public capital spending on housing is to decline in real terms as we enter the 1990s, local authorities' share of this falling total is to be reduced still further, and the overall proportion to be devoted to new construction of rented housing is on the wane. The Government has left itself with just two routes of expansion.

First, the Government hopes that public expenditure on new provision by housing associations will be added to substantial private investment, either in the form of low-start mortgage finance (e.g. index-linked and deferred-interest loans) or as stock issues raised by intermediaries on behalf of housing associations. Not all housing associations will want to, or be suitable to, participate in such mixed-funded ventures. The intermediaries will mainly deal with the larger associations who wish to borrow substantial sums, often for schemes which are in fact wholly privately funded and involve low cost home ownership sales. Many associations will not have the asset base, reserves, or confidence to become involved. The problem for the Government is that it cannot guarantee either low enough interest rates now and in the future in the market place, or high enough income support through housing benefit to ease the entry of associations into this area by lowering the risks involved, and to enable the capital grants to be 'stretched' far enough to have a significant impact. In the light of the low incomes of housing association tenants[4], the Government must be prepared to continue to pay high rates of capital grant to housing association schemes, albeit a little lower than those paid in the past.

The other area in which the Government is looking for expansion is in the private rented housing market. To achieve this, its main instruments have been the deregulation of rents for new or newly vacated units and the extension of the Business Expansion Scheme to provide tax relief as an incentive to investment[5]. Once again, an obstacle to the proposals is the housing benefit scheme. The high marginal tax rate involved in the revised scheme introduced in April 1988 (i.e. the fast rate at which benefit is withdrawn as incomes rise) will limit the effective economic demand for new lettings, particularly from young single people who are a major market for private renting and yet are among the hardest hit by the housing benefit changes. A restructuring of housing benefit is required if the expansion of private renting is to extend beyond the luxury market. Moreover, the ease and frequency with which government adjusts housing benefit regulations to suit expenditure plans does not offer the confidence of stability to private landlords who might provide lettings for low income households.

Similarly, although the use of the business expansion scheme (BES) for rented housing investment is to be welcomed, it is unlikely to be sufficient to provide a major boost to the private rented sector. There are two obvious constraints. First, there are a limited number of investors interested in this type of venture, and although the cost of the tax relief in its first year (around £200 mn) was more than the Government expected, there was an excess of BES share issues over investment finance available. Second, even with the subsidy of tax relief on investment, the rents in BES company lettings will be high, which limits the number of prospective tenants.

The scheme is indiscriminate as to what type of housing is provided and early indications are that a large share of the tax relief will go to the provision of luxury rented homes (often in competition with hotels) rather than to 'popular' lettings. The other main area of activity has been in sheltered housing for former owner occupiers. After the passage of the statutory five years during which shares have to be held, the easiest exit route for investors, and the most attractive (not least because prospective investors would be better off buying new shares rather than second hand ones in order to get capital gains tax relief on first disposal), will be for the company to sell its properties. This has two consequences: it will restrict the choice of tenants to those with fixed term renting requirements; and there will be a rapid turnover of BES companies rather than net new additions to the stock of rented housing through the scheme in subsequent years, although early entrants to the 'executive rentals' market may be an exception to this. Despite the Government's intentions, and the BES regulations, there is a likelihood that the scheme will be used primarily for its initial tax advantages rather than (through the provision of venture capital) to stimulate the growth of new rented housing companies, which have long term intentions to stay in the market.

The regrettable fact is that the housing finance policies now being advanced, if moving in the correct direction, still fail to offer equity and efficiency as a foundation for consumer choice and satisfaction. There has been a sustained move away from 'bricks and mortar' subsidies and towards personal subsidies, but without equitable treatment between housing benefit for those renting and mortgage interest tax relief and exemption from capital gains tax for those owning their homes. The problem is not so much that of devising a method of phasing out mortgage interest tax relief,[6] but of finding the political will to see renting as a legitimate, sensible housing option which should be as available to all those who want to choose it, as owner occupation is. This still leaves the question of what to replace mort-gage intest tax relief with, for which some of the options are reviewed in Berthoud (1989). However, to achieve a satisfactory situation, once the will is there, would necessitate the introduction of a uniform, progressive system of assistance with housing costs which applies across all tenures, is explicit about its affordability assumptions, and overcomes the problem of non-take-up.[7] Furthermore, the expectation in the move away from direct 'bricks and mortar' subsidies that existing tenants of local authorities and housing associations should contribute through the generation of rental surpluses towards the costs of new provision is also inequitable, placing a burden on tenants which does not relate to their own housing consumption.

Finally, we have tried to demonstrate how all public expenditure on housing have regional impacts which need to be recognised and assessed. The use of public housing investment and subsidies in the future as part of a coherent regional policy would be a significant advance in the development of co-ordination across government policies. Housing should be recognised as having an important role in the provision of infrastructure necessary to a thriving economy,[8] in the generation of employment and labour market flexibility and in ensuring that Britain is not left with a dependent, demoralised underclass. Public expenditure on housing, and the financing of the house organisations of the future, should therefore reflect the fact that our quality of life depends heavily on the quality of our housing.

Notes

1 Historic cost accounting, unsystematic pricing and rent pooling throughout the social rented sector means that it is impossible to equate current subsidy spending with the real levels of true housing subsidies (defined as the gap between market and actual rent levels).

2 Gross capital spending constitutes the sum of borrowing permissions for land acquisitions, new construction, grants etc. plus that portion of receipts from sales of public houses which local authorities and the Housing Corporation are allowed to use in a given fiscal for new housing investment. This gross spending total indicates the extent of the housing investment programme undertaken. Net spending represents new additions to the Public Sector Borrowing Requirement.

3 Maclennan Report

4 A number of surveys in the sector have, despite the use of different methods of assessment, shown with remarkable consistency that housing association tenants are poor, with two thirds of them on housing benefit and typically three quarters on net incomes of £100 or less per week. See for example the following reports: *Who do we house?* Scottish Federation of Housing Association (1988); *Census of new tenants*, National Federation of Housing Associations (1988); *Talking back*, New Islington and Hackney Housing Association (1988); and *Rents and incomes*, Circle 33 housing trust (1988).

5 For a detailed discussion of the Government's proposals for the private rented sector and a review of the critics' view of them see Kemp (1988).

6 See Fraser and Platt (1988) for a discussion of some of the available options for removing mortgage interest tax relief.

7 A review of the research to date on the causes of non-take-up of benefits is contained in Craig (1988).

8 Glasgow is a very good example of the part which housing investment can play in the revival of an urban economy. This process is
described in Maclennan and Gibb (1988).

References

Atkinson A., Hills J. and Le Grand J. (1987) The welfare state in
Layard, R. and Dornbusch R. (eds) The performance of the British
Economy Oxford: Clarendon Press.

Berthoud R. (1989) Social security and the economics of housing in
Dilnot A. and Walker I. (eds) The Economics of Social Security
Oxford University Press.

Craig P. (1988) Costs and Benefits: A Review of Recent Research on
Take up of Means Tested Benefits, forthcoming

DoE (1987) Finance for Housing Associations: the Government's
Proposals London; Department of the Environment.

DoE (1988a) Capital Expenditure and Finance. A Consultation Paper
London: Department of the Environment.

DoE (1988b) New Financial Regime for Local Authority Housing in
England and Wales. A Consultation Paper London: Department of
the Environment.

DoE (1988c) Improvement Grants. Consultation Paper London:
Department of the Environment.

Fraser R. and Platt S. (1988) Breaking the link without breaking the
bank in Roof, September and October London: Shelter.

Hills J. (1987) When is a grant not a grant? The current system of
housing association finance Welfare State Programme Discussion
Paper Number 13 London: STICERD, London School of Economics.

Hills J (1988) twenty-first century housing subsidies: durable rent fixing
and subsidy arrangement for social housing Welfare State
Programme Discussion Paper Number 33 London: STICERD,
London School of Economics.

Joseph Rowntree Foundation (1991) Inquiry into British Housing
Second Report (1991) York: Rowntree Foundation.

Kearns A. (1988) affordable rents and flexible HAG. New finance for
housing associations Centre for Housing Research Discussion Paper
Number 17 Glasgow: University of Glasgow. p 60 Kemp (1988)

Leather P. and Murie A. (1986) The decline in public expenditure in
Malpass P. (ed) The Housing Crisis London: Croom Helm p 52
Maclennan D. (1986)

Maclennan D. and Gibb A. (1988) From no mean city to miles better
Centre For Housing Research Discussion Paper Number 18
Glasgow: University of Glasgow.

Maclennan D., Gibb K. and More A. (1991) Fairer Subsidies, Faster
Growth York: Rowntree, Foundation.

Maclennan D. and O'Sullivan A. (1987) British housing policy:
equitable or efficient in Van Vliet H. (ed) Housing in Conditions of
Fiscal Austerity.

Part 2
Looking ahead

Chapter 3
Organising effective housing management

Introduction

The purpose of this chapter is to examine organisational structures and processes appropriate for housing management organisations, whether local authorities, housing associations, trusts, private landlords or other kinds of landlords. The intention is not to lay down one ideal organisational form — landlords face different problems and have different objectives and, therefore, may need to organise themselves differently. Rather, the key argument of this chapter is that organisational effectiveness is the touchstone by which organisational forms and practices should be judged. Information in the chapter is based on a study carried out by the Centre for Housing Research for the Department of the Environment (DoE) into the nature and effectiveness of housing management in England (Maclennan et al. 1989). The next section examines some of the issues and problems which were associated with this study and any other attempt to measure the effectiveness of housing management. Bearing these in mind the following sections look at two organisational variables (organisational structure and staff motivation) using information from the above study of housing management to relate the current practices of landlords to organisational effectiveness. In the penultimate section the steps taken by landlords to monitor their own effectiveness through 'responsiveness' to their environment are discussed using information from the DoE research. Finally, some concluding comments are made about the consequences of the findings of this chapter for debates about the nature of housing management.

The emphasis in this chapter on effectiveness as a touchstone for organisational design is not one which is currently widely held. The most commonly used method of assessment at the moment is comparison of what happens in practice with an ideal form derived from a theoretical base. This entails the choice of one particular theory from at least three major theories which are commonly used in the literature on organisations; classical; human relations; and systems approaches. The last of these is by far the most popular at present because of its emphasis on the responsiveness of organisations to the outside world. In the present circumstances of rapid change in the environment facing housing organisations this concern is not unexpected, although it may be transitory, because popularity is largely the product of fashion, and fashions continually change as circumstances alter. Each of the three theories are partial in that they each stress one or two features of organisations to the neglect of others. An over-reliance on the tenets of one particular theoretical perspective is likely to result in the neglect of other important organisational variables and is not righted by jettisoning one approach and accepting whole-heartedly another which has tended to happen when circumstances change. Theories of organisations should be viewed together as offering important clues about the key variables which should be taken into account in evaluating organisational structure and process, rather than as 'off the peg' solutions to organisational problems. This pragmatic approach is the one adopted in this chapter.

Recourse to fashionable theory has been the predominant approach in the absence until recently of any attempts to assess the effectiveness of different organisational structures and processes. This applies to many types of organisations but particularly in the housing field where there is little information about the relative effectiveness of different organisations or different policies and practices. Given this lack of information, it is no surprise that recourse has been made to fashionable theories, most of which were not formulated in a public sector or housing context, or to homespun management maxims which are passed on by 'successful' managers.

The approach adopted here is to relate organisational design to effective performance. Organisational factors should then be seen as variables whose justification is not their relationship to a particular theory, but their influence on effective performance. They are means to a particular end and not ends in themselves. Because of the key importance of performance measurement, some of the key issues and problems involved in attempts to measure effectiveness are discussed in the next section

The effectiveness of housing management

The few studies of the effectiveness of public services which have taken place have largely been concerned with achieving reductions in costs; for example, Heald (1983) criticises the approach of Lord Rayner, who instituted a system of 'scrutinies' of areas of public expenditure, for being solely concerned with reducing the inputs required to achieve the same output. The major concern has been with efficiency (the relationship between inputs and outputs) whilst ignoring questions of effectiveness (the relationship between inputs and the quality or appropriateness of the output).

The Audit Commission's (1986) report on local authority housing management can also be criticised on these grounds. It concentrated on opportunities for reducing costs by, for example, changing the methods of rent collection or reducing the numbers of empty houses. Little attempt was made in the study to assess effectiveness by looking at the impact of the services provided for tenants. However, this is not surprising given the difficulties involved both in deciding what measures of effectiveness should be used and in collecting the relevant information.

Where limited attempts have been made to measure effectiveness, in the Audit Commission work and elsewhere, recourse has usually been made to a limited number of statistical indicators, the most commonly used being the proportion of properties which are void and the level of rent arrears.

However, there are many problems with an approach which relies on the use of statistical indicators. First, the indicators must be relevant in that they should relate to the objectives of the particular programmes. This raises the question of whose objectives should be taken. In a local authority housing department should it be the objectives of the ruling political party, or those of professional housing managers or the customers? And are the tenants the main customers, or those on the waiting list, or the poll tax payers? Sometimes their objectives may be the same but often they will not be. It is not possible to ignore objectives because otherwise one does not know what to monitor as the field of possible measures is vast.

Second, there has to be a causal relationship between the input and the output. Otherwise, many other factors may be causing variations in the output indicator such as levels of unemployment influencing the level of rent arrears. It is important to know the degree of influence the input has on the performance of the service being measured.

Third, it is very difficult to measure the output of a particular policy. The reliance on indicators can only be useful where output is tangible and they offer little help in measuring the quality of housing management, for example. The difficulty in finding measurable indicators means that in practice 'intermediate' outputs are often used. These are usually indicators of service output such as the number of lettings made or the number of repairs carried out. The problem with these measures is that their relationship to the efectiveness of the service and its quality have to be assumed. Were the repairs carried out to the satisfaction of the tenant and in such a way as to ensure the structural integrity of the building? Will the lettings made result in a stable community and satisfied tenants or in numerous allocation requests and serious neighbour disputes? Final output measures are almost always subjective and depend on the subjective evaluation of a service whether by producer or consumer. Therefore, it is necessary to supplement or even supplant objective output measures with subjective measures of performance, although their use is also dogged with problems.

The first problem is to decide whose subjective assessments should be taken as this depends on the view which is taken of the role of the landlord. For example, should the housing management performance of local authorities be assessed by tenants or by housing managers or by councillors? The answer will depend on whether council housing is seen as a form of charity, a form of social control, or as a service which is paid for on a contractual basis. The implicit assumption of Maclennan et al. (1989) is that there is a contractual customer–landlord relationship in housing management and, therefore, that tenants as customers of the service are the appropriate arbiters of its quality. This approach, which is the one adopted in this chapter, does have some drawbacks. For instance, the discussion of allocation policy is necessarily constrained because the customers of this service are not just existing tenants but also prospective tenants. Nevertheless, if the social control and paternalism inherent in the past practices of many public sector landlords are rejected, as they should be, then it is appropriate to view tenants as customers of a housing management service received in return for the payment of rent.

However, there are problems in attempting to gain a customer assessment of housing management. The first problem is in relating general feelings of satisfaction or dissatisfaction to the output of a particular housing management service. For example, tenants may be satisfied with housing management because there are few problems of vandalism but this may be due to the socio-economic profile of their neighbours or the general attitudes of the tenants or the action of the police, rather than the activities of housing managers. However, the problem occurs just as much with objective indicators and the only way to offset it is to standardise wherever possible for other factors which may influence the outcome.

In Maclennan et al. (1989) this was attempted by devising a measure of the 'context' of housing management designed to give an indication of the 'degree of difficulty' faced by the housing management service. It was constructed from measures of the adequacy of the housing stock, perceptions of the degree of neighbourhood problems, and indicators of the socio-economic and demographic profile of tenants.

The second problem is that citizens may have opinions about services which they know little about. This problem can be avoided by concentrating on the views of users of a service (for example, people who have recently had a repair undertaken) rather than the views of tenants as a whole.

The third difficulty is that, in housing management, because of the existence of revenue subsidies and rent pooling, there is sometimes little direct relationship between the housing management service received by tenants and what they pay in rent. There is a danger that ratings of performance can be made without an understanding of the relative costs of different service levels, and with a recognition by tenants that increases in costs may not be borne by the tenants themselves. This can be a major drawback to the use of tenant assessments of service provision, although the recent severe cut-backs in revenue support for local authority housing and reforms such as the 'ring-fencing' of council housing revenue accounts and the recasting of housing association finance have strengthened the link between the rent paid and the service received. The major continuing problem in this context is the large number of tenants in all tenures who are in receipt of housing benefit.

The fourth difficulty is that many tenants will only have experience of one landlord and, therefore, will have no means of assessing their performance relative to other landlords. Ratings of satisfaction can be compared for those who have had only one landlord and those who have had more than one. The fifth difficulty is that, in some areas — allocation policy for example — people may assess the service in relation to their position in the queue. People at the head of any queue are likely to be more satisfied than those at the back. This factor may also have to be controlled.

Even if the assessment of effectiveness results in concern about performance in a particular service or in a particular geographical area, the reasons for this state of affairs need to be identified if corrective action is to be taken. Organisational structures and processes are just one of the many possible factors which could be creating difficulties. Even if apparently organisational problems such as low morale, a high degree of conflict amongst staff or a high turnover of staff are found to exist, these may be due to factors outside the control of the individual housing authority, such as underfunding of the service or low national salary scales. Alternatively, they may be due, at least in part, to an inappropriate management style or an inappropriate division of responsibility between staff. It is not possible to say in general terms how important such factors may be because this will vary from case to case.

The difficulties outlined here make any comparative assessment of the effectiveness of housing management services from different organisations of limited value. Nevertheless, it can be of some value if used, as in this chapter, to identify factors which are worthy of further examination. Before describing in more detail the research on housing management which forms the basis of this chapter, it is important to introduce a point which will be expanded later, namely that many of the difficulties can be overcome by individual landlords monitoring their activities over time. Regular monitoring using a variety of methods or techniques can give landlords (and tenants) invaluable information about the impact of the service provided. Comparisons with other similar organisations and changes over time can offer important pointers towards areas where improvement can be made. Careful evaluation at the level of the individual organisation enables the data to be interpreted using a detailed knowledge of local circumstances. A cautious approach to the data coupled with emphasis on changes over time can help to alleviate many of the difficulties outlined here. However, as will be shown in a later section few landlords have monitored the impact of their services in this way.

The discussion in this chapter is based on the most comprehensive attempt to date to measure the effectiveness of housing organisations. This was a study carried out for the Department of the Environment looking at the effectiveness of housing management in housing associations and local authorities in England (Maclennan et al. 1989). The research consisted of a survey of 139 local authorities and 84 housing associations in England intended to elicit information about their expenditure on housing management, and their management policies, and also to collect some relatively simple measures of performance (such as number of void properties, level of rent arrears, number of offers of accommodation refused). From this overall sample, nine local authorities and nine housing associations of different sizes and types were chosen for further examination. Here questionnaire surveys were carried out with tenants and staff of the organisations. In addition, a house condition survey of a small proportion of the properties was carried out, tenant discussion groups were held and interviews were carried out with key staff at all levels.

The aim was to compare the costs of housing management in different organisations with levels of performance which was measured both by the use of objective management indicators (such as amount of rent arrears as a proportion of total rents) and tenants' subjective perceptions of the service. To allow for external factors which could influence the management task, a measure of 'context' was derived (this included measures of the socio-economic status of tenants, the relative occurrence of neighbourhood problems and a measure of the physical standard of the dwellings). In this exercise it was possible to overcome some of the problems identified earlier but others were more difficult to solve. For example, tenants' views of the service were taken at face value despite the problem that the reference points of groups of tenants may be different, as may their knowledge of the service provided. The management indicators used were essentially arbitrary and could sometimes be influenced in perverse ways. For example, during the period of the study one local authority decentralised its jobbing repairs service which resulted in a larger number of repairs being carried out. However, at the same time the number of repairs reported increased as tenants began to see the prospects of repairs being carried out improving. On this occasion, an increase in the level of service resulted in the proportion of repairs outstanding (our management indicator) worsening. This example points to the importance of interpretation of the performance information and in a study of the size reported here there was little opportunity to examine the local factors which influenced individual indicators.

Despite these reservations, the research offers a reasonable starting point for analysing the organisational factors which influence housing management performance. Variation in performance between the housing organisations studied was marked. For example, the proportion of tenants who rated their landlord as efficient varied from 50 per cent in one local authority to 85 per cent in one housing association. Further, there were systematic differences in costs and performance between different sizes and kinds of housing organisation, although there was substantial variation even among organisations of similar size and type. The aim of this chapter is to explore some of the organisational factors which influenced these variations in performance.

Key organisation variables

Although theoretical approaches to organisations cannot by themselves offer blueprints for the design of effective organisations, they can provide some ideas on the important variables which may influence organisational performance. The major theoretical approaches are well covered elsewhere and so will be explained briefly here. Readers requiring more information on the approaches are referred to Haynes (1980). The emphasis in the classical approach to organisations is on the formal organisational structure. Key issues include the need for a clear and appropriate division of responsibilities, an effective managerial span of control, the right mix between generalisation and specialisation, and staff and line functions. These issues generally refer to the shape of an organisation, i.e. the formal distribution of the responsibilities and tasks.

The human relations approach, as its name implies, is more concerned with the relationships between people within organisations. The emphasis is shifted form the classical pre-occupation with the formal structure to the informal functioning of organisations. Key issues include the motivation and morale of staff and the organisational factors which influence them.

The systems perspective places emphasis on the functioning of an organisation as a whole, and the relationships between its constituent parts. In particular, the systems approach draws attention to the relationship of an organisation to the outside world and its responsiveness to this environment. Stress is placed on the importance of concentration on the information which an organisation receives about the services it is providing and how this impacts on policy-making.

These three main factors, organisational shape, motivation and morale of staff, and the relationship between an organisation and its environment will now be considered in turn and their influence on performance assessed.

Organisational shape

Classical organisation theory tends to be associated with a pyramidal, hierarchical structure, which Burns and Stalker (1961) have called mechanistic. They contrasted this with an organic structure which is less formalised, more flexible and has more developed horizontal communication than the mechanistic form with its hierarchical structure and its emphasis on vertical rather than horizontal communication. Most of the housing organisations studied, corresponded more closely to the mechanistic rather than the organic form. The only exceptions to this general rule were the smallest organisations which were housing associations with 1000 or fewer properties and a dozen or fewer staff. Although still hierarchical in structure, these tended to have relatively flexible structures of responsibility and more informal procedures and working practices.

The impact of organisational size on the costs and effectiveness of housing management was pronounced. Apart from the type of organisation (i.e. housing association or local authority) it was the most important determining factor. In general, small size led to higher costs but more effective performance, whereas large size led to lower costs but less effective performance. Nevertheless, organisations of the same size still showed considerable differences in costs and performance

Comprehensiveness and decentralisation — two major features of organisational structure which feature prominently in the literature on organisations in general as well as in recent debates on housing management — were examined in order to see whether they accounted for differences in performance. Each of these will be covered in turn.

Comprehensiveness
Comprehensiveness has two major meanings in this context. Local authorities have been cajoled since the 1960s into providing a comprehensive housing service, by which is usually meant providing a service to all inhabitants of the area and not just to those in council housing. Linked to this has been the move to a comprehensive housing department where all housing functions are controlled and sometimes carried out in the housing department.

Local authorities varied in their attitude to these dimensions of comprehensiveness. Almost all did not confine their activities to council housing, but the relative emphasis on other functions varied considerably. Housing associations, of course, did not have as wide a spread of functions as local authorities because of their concentration on the development and management of their own stock. There was no evidence to show that comprehensiveness in this sense influenced housing management performance.

Comprehensiveness in the sense of carrying out housing management functions in the one local authority department was relatively rare. A majority of departments did not carry out functions such as the payment of housing benefit, repair work and computing activities. 31 per cent did not collect rents themselves; 40 per cent did not carry out rent collecting; and 29 per cent did not carry out the administration of repairs. In general, the large metropolitan authorities tended to be more comprehensive in this sense, whereas the smaller district councils tended to split responsibility for these functions between different departments.

Housing associations were comprehensive in the sense that they were responsible for all housing management functions, but in a small number of instances they contracted out the work itself to another organisation. For example, some contracted out repair work, computing services or staff training.

The degree of comprehensiveness did not seem to influence housing management performance. For comprehensive organisations, the primary management task was to ensure effective communication between staff with different professional backgrounds and different specialist skills. For non-comprehensive organisations, the primary management task was to ensure control over functions they did not themselves carry out. The sample in the DoE research contained examples of organisations failing in this task, leading to unco-ordinated policies and working practices which caused confusion and conflict.

However, there were also examples where functions were successfully carried out by another department or agency in a co-ordinated and effective service with all agencies working to common objectives and where communication between them was good.

On this evidence, the emphasis (much apparent in recent years) on a comprehensive housing department seems to be a mistaken one. Although the comprehensive and non-comprehensive approaches pose different management problems, they can be overcome. Therefore, comprehensiveness does not necessarily lead to effective housing management unless it is managed well, and the same is true of non-comprehensiveness. Both structures can be made to work effectively.

Centralisation and decentralisation

There has been much written in the past few years about decentralisation and many local housing authorities are moving, at varying speeds, in this direction. The topic will be dealt with more fully in Chapters 7, 8 and 10. Suffice it to say here that decentralisation has many different dimensions. It can involve service delivery only — which might better be termed 'deconcentration' — or it may include planning, budgeting and policy-making on varying scales. It may transfer significant powers to representatives of the customers, or it may offer them no more than opportunities for consultation.

In the DoE research there was substantial variation in the scale at which front-line housing management was carried out. Local authorities with area housing management offices varied in the average number of dwellings which were managed from these bases, from 1700 for local authorities with less than 5000 stock, to 7416 for those with more than 30,000 stock. 12 per cent of authorities had neighbourhood offices which administered, on average, 1000 dwellings. Housing associations operated at a smaller scale with 583 dwellings on average per area housing office. Therefore, even decentralised local authorities operated their front-line management at a larger scale than almost all housing associations.

The scale of front-line housing management was associated with the amount of contact between staff and tenants. For example, in decentralised local authorities 70 per cent of tenants said that they had contacted housing management staff in the past year — a figure similar to that of housing associations (73 per cent). However, for centralised local authorities the proportion was approximately half this figure.

The average scale at which front-line housing management operated was associated with the overall size of the housing organisation, i.e. the larger the organisation as a whole the larger the scale of front-line management. Therefore, it was difficult to disentangle the influence of these two different factors on performance. There was substantial variation in the scale of front-line management between organisations of similar overall size, but it was difficult to find any consistent relationship with performance. For example, a number of large metropolitan authorities had decentralised their housing management to the neighbourhood level and some of them performed better than other similar non-decentralised authorities. However, one large metropolitan authority with a decentralised neighbourhood management had the least effective performance (on the indicators used) of all 18 organisations examined.

From this research and a similar study of the management effectiveness of housing co-operatives (Satsangi and Clapham 1990) it is clear that smaller housing management organisations are more effective and more expensive providers. It would seem logical that large scale providers could achieve more effective performance by creating small scale housing management organisations through effective decentralisation and devolution. However, whether the increase in performance can be achieved through more administrative decentralisation, which is the most common form, is open to question. Certainly the evidence from the research is that decentralisation will not automatically transform a poor service into a good one.

Staff motivation

Despite the widespread importance attached by many writers on organisations to staff motivation, and their view that it has a major influence on organisational performance, there has been little attention paid to this aspect of housing organisations. How well motivated are housing staff and how can motivation and, therefore, performance be improved?

There are many differences in approaches towards the motivation of staff and towards ways of improving employee attitudes towards the organisation and their role within it (for a review see Dawson 1986). The earliest approaches of 'scientific management' saw employees as dominated by their economic needs, so that linking pay with performance was all that was required to achieve efficiency. When the importance of economic reward was found to be over-emphasised, social psychologists began a search to identify other universal goals of workers. Following the 'Hawthorn experiments' attention focused on social relations at work and the role of supportive and helpful supervisory practices in increasing productivity.

Others searched for more complex explanations of worker motivation based on the hierarchy of needs devised by Maslow (1943, 1954). He argued that people first sought to satisfy lower-order needs of physical survival, security and affiliation, but once these were satisfied they sought to achieve higher goals of self-actualisation and self-esteem. Herzberg (1966) refined this idea by distinguishing what he called 'motivators' from 'hygienic' factors. The latter, which were similar to Maslow's lower-order needs, only served as sources of dissatisfaction, and once relatively satisfied did not motivate workers to better performance. Positive motivation came from higher level needs or 'motivators' such as achievement, responsibility and recognition.

The problems with such theories are first that they postulate a universal set of motivating factors which have been found not to exist in all situations. In other words, the factors which motivate a particular group of staff in a particular situation must be empirically determined and not assumed. Second, the assumption is made that there is a direct link between satisfaction and performance — that a happy worker is a better worker. However, this may not be the case if, for example, staff do not perceive that appropriate rewards follow from improved effort or performance. Therefore, the link between job satisfaction and increased performance needs to be investigated in each instance rather than simply assumed to exist in all circumstances. Theories of motivation offer some guidance on the factors which may possibly influence staff motivation and performance and which are examined here. Information in this section is largely drawn from a questionnaire survey of 272 staff in 16 of the 18 case study housing organisations. The staff were at all levels of the organisation, although all were directly involved in housing management.

The relationship between job satisfaction and performance in housing organisations is not necessarily a straightforward one. On an organisational level, the average staff ratings of job satisfaction did not show a direct relationship to levels of organisational performance. However, this may be explained by the fact that the motivation of staff is only one factor which influences performance. There was a close relationship between an individual's own rating of job satisfaction and their rating of their own performance. Overall, 27 per cent found their job very satisfying and 61 per cent found it satisfying. Only 13 per cent found their job dissatisfying. However, 51 per cent of those who said they were very satisfied with their jobs rated their own performance in the past year as very good, and 37 per cent rated their performance as good.

In contrast, only 12 per cent of those who were quite or very dissatisfied with their job rated their performance as very good. 27 per cent rated it as adequate, and 15 per cent as poor. Thus, there is some evidence that, in housing organisations, a satisfied worker is a motivated worker.

The factors which led to high or low job satisfaction were many and varied. As predicted by Herzberg, the 'hygienic' factors such as conditions of work and levels of pay seemed to be associated with job dissatisfaction but were not associated with high job satisfaction. 49 per cent of those dissatisfied with their job rated pay as bad, but only 24 per cent of those very satisfied with their job said that the level of pay was very good.

Higher-level needs, such as those associated with social relations at work, were associated with high job satisfaction. Factors such as feeling part of a team, enjoying the company of workmates, and high ratings of morale in the immediate work section were all closely associated with high job satisfaction. Other 'motivators' were measures of 'self-actualisation'; highly satisfied staff were likely to feel stretched by their job and to rate highly the content of the work itself.

Supervision and management control were also important factors. Highly satisfied workers were more likely to rate highly the performance of senior staff in general and the quality of the supervision *they* experienced in particular. They were likely to feel that senior staff gave them sufficient support and encouragement and understood the problems they faced. In addition, highly satisfied staff were more likely to feel that they were consulted about changes in the organisation and that their views were taken into account. In other words, the supportive, democratic supervisory practices stressed by the 'human relations' theorists were important in creating job satisfaction in a housing context.

The extent and type of management control was associated with high job satisfaction and it was also important in determining the strength of the relationship between job satisfaction and motivation. High job satisfaction was associated with management monitoring of performance. Although most monitoring of staff was merely concerned with ensuring that they were at their desks at appropriate times, where monitoring of effort, output and the quality of work took place, it was associated with high job satisfaction. When targets for work activities were set and when staff felt that senior management were concerned about the standards of service provided, job satisfaction was high.

The link between the need for adequate monitoring of the performance of staff and motivation is clear. Staff need to know how well they are performing if they are to be motivated to improve their performance. They must also believe that improved performance will be noticed and will be rewarded. At the moment, few housing organisations monitor the performance of their staff and give them systematic and regular feedback about the level of their performance. 53 per cent of staff in the survey felt that the quality of their performance was not assessed by supervisors and 67 per cent felt that their output was not assessed. 61 per cent felt that the effort they put into their job was not assessed.

The extent of performance monitoring of staff varied considerably between different types of organisations, with housing associations being much more likely to monitor performance than local authorities, and this may be an important factor in their better general organisational performance in housing management. Of course, the monitoring of the performance of individual staff is linked to monitoring of the whole organisation's performance to which we turn in the next section.

In summary, satisfied staff in housing organisations were more highly motivated staff. The factors which created job satisfaction were the 'motivators' highlighted in general theories of motivation such as good social relations at work and self-actualisation. Supervisory practices and management control were important both in leading to higher job satisfaction and in transforming this into better staff performance. These factors have received little attention in housing organisations, but where they have, performance of individual staff and the organisations as a whole were high. The lesson for housing management practice is clear.

Responsiveness

In the systems approach great stress is laid on how organisations interact with their environment. This has been a key feature of much writing in local government management since the early 1970s (see, for example, Stewart 1971 and 1974 and Hambleton 1978), and these ideas have recently been specifically related to housing departments (Stewart 1988). Interaction with its environment is necessary if an organisation is to have an accurate perception of the demands and needs in the environment and the impact of services provided by the organisation. In other words, responsiveness is a key element of performance assessment.

For many local authority housing departments, responding to the environment has largely consisted of keeping councillors happy on the one hand and reading government circulars and legislation on the other. On the whole, judgments about performance were left to councillors. In some cases they had very close links with consumers of the service or were consumers themselves, but in others no such links existed, and the consumer perspective was unheard. Statistical indicators of performance were also few and far between because of poorly developed information systems.

During the 1980s many housing managers and councillors have perceived council housing as being under threat, a view which has been particularly prevalent since the passing of the 'tenants choice' provisions of the Housing Act 1988. The threat posed by this legislation has reinforced the trend towards the definition of tenants as customers and the realisation of the need to ensure that they are satisfied with the service they receive. At the same time, financial pressures on the sector have increased the need to maximise rental income by reducing the number of void properties and keeping rent arrears to a minimum. The result has been increasing interest on the part of housing authorities in monitoring their performance both in order to gain information about the tasks which need to be undertaken and also to gauge how well they are currently performing the tasks and meeting the needs of tenants.

Information of this kind can be gained in four major ways. First, housing agencies are increasingly adopting formal systems of tenant participation in order to improve communication and to gain feedback on performance. Housing organisations in England have a legal duty to counsult tenants on some housing management matters, but many relied on impersonal methods of communication such as letters to individual tenants and through posters, notices or advertisements (Cairncross, Clapham and Goodlad 1990b). While these methods may be effective in providing information to tenants, they are not effective means of eliciting the views of tenants (Cairncross, Clapham and Goodlad 1990a). More personal face-to-face means of communication are needed to achieve this, such as meetings between housing management staff and tenants representatives. In the DoE research, 61 per cent of local authorities and 76 per cent of housing associations had irregular discussion meetings of this kind. About one third of local authorities had a more formalised structure of consultation involving regular discussion meetings or co-option of tenant representatives on to council committees or sub-committees. It was clear that the number of local authorities pursuing tenant consultation had increased substantially in the previous ten years (Cairncross, Clapham and Goodlad 1990b).

Many organisations have sought to consult with tenants but few have attempted to help the tenants movement in order to extend the number of tenants represented or to improve the level of discourse. Only three out of 84 housing associations and 15 per cent of local authorities employed specialist staff to improve tenant participation. Two housing associations and the same number of local authorities provided any kind of help for tenants' groups including premises, starter grants and training.

Tenant participation is not the only way to find out the views of tenants on the standard of service. As in the research reported here, questionnaire surveys of tenants can be useful in identifying problem areas and gauging general views, and discussions with small groups of tenants can provide insight into tenant attitudes. Of course, some staff, particularly those at the lowest organisational levels such as counter clerks and receptionists, are in constant proximity to tenants. Most housing organisations have yet to attempt to channel feedback from low-level staff to management. As a consequence, those who know most about problems when they first arise have no power to improve the situation, and those who have the power are often starved of information until the issue becomes critical.

If information about the effectiveness of services is to influence performance, it has to be communicated to those with the power to change services. In most housing organisations power is held by those at the top of the hierarchical structure, but most communication is from the top down rather than from the bottom up, despite the fact that some of those at the bottom of the hierarchy are more likely to have information about performance because of their greater contact with consumers. However, even their perception is likely to be partial because of the horizons imposed by the limits of their jobs and the lack of horizontal communication between people at similar levels in different parts of the organisation.

Another more traditional source of feedback is through the local authority housing committee or the housing association committee.

Some district councillors have regular contact with tenants. Indeed, some councillors are themselves tenants. Likewise, but to a lesser degree, some housing association committee members can perform a similar function as an important source of negative feedback, for example, by taking up the complaints which are put to them. If problems are dealt with by a committee member on an *ad hoc* basis, the impact on the organisation will be minimal. However, if complaints are used by them to demonstrate the need to change policies then, given the potential power of committee members, this can be one of the most important sources of feedback.

Despite the increasing interest by housing organisations in finding out how tenants view the service provided, it is still apparent that few housing staff have an accurate perception of tenants' views. Moreover, staff working in some kinds of organisations are more likely to have an accurate perception than staff working in others. On average, staff in all kinds of organisations felt that tenants had a less favourable view of the performance than they actually had; perhaps because the only feedback many staff receive is in the form of complaints about the service. However, staff themselves rated the performance of their organisation more highly than did tenants. The exceptions were national and regional housing associations where staff had a more critical view of their organisation's performance than did tenants. In general, staff in small organisations were more in line with tenants' views than staff in larger organisations. These findings emphasise the fact that housing organisations have a long way to go before the rhetoric of 'keeping close to the customer' is put into practice.

Most attention in this section has been focused on tenant assessments of performance, but, as outlined at the beginning of the chapter, there are many statistical indicators which housing organisations can use to gauge their own performance in relation to other organisations and to chart changes over time. Computerised information systems can be programmed to provide regular statistics on matters such as void rates, rent arrears levels, numbers of repairs carried out, numbers of repairs outstanding, and refusal rates for allocation offers. However, in the DoE research it was unusual to find examples where a wide range of information was routinely collected and fed into all levels of decision-making. One exception to this general picture was a regional housing association which used a wide range of such information to monitor performance regularly and to form the basis of performance targets set for work sections and for individual staff. This system improved communication within the association as well as providing feedback on performance to the organisation as a whole and to individual members of staff.

The research reported in this chapter was a first attempt to assess the performance of a wide range of housing organisations. It suffered from a number of problems mostly arising out of its wide scope. Nevertheless, it has provided evidence that performance monitoring is possible and can give important feedback to housing managers. If housing organisations wish to improve their performance to be responsive to changes in their environment, they will need to carry out such exercises as an integral part of their management processes. The many problems inherent in attempts to monitor performance were outlined at the beginning of the chapter, but it was argued that many of these could be overcome by housing organisations if they used a wide variety of methods to gain feedback on performance and treated the results with caution. Performance measurement is not an exact science, but it can provide information which, interpreted correctly, can enable a housing organisation to identify areas where its service can be improved and to keep in touch with the changing needs and demands of consumers.

Conclusion

In his discussion of the 'new management' which he claims is needed in local authority housing departments, Stewart (1988) argues that housing managers as a whole have shown too much concern with advancing the professional credentials of housing management. This was a pursuit thought necessary to improve the image and standing of housing management in local government where it was competing with more established professional groups such as engineers, architects and accountants. Stewart puts forward the view that housing management has no clearly identified professional role and no distinctive professional knowledge. Therefore, he argues that the case for a strong professional identity for housing management should emphasise *management* rather than traditional *professionalism*. However, even the brief review of management outlined here shows that there is a long way to go before this claim will form a strong basis for an increase in status.

Housing organisations have in the past placed little emphasis on management skills. Some attention has been paid to the organisational structure of housing management, particularly through recent moves towards the decentralisation of service provision. However, this emphasis seems to be misplaced because there is no evidence to show a link between organisational structure and performance, and organisations with very similar organisational structures show great differences in their level of performance. In addition, organisational change, through for example the introduction of decentralisation, does not seem to transform automatically a bad service into a good one in the eyes of tenants. This does not mean that in some circumstances organisational structure cannot hinder or help certain management processes. However, a concern with organisational structure without a corresponding concern with organisational processes is not likely to lead to improved service performance.

In this chapter, areas have been highlighted which have received less emphasis in the past. In particular, most housing organisations have paid little attention to the management of their staff resources. Although the commitment and morale of many staff are high, their performance in many cases is hampered by a lack of effective management control and by the absence of feedback on their performance. Many staff did not see a strong link between extra effort on their part and the rewards of promotion or increased organisational performance. In consequence, staff motivation was not as high as it could have been.

Also, despite recent attention directed at the need for housing organisations to 'stay close to the customer' and to monitor performance, many organisations did not have an accurate perception of tenants' views on the standard of service or regularly monitor their performance through the collection and use of statistical indicators.

The need for housing organisations to monitor their performance is the central theme of this chapter. It is essential if housing organisations are to meet the difficult challenge which now confronts them of managing a deteriorating housing stock in the face of severe financial constraints and a changing political climate. Without a full knowledge of how well the organisation is performing and how it is perceived by its tenants, a housing agency does not have any yardstick by which to judge the effectiveness and appropriateness of its organisational structures and management processes. The appraisal of organisational performance is not an easy task. There is no unique 'scientific' way of doing it and, as outlined earlier, there are many problems involved in using the various techniques. Nevertheless, it can be done and is vital if rented housing agencies are to confront the challenge which now faces them.

References

Audit Commission (1986) *Managing the Crisis in Council Housing* (London: HMSO).

Burns T. and Stalker G.M. (1961) *The Management of Innovation* (London: Tavistock).

Cairncross L., Clapham D. And Goodlad R. (1990a) *Tenant Participation in Housing Management* Coventry/Salford: Institute of Housing/Tenant Participation Advisory Service (England).

Cairncross L., Clapham D. And Goodlad R. (1990b) *Patterns of Tenant Participation in Housing Management.* Discussion Paper No 31 Glasgow: Centre for Housing Research.

Dawson D. (1986) *Analysing Organisations* London: Macmillan.

Hambleton R. (1978) *Policy Planning and Local Government* London: Hutchinson.

Haynes R. (1980) *Organisation Theory and Local Government* London: George Allen & Unwin.

Heald D. (1983) *Public Expenditure* Oxford: Martin Robertson.

Herzberg F. (1966) *Work and the Nature of Man* World Publishing Company.

Maclennan D., Clapham D., Goodlad R., Kemp P., Malcolm J., Satsangi M. and Whitefield L (1989) *The Nature and Effectiveness of Housing Management in England* London: HMSO.

Maslow A. (1943) A theory of human motivation *Psychological Review* **50**, 370–96.

Maslow A. (1954) *Motivation and Personality* New York: Harper and Row.

Satsangi M. and Clapham D. (1990) *The Management and Effectiveness of Housing Co-operatives* London: HMSO.

Stewart J. (1971) *Management in Local Government* London: Charles Knight.

Stewart J. (1974) *The Responsive Local Authority* London: Charles Knight.

Stewart J. (1988) *The New Management of Housing Departments* Luton: Local Government Training Board.

Chapter 4
Housing allocation and the role of the public rented sector

Introduction

The allocation of housing stock is one of the major housing management tasks facing any housing organisation and one which has received considerable attention from housing managers and outside observers, including academics and pressure groups. During the 1970s there was even a consensus about the appropriate approach to take, that is allocation of housing on the basis of need (even though there is little agreement about what this means in practice).

However, recent changes in government policy towards the rented sector, particularly the contents of the Housing Act 1988, and the Housing (Scotland) Act 1988, have again brought the issue of housing allocation to the fore. Government policy is intended to break the virtual monopoly of local authorities over rented housing and to create a pluralist rented sector made up of a variety of bodies with a range of objectives and interests. The range of landlords envisaged includes housing associations, residents' co-operatives and housing trusts, as well as some private companies. It is likely that some of these bodies will have quite different objectives from local authorities in terms of their preferred tenant group while others will be driven by activities, such as area renewal, which will affect allocation policy. Therefore, the variety of allocation policies is likely to increase within the rented sector, and the debate about alternative methods of allocation will reopen.

The growing diversity of the rented sector also raises questions about how local authorities can fulfil their legal obligations towards homeless people and satisfy the housing needs of people in their area in a situation where they directly control a declining proportion of the rented stock and, in some cases, own on stock at all.

The aims of this chapter are then first, to examine different approaches to allocation policy in the light of different organisational roles and second, to examine the emerging strategic role of local authorities in taking an overview of allocation policies in a diverse public rented housing sector. The discussion is limited to the public rented sector, by which is meant local authorities, housing associations, co-operatives and quangos such as Scottish Homes and the Northern Ireland Housing Executive — what in other chapters is described as 'social rented housing'. This is partly because of the different objectives held by private profit-making organisations which warrant treatment on their own, but partly because of our belief that, in spite of recent government policy changes, most rented housing will still be provided by public non-profit making bodies. It would be quite unrealistic, however, to regard housing organisations as having complete freedom with respect to allocations. Housing organisations in the 1990s will continue to operate within a variety of constraints concerning their stock and their tenants.

For local authorities, the 1980s has seen the diminution of their stock, especially the more popular types of houses in the better areas. At the same time financial restrictions have limited the ability of authorities to reinvest in older housing and there are a considerable number of properties in need of essential repairs (Cantle 1986). These difficulties, together with house size constraints, mean that it is often difficult to meet the requirements of certain types of applicants. Housing associations, in contrast, have enjoyed an expansion of their property holdings. But individual associations, even if they intend to cater for 'general needs' are rarely in a position where their stock exactly matches the needs of applicants, because of the often opportunist nature of association developments.

The role that housing organisations perform really comes down to what sorts of people they house. Overall demand, and the social structure of applicants, is influenced by what else is available to households of different income groups. It is now quite clear that few households make explicit choices after a comparison of prices and quality in rented housing and owner occupation (Clapham, Kintrea and Munro 1987). Instead, those who can afford it opt almost automatically for home ownership. In these circumstances, providers of public rented housing will tend to attract those on quite low incomes. The exception may be in areas of very high prices in the south east, where housing associations are now seen to have a role in housing wage-earners who would certainly become home owners elsewhere in the country.

These constraints, however, do not mean that there are no choices to make. The continuing excess of demand over supply in most districts and the shortages of certain housing types and sizes already referred to mean that housing authorities and housing associations must implement some sort of rationing, or allocation, system to determine who will be housed.

Approaches to allocation policy

In developing allocation systems, housing organisations are able to exercise a considerable degree of freedom. Local authorities are subject only to the vague wordings of the Housing Act 1957 (in England and Wales) and the Housing (Scotland) Act 1966. Additionally, in Scotland the Tenants' Rights etc. (Scotland) Act 1980 (as amended by the Housing (Scotland) Act 1986 means that authorities must not exclude people from outside their districts and must take no account of the age, income and marital status of applicants, and must disregard ownership of property, in both admitting applicants to the waiting list and in letting houses. Experience of the implementation of the Scottish legislation indicates that differences in law between different parts of the country are not very important and that legislative provisions are often evaded (Shelter (Scotland) 1982).

The most important constraint on local authorities is the Housing (Homeless Persons) Act 1977 (now re-enacted in the Housing Act 1985, and the Housing (Scotland) Act 1987). Although there are important differences in practice between authorities, the legislation places a duty on the authority to house certain categories of homeless people. Because the authority's own housing stock is still usually the most readily available permanent accommodation, the need to rehouse the homeless constrains the authority in the use of its stock. Clearly, the strength of the constraint will vary between authorities and over time according to housing market conditions. In times of scarce and expensive private housing, high rates of poverty and joblessness, and low rates of turnover and new building in the public sector, some authorities have been forced to allocate all or most of their vacant houses to the statutorily homeless. This is particularly the case in inner London where few lettings are now made to people from the waiting list.

Nevertheless, allocation policy and practice are still highly significant in most authorities and in other housing organisations, both in determining who enters the sector and, with increasing importance for tenants as the quality of the stock diversifies, also in determining which households are to get the high quality dwellings and which are to get houses on the 'difficult-to-let' estates. These processes have been described as 'primary' rationing (who enters the sector) and 'secondary' rationing (who gets which house). They can be complex and are often resolved simultaneously in that entry to the sector for any given household will depend upon their willingness to accept the house offered. The outcome of housing allocation systems depends on three inter-related factors: the formally stated policy of the organisation; the way that policy is translated into practice; and the interaction between the household and the allocation process (Clapham and Kintrea 1984). However, in spite of much official advice and academic research on allocation, few housing organisations have given much thought to this area of policy which is crucial in determining the role of the rented sector.

Four main types of formal allocation scheme are usually identified (Shelter (Scotland) 1982, Spicker 1983). These are first, 'merit' schemes where lettings are made on the basis of personal knowledge of each applicant's circumstances, and second, 'date-order' schemes, where houses are let to applicants in chronological order of application. The third type of scheme is 'group' schemes where the waiting list is subdivided into groups of households in similar circumstances with a proportion of lettings going to each. Group schemes are usually combined with a date-order ranking or with the fourth main type, 'points' schemes. Under points schemes, applicants are awarded a number of points according to their housing circumstances. For example, points may be awarded for overcrowding or lack of basic amenities, and applicants are ranked by counting their points.

It is this last type of scheme which has been consistently recommended by official reports (see, for example, Central Housing Advisory Committee 1969, Scottish Housing Advisory Committee 1980, Housing Corporation 1988) and by pressure groups. The argument is that housing need should be paramount, and that by awarding points for different aspects of housing circumstances, a variety of needs can be taken into account systematically in allocation. Merit schemes may reflect need but are rejected because they can be arbitrary and unfair and they lack visible justice. Date-order schemes are rejected because they are not a means of measuring housing need, while group schemes are not favoured because they are often considered to be difficult to implement and to understand, particularly where the number of groups is large.

The discussion about the advantages of these different systems has rarely been associated with any consideration of the role of the housing organisations, even though allocation systems heavily influence it. An exception is the discussion by English (1982), who has suggested that the ultimate logic of the move towards allocation according to need by public housing agencies is the emergence of a purely welfare role for the public housing sector, whereby it will only shelter households who are unable to get any other type of housing. He argues that, in order to maintain a sector which has an ability to attract a wide range of social groups, allocation according to need should be tempered by the allocation of acceptable accommodation on demand to households with the ability to choose. This would imply wide differences in rent levels so that households with higher incomes would be able to choose to rent an attractive dwelling in the public sector. Other authors, particularly from within the Labour Party, have also argued for the strengthening of public housing by an increased emphasis on choice (Raynsford 1984).

Another view of the future of allocations policy has emerged from ideas about decentralised housing management and tenant participation which are coming to the fore in several large authorities. This view is that the unpopularity of local government services, including council housing, derives from rigid, centralised, uniform policies which cannot meet the requirements of different neighbourhoods and communities within large cities. Instead, it is argued that local authority functions must be decentralised to an estate or neighbourhood level. Allocation policy should therefore be devised and implemented at the local level and respond to the needs and preferences of residents of those areas.

Each of these three versions of desirable allocation policy (allocation according to need, allocation on demand, and local lettings) are now considered in turn.

Allocation according to need

In the 1980s, by means of a combination of housing market changes and policy changes at national and local level, the public sector, and particularly local authority housing has been seen to be moving towards becoming a 'residualised' or welfare sector, because it is seen as the prime means within the housing system of catering for need (Forrest and Murie 1983, Malpass 1983, Murie 1983). To some extent this may be considered to be desirable in that the least well-off people are provided with basically sound housing with all amenities. If meeting the needs of the less well-off is considered to be the main role of the public sector, it can be argued that allocation must be made purely on the basis of need which, indeed, is a principle that commands wide agreement.

Although there are many organisations which still operate merit and date-order allocation schemes which are not systematically based on need, over the past twenty years there has been a gradual shift to needs-based systems by local authorities. The majority of councils in a survey conducted by Spicker (1983) in England and Wales used a points or groups plus points system based loosely on need, the exceptions being a handful of rural authorities controlling a very small housing stock.

In a survey carried out for the DoE (Centre for Housing Research 1989) it was found that 55 per cent of local authorities used a points scheme and 10 per cent used a groups plus points system. The majority of the others used a system based on date order. However, housing associations have been slower to adopt points schemes. In the same survey it was found that only 22 per cent of associations had a points scheme and only 4 per cent had a groups with points system. 43 per cent had less formal allocation systems which, although usually intended to be based on housing need, were discretionary or merit systems which depended on decisions by housing managers on the basis of the circumstances of each individual case.

Despite the popularity of the concept of need in allocation policy, difficulties arise when it is put into practice. First, there is the question of how housing needs are defined and identified. Households' circumstances are usually assessed according to professionally-designed criteria which can be readily measured, such as the degree of overcrowding or the lack of basic amenities. In most cases little account can be taken of how the household views its own circumstances, even though it may place rather different values upon the same set of circumstances. In other words, the assessment of need for allocation purposes derives from the concept of 'normative' need rather than 'felt' need, to use Bradshaw's (1972) terminology.

Second, there is a difficulty in creating a balance between the different needs experienced by different households. As Raynsford neatly illustrated:

> How does one decide the respective degree of need between a person who has been living for a month in deplorably overcrowded conditions and another who has endured slightly less severe overcrowding for ten years? ... Should one give priority to a tenant living under the potential threat of homelessness in an insecure private sector letting, or to a secure tenant whose life is made miserable by subtle harassment and poor conditions?
>
> (Raynsford 1984, p121)

These dilemmas often lead to apparently arbitrary decisions about the weighting of different aspects of need and, as Spicker (1983) has demonstrated, households in identical circumstances will be very likely to be given different priorities by different landlords. As Spicker concludes:

> Points schemes are a method of achieving consistency while taking different factors into account but they are not themselves a guarantee of fairness.
>
> (Spicker 1983, p 17)

The third problem is that allocation according to need takes no account of the circumstances of individual neighbourhoods. For example, a neighbourhood may already have a large number of particular household groups, such as young families or older people, and it may not be for the good of that area to further increase these numbers by letting yet more houses to families or to older people. Very few allocation schemes formally take into account the local social structures that are created by their operation, even though all allocation systems have social consequences.

Finally, many housing organisations do not wish to house only those most in need. Even in council housing, although it is increasingly residualised, it is not yet performing *merely* a welfare role. In many local authorities, the broad range of social groups already in council housing belies total residualisation. Early commentary on the residualisation thesis explicitly or implicitly compared the British situation with the public sector in the USA (for example, Karn 1982), but it is clear that British council housing is not yet entirely a stigmatised ghetto for the very poor as it is in the USA. There are some people entering the sector who have a degree of choice and want to live in a council house, and there are many who are already council tenants and who have aspirations to move to a better house or neighbourhood within the public sector. Allocation according to need alone overrides these significant considerations. Furthermore, apart from the difficulties in establishing a needs-based allocation policy, major problems also arise in the practice of allocation according to need, which can be illustrated by a discussion of allocations in Glasgow.

Glasgow District Council operates a computerised allocation scheme based on points which was introduced in 1980 'in order to allocate houses fairly and efficiently according to housing need' (Glasgow District Council 1984, p 51). Applicants are allowed to express preferences both for the type of house and the area they want, and there are 36 permutations of house type and the area available to each applicant. In effect there is a queue for each housing type and each area with applicants listed in order of number of points. When a particular property is ready for letting, the appropriate queue is called up through the computer system and, in principle, the house is offered to the first applicant on the list, that is the applicant with most points. This arrangement is complicated by the presence of nine priority categories which override the priorities afforded by the general waiting list. These categories include applicants with exceptional needs, such as rooflessness, and applicants whose transfer would result in a 'gain' for the local authority, such as the vacation of a popular dwelling. Applicants may reject as many offers as they wish without affecting their place in the queue. The Glasgow scheme has been likened to a market with points as currency and is very close to the type of allocation scheme which the Labour Party (1981) has argued should be 'carefully examined' by other local authorities.

At first sight the system appears to be a good attempt at reconciling allocation according to need with the ability of applicants to exercise some choice about their housing. However, at a formal level the Glasgow scheme falls short of the idea of allocation according to need on two counts. First, points are given for 'local connection', that is previous residence in a particular area of Glasgow, a policy which is designed to strengthen communities. Second, the allocation scheme gives a considerable number of points for waiting time. New applicants are awarded points for the length of time they have been on the waiting list and transfer applicants for the length of time they have lived in their present accommodation. In some cases waiting time reflects the length of time spent in housing need and as such can be considered to be a legitimate concern, but because waiting time points may be accumulated by any applicant this is by no means always the case.

The Glasgow scheme essentially serves to determine the secondary allocation of dwellings, because the points held by a household effectively indicate the quality of housing it can hope to achieve. The queues for each combination of house type and area vary considerably in length and in the number of points held by applicants at their head. If a household has a high number of points it can join the queue for a popular house type and area with an expectation of reaching the head of the list. On the other hand, a household which has a small number of points will not join a popular queue unless it is able to wait for a very long time before being rehoused. In most cases a well-informed household with few points will tend to join a queue for a less popular house type or area where the chances of being rehoused in the short run are greater.

In a system like this, existing council tenants who want to transfer to another house and new applicants are treated in broadly the same way. Both of these groups are assessed according to their housing situation and awarded points accordingly; they both express their preferences for area and house type and join the queue in competition with all other applicants. However, if transfer applicants were treated *exactly* the same as new applicants, the points totals of those wanting to transfer would tend to be rather low because, by definition, all transfer applicants are already householders in the public sector and the house in which they live is usually considered to be adequate, however unpopular particular houses or estates may be. Small points totals, perhaps reflecting a changed household since the original tenancy was taken up would only give them the option, in most cases, of a transfer to another unpopular area. Meanwhile, those in greatest need not already in the council sector with a high level of points would exclusively attain the most popular estates. In addition, people wanting council tenancies, but not in great need, would be deterred from taking a house if they had little chance of moving to a better area or house in the future.

In Glasgow, because of the potential difficulties of a system based primarily on need, residents of some of the less popular areas have exerted pressure through the political system to ensure their points totals are sufficient to enable them to make up-market transfers. The consequence of this pressure is the inclusion of factors which many would not regard as housing need in the points calculation, particularly 'local connection' and waiting time, with the result that transfer applicants are able to compete for the better quality dwellings. In a survey carried out in 1983 (see Clapham and Kintrea 1986a, 1986b) 43 per cent of successful new applicants and 56 per cent of transfer applicants had points for waiting which made up more than half of their total points. Indeed, since the time of the survey, the system has been revised to give even more priority to long-standing council tenants seeking a transfer, and it was reported that, in 1985, as many as 99 per cent of transfer applicants were claiming waiting time points compared to 32 per cent of new applicants (Glasgow District Council 1986). In a review of the allocation system in 1987, among other changes, it was suggested that even more priority should be given to transfer applicants. So far this has not been implemented because of opposition, both from within the council and outside, from those who believe that it would severely disadvantage new entrants. But as Cooper (1988) argues there is likely to be a general trend towards policies which favour existing tenants. The 'tenants choice' provisions of the 1988 Housing Acts may encourage landlords to adopt such policies to please and retain their tenants and, with them, their stock. Of course, such a strategy could backfire if tenants became so pleased that they decided to exercise their right to buy.

The Glasgow District Council allocation scheme, like many others, is both a compromise between different concepts of need and between the needs and aspirations of various groups of tenants or would-be tenants. It illustrates that political pressures and a recognition of the legitimate aspirations of existing council tenants may make pure needs-based allocation systems impractical. Indeed, the Scottish Housing Advisory Committee (1980) and Raynsford (1984), among others, have stressed the desirability of allowing for preferences as well as need in allocation schemes. In a purely needs-based system, where the number of points determines secondary rationing, in theory those most in need would get the best houses. This is intellectually as well as politically problematic unless it can be successfully argued that those living in the very worst circumstances should be compensated by being awarded the best council houses. Furthermore, such a system, because of its complete reliance on measures of normative need, could be seen as inherently paternalistic giving no weight to the needs felt by applicants.

The second main obstacle to an allocation policy based entirely on need is that, even if such a policy could be agreed, it is unlikely that it would operate in the intended way in practice. First, in Glasgow there is a tendency for many of those most in need to ask for less popular areas (Kintrea and Clapham 1986). Second, as Henderson and Karn (1984, 1987) have shown from their study of Birmingham, allocators tend to make discriminatory allocations based on suppositions about applicants' status and behaviour in order to match vacant dwellings with suitable applicants. Third, unless rigid restrictions are imposed, those in a small degree of need will turn down unsuitable houses and wait for better opportunities in other areas. Fourth, from the landlord's point of view, there is a compromise to be found between the efficiencies of the letting process, and the basis of the allocation scheme. A recent study of housing management has shown that needs-based points systems are associated with higher rates of refusals and higher administrative costs than other allocation systems (Centre for Housing Research 1989). Discretionary systems, often based upon a list of relevant needs as used by many housing associations, were found to be cheaper to administer and were associated with lower refusal rates. The reason for this seems to be their capacity to match the needs and aspirations of tenants more closely with the available stock. In housing organisations which have marked variations in the quality of stock available, there is always a requirement to find tenants for the less popular areas, unless there is a disregard of any priority to minimise vacancies. To offer tenancies on run-down estates, with little possibility of subsequent transfer, to relatively comfortably housed applicants who are not in a high degree of need would be likely to result in slow re-letting rates and increasing vacancy levels.

The third main problem with allocation according to need by means of points systems is that the most developed systems which attempt to cater for a great range of types of need, and create a balance between competing applicants can be overly complicated. To use the example of Glasgow again, it was acknowledged by the Council that:

our system has become extremely complex and difficult to understand, particularly for our customers.

(Glasgow District Council 1987 p1)

A corollary of such convolution and lack of understanding is that tenants do not view such points systems as fair. In a recent study of housing management points systems, they were seen, on the whole, as less fair than other types of system (Centre for Housing Research 1989). This is likely to further enhance political difficulties in promoting the position of new applicants in need over that of those requesting transfers.

In essence then, 'allocation according to need' is always likely to be a slogan rather than an actuality because, in practice, it is tempered by the requirements of political compromise and administrative efficiency. However, compromise tends to lead to an allocation system with a variety of aims, some of which may be unstated. These systems tend to be difficult to understand and often produce an outcome which is difficult to justify according to any conception of fairness.

Given the bad housing circumstances of many low-income people, it would be unacceptable for public organisations to abandon the position of allocation according to need. Nevertheless, in an organisation where the social composition of the tenants indicates that it is still performing more than a residual role, and for supporters of public rented housing who believe that the housing circumstances of the poorest people will be irreparably damaged if public rented housing becomes solely a welfare sector, to continue to pursue solely the goal of allocation according to need is surely misconceived. At present, a further push in this direction can only confirm the view that public housing is only for the most deprived and will do nothing to assist the aspirations of better off tenants.

Public housing on demand

If administrative allocation based on need is seen to be a mechanism which tends to confirm the welfare role of council housing, the idea of public housing on demand is held to be able to counter the trend towards residualisation. In this there are two main approaches. First, the view that administrative allocation schemes should be replaced by price rationing and, second, that administrative schemes should be reformed to increase the degree of choice available to the consumer. Advocates of price rationing (Grey, Hepworth and Odling-Smee 1981, English 1982, Webster 1981) argue that rents in most authorities bear little relationship to housing popularity and should be reformed in order to reflect differential demand. This implies that the rents of the most popular houses would be raised until all excess demand was eliminated while the rents of 'difficult-to-let' property would be decreased until the house could be let. Thus the perverse situation would be ended where some relatively highly rented but unattractive houses lie empty while there are long queues for more popular houses at lower rents. Households would be free to select the particular type and location of house that best suited their aspirations and their income.

It is not suggested by its proponents that market pricing should be implemented without a package of housing finance reforms. These would be aimed at reforming the distortions created by differential subsidies to the owner-occupied and public sectors, and at protecting low income households from some of the disadvantages they would suffer in any system of allocation based on ability to pay. Thus it is envisaged that there would be a 'tenure neutral' finance policy and a means-tested and needs-related housing allowance scheme for all householders, including owner-occupiers (see National Federation of Housing Associations 1985).

Since allocation under a pricing scheme would be based on choice, a housing allowance system would have to be devised to ensure that even the least well-off would receive less than 100 per cent of their housing costs, unlike the present housing benefit system. It is suggested that, for the poorest households, rent up to a basic level (for a given household size) would be fully rebated, while rent above this level would be paid directly by the tenant. Otherwise, a large percentage of households would be able to meet any rent cost, however high, and outbid everyone else, thereby making nonsense of price rationing.

Currently, changes in financial regimes for both local authorities (in England and Wales) and for housing associations are likely to introduce an element of differential pricing within housing organisations' stock, and with it the possibility that ability to pay may begin to play a part in the allocation process for public housing.

For local authorities the Housing and Local Government Act 1990 introduces a single subsidy to replace housing subsidy, rate fund contributions, the housing element of rate support grant and housing benefit subsidy. The new subsidy will take into account a notional rent increase and it is clear that part of the Government's intention is to persuade local authorities to set rents which more closely reflect market values. Indeed, any substantial upward movement of rents inevitably pushes local authorities to justify their rent schemes, and seems likely to result in greater rent differentials. Ultimately this means that some council housing will be priced out of reach of those low-income tenants who are not protected by housing benefit.

In the housing association sector there is similar pressure. Since the inception of mixed-funding arrangements for the finance of new developments in the housing association sector, housing associations now establish their own rents, partially reflecting the costs of development. One factor in obtaining approval for new projects from the Housing Corporation, Scottish Homes or Homes for Wales is that rent structures are scrutinised by the funders with a view to their appropriateness. This has opened up a debate about differential pricing within the association sector, with property points systems and capital values being the front-runners as methods of setting rents. It is possible, therefore, that in tandem with the general increase in rents expected under mixed-funding, there will begin to emerge a degree of price-rationing in the housing association sector as higher amenity properties begin to have their rents pushed up. As with local councils, this may result in some applicants on low incomes but without a cushion of housing benefit finding rents difficult to afford.

The overwhelming criticism of market schemes, whether achieved as a deliberate result of policy by housing organisations or by means of subsidy manipulation by government, is that they would inevitably strengthen the relationship between housing quality and income. Therefore, although a public sector containing a broader range of income groups might be created, even greater social segregation between areas of different popularity would be likely to occur. It is already the case under administrative allocation schemes that there is a strong relationship between income and housing quality (Clapham and Kintrea 1986a, 1986b). English (1982) argues that a continuation of this is the price which would have to be paid for retaining and attracting tenants with higher incomes, but there are many who would oppose such blatant institutional inequality within publicly supported rented housing that has done so much to break the link between housing quality and income.

Raynsford (1984) accepts the analysis of the proponents of market pricing with regard to the difficulty of meeting both needs and aspirations within a rental sector. However, this approach is to argue for the incorporation of a greater degree of choice within administrative rationing systems. This stems from the desire of the Labour Party to offer policies which can compete with the Right's view that only market systems of resource allocation can offer real freedom of choice. Indeed, the fact that a poll found that 45 per cent of respondents believed that councils should provide housing for anyone who wants it suggests that this ought to be a popular policy (Griffiths and Holmes 1985).

It is argued that a greater degree of choice could be achieved in public housing by opening every authority's and association's waiting list to all, by offering all households, even those in severe need, including the homeless, a real range of houses to choose from, and by allowing an unlimited number of refusals to be made without penalty. For existing tenants, choice could be increased further by enabling a transfer to take place to any other vacant house both within and outside the local authority's or association's stock. An additional suggestion is made by Harrison (1983) who argues that prospective tenants be offered several houses simultaneously rather than being able to turn down houses sequentially with no knowledge of what may be available from future offers. These administrative changes would be supported by a realignment of the relationship between the landlord and its tenants which should pervade all aspects of the housing system:

> The aim should be that the applicant/tenant is seen as the customer whose needs and aspirations are to be met by the public authority providing the service rather than as a supplicant who should be grateful for whatever home the authority has decided is appropriate for him or her.
>
> (Raynsford 1984, p 127)

Although this approach is intuitively appealing, it is only likely to be feasible in areas where there is a large public sector, with a considerable range of house types and locations and a considerable turnover of lettings. Even in very large local authorities or housing associations, where some degree of choice could be offered, the proposals fail to provide a realistic solution to the conflict between needs and aspirations that is a central issue in most allocation systems. Indeed, the increased emphasis on choice will surely mean that those who are least able to choose, notably the poor and badly housed, will be disadvantaged. In our research on the allocation system in Glasgow (which is open to all, incorporates a high degree of choice of house and location, and allows households to reject an unlimited number of offers) it was found that choice could be more readily exercised by some households than others. Higher income households, and those who were better housed prior to moving, were able to wait for a long period and reject offers of houses that they considered to be unsatisfactory. The result was that they achieved better quality accommodation than badly housed and poorer households who waited for shorter periods and accepted offers more readily (Clapham and Kintrea 1986a). It is difficult to conceive of an allocation system which would offer more choice without intensifying this situation.

A further set of ideas that emerged from the Labour Housing Group and is relevant here is the 'right to rent' (Merrett 1985, Griffiths and Holmes 1985), a slogan which was later adopted by a Conservative Housing Minister to promote a totally different package of policies. In its original conception its proponents proposed that there should be a statutory right to rent a house in the local authority sector, which could be exercised by most private tenants and owner-occupiers by insisting on the municipalisation of their houses and, through a considerable extension of the current homelessness legislation, by households in severe housing need.

These proposals are innovative and far-reaching but lack practicality. They would be likely to have the result of putting considerable strain on the council sector while drying up the supply of private rented housing, and could only work following a great expansion of public building or acquisition. Although the 'right to rent' could improve access to good housing for some people, there is a danger, shared with all other concepts of 'normative need', that others would be relegated to a long waiting list while the authority's efforts were absorbed in rehousing those in statutorily defined need.

More important, the 'right to rent' is unlikely to be able to solve some of the most pressing issues in housing allocation. Because the municipalisation of privately rented and owner-occupied houses would be led by existing householders, it would not increase the supply of lets for others in housing need. Thus the purpose-built council sector would still be the general destination for the homeless and other severely deprived groups, a situation which would do nothing to alleviate the 'residualisation' of the traditional council sector. Moreover, proponents of the 'right to rent' have avoided the question of secondary allocation and the aspirations of transfer applicants, which are two of the most important areas to be tackled in the consideration of allocation policy.

All of the proposals for housing on demand, then, depend on major changes in the provision of housing but it is also far from clear, even if such changes could be implemented, that allocation on demand would be realistic and fair.

Local lettings

Over the past ten years there has been a growing body of opinion which has argued that services, and public housing in particular, are not best organised in a centralised way (Donnison 1983, Wright, Stewart and Deakin 1984, Labour Co-ordinating Committee 1984, Power 1987). Instead, it is argued that housing management should be carried out at local level and that residents should exercise more control over their own housing.

The case for local lettings is based on the idea that, instead of futile attempts to meet the requirements of the whole of a local authority's area or all of the stock of a large housing association, allocation policy should be decentralised to meet the needs of particular local areas, or even particular streets or buildings. At present, the social consequences of allocation policy are usually the concentration of similar types of households in particular areas. In a system of local allocation the varying roles which the public sector plays in different localities could be taken into account and, in line with much current thinking, the process of defining policy could have a much greater local input from tenants. The precise way in which a local allocation policy is achieved is, then, likely to vary markedly because of the different circumstances of individual areas and the varying ideas of their residents.

Adoption of the practice of local lettings is not necessarily associated with particular kinds of housing organisation. In other words, the creation of a pluralistic public rented sector with more housing associations may not necessarily lead to more 'local lettings' because these agencies may not adopt allocation policies which are adapted to the needs of local areas. On the other hand, a large local authority or housing association may decentralise allocation policy in such a way as to allow local lettings. It is the local scale of management decision making which is the important precondition for local lettings rather than the type of housing organisation. Also important is the commitment of the organisation to the ideas of 'neighbourhood' or 'community', and the desire to respond flexibly to the needs of local areas through the provision of an appropriate service.

There are several variants of local allocation which are now being developed. They include the local administration of lettings on 'difficult-to-let' estates, the use of computer technology to decentralise lettings to local offices with the ability to fine-tune a centralised policy and, most importantly, the development of separate lettings policies for local areas. These will now be considered in turn.

On many deprived and run-down estates, including some of those which are part of the government sponsored Priority Estates Project (Power 1982, 1987), the administration of lettings is carried out in an office on the estate. The principal aims are to accelerate the letting process, to eliminate vacancies and to reduce turnover: in a situation of very low demand it makes little sense to adhere strictly to an allocation policy which is designed to distinguish between competing needs and demands. With the abandonment of the formal policy, empty houses are available quickly to anyone who wants them, including those who would be excluded by the ordinary allocation system. Other advantages that are claimed for the landlord are cost savings, an increase in rental income and a reduction in vandalism. The local administration of lettings also cuts out the doubt that applicants may have about the type or quality of housing that will be offered and the landlord's misgivings about whether offers will be accepted. Local lettings on a particular estate provide a safeguard in that those who apply will actually want to accept a house there, thus easing administrative problems and strengthening commitment to the estate.

Several local authorities have used computerised administration systems for rents, repairs and allocations to enable a centralised system to be operated from local offices. The 'going local' policies at Walsall and Islington, for example, rely on the use of such systems. Glasgow District Council has operated a computerised allocation system since 1980 and all aspects of housing allocation are handled by area offices, although the council has not decentralised to the same degree as some other authorities. However, Glasgow moved away from a totally unified allocation system and refined its information base about particular estates or letting sub-areas, so that variations on the centrally-defined policy can be incorporated. Rules defined by local management about allocations, such as the definition of dwellings not suitable for older people or for young families, are incorporated in the computerised system in order to match applicants more closely with suitable dwellings and to influence the population mix in particular areas. While this modification is a useful management tool, its drawback is that it has made an already complex allocation system even more difficult to understand.

The third and most interesting variation on local allocation is the development of allocation policies, in consultation with residents, which operate only in particular small areas. In the West of Scotland local control in this way has been led by the community-based housing associations whose main task has been to rehabilitate nineteenth century tenements within closely defined Housing Action Areas (Armstrong 1983). Allocation policies, and all other areas of activity, are determined by an elected management committee of local residents and, although concern was expressed previously that many associations had not established a formal allocation policy, this situation has now been remedied. A review of the subject (Nugent 1985) shows that the allocation policies of community-based housing associations are generally based on two main criteria, the applicant's housing need (mostly defined by normative physical conditions) and his or her connection with the association's area. Because local connection is usually used as a balancing factor where needs are similar, such policies as these not only meet the housing needs of applicants but also ensure that most of those who become tenants have a commitment to the association's area.

In the local authority sector in Glasgow there have been several attempts to develop local lettings initiatives (Glasgow District Council 1984). Some of these are management initiatives aimed at increasing the take-up of lets on run-down estates, but there are also some interesting examples of local lettings where residents have been involved in determining policies aimed at creating more balanced communities and building close family and neighbourhood ties. This is a reaction to the city-wide policy in which local connection does not feature strongly and which tends to lead to concentrations of similar types of households in each housing scheme. Some of the most interesting of the local lettings schemes devised so far are the types developed by the residents of tenant management co-operatives. The Whiterose Co-operative in Glasgow's East End is an example. Whiterose is a popular estate of tenement flats built in the 1920s where, under an agency agreement with the council, a tenants' co-operative is responsible for the management of the housing stock. This not only includes day-to-day repairs but also taking decisions on the allocation of 50 per cent of the dwellings that become vacant on the estate. The objective of the co-operative's policy is to increase the number of young people on the estate (70 per cent of residents were pensioners) in order to add drive and vigour to the community and to provide support for older people. Under the city-wide allocation scheme, flats in Whiterose were not readily available to young people with relatively few points. Instead, they were forced to move away from their parents on the estate with the result that the older people often felt isolated and lonely. Under the new scheme priority is given to strengthening community ties: 70 per cent of co-operative's lettings are made to people with an immediate family connection in the area, 30 per cent to others. To ensure that lets are made fairly, all applicants from each of these groups are taken in points order from the council's waiting list.

A less successful example of locally controlled lettings in Glasgow is illustrated in the case of the Kingsridge-Cleddans initiative in Drumchapel where, since 1983, allocations have been made by a local management committee consisting of officials and residents. This was the first of a handful of local lettings policies designed to respond to local needs in less popular areas of the city. In Kingsridge-Cleddans the difficulty was partly the opposite to that of Whiterose because there were many lets made to young people, high child densities and many difficult-to-let flats. There were, however, similar concerns about population imbalance and a lack of neighbourhood ties.

Under the local policy the council's points system is retained as the means of ordering the queue for flats but two thirds of vacancies are allocated to applicants from the Kingsridge-Cleddans area. In addition, there is an attempt to create a balanced community within tenement buildings. When a vacancy arises, the management committee reviews the present household composition of the building and decides what sort of household would be a suitable complement. The difficulty that emerges is that, in spite of considerable physical and management changes in Kingsridge-Cleddans, it remains an unpopular area so that in many cases it is not possible to find suitable tenants. For example, many long-standing residents looking for a transfer have enough points from the city-wide allocation system to move to a more popular area. Although there has been a substantial reduction of lets to homeless people, the local lettings policy has not been entirely successful in altering the social balance of the area and is unlikely to make such progress without further measures to increase demand.

A case often made by critics of local lettings is that residents will work to exclude 'problem' tenants and create elitist ghettos. The examples of local lettings schemes we have discussed all have the safeguard that a proportion of lettings continue to be made through the city-wide system. The council has nomination rights for a negotiable proportion of housing association vacancies, and a proportion of lets at Whiterose and Kingsridge-Cleddans is still made to non-locals. Furthermore, the charge that the decisions of local residents will be necessarily discriminatory is in no way proven: it is clear that these local letting schemes have been intended to operate within an overall framework of allocation according to need.

So far, local lettings only affect a very small proportion of the housing stock. Therefore, they do not yet compromise the ability of housing authorities to meet housing need or their statutory obligations to rehouse the homeless. However, as the number of local lettings schemes multiplies and there is an increase in new forms of rented housing created from former council housing, such as housing trusts and co-operatives, new difficulties may emerge. The danger is that, unless nomination rights are agreed with the new landlords, the ability of the homeless or those without local connection to get good rented housing is likely to be threatened.

In conclusion, these difficulties are not insuperable and local lettings schemes are an important new development and an essential part of any plan to bring about real local control and resident involvement in housing management. Because of the role of allocation policy in determining the character of neighbourhoods it is important that policies are devised which reflect local concerns and needs.

The need for monitoring

The previous sections have illustrated three ways in which public housing can be viewed, and the appropriate allocation policy for each of these roles has been discussed. The aim has not been to provide an exhaustive list of all possible roles or to recommend a best allocation policy for each. Rather the aim has been to show the important links between ideas about the role of the sector and the types of allocation policy, and to encourage discussion of both together.

Whichever form allocation policy takes, there is a need for housing organisations to monitor the operation and the outcomes of their policies. Otherwise, policy making will continue to exist within a framework of uncertainty and obscurity, which is no basis for re-forming allocation policy with positive objectives in mind. There has been long debate about ethnic monitoring in local authority allocation policies, but research suggests that many local authorities and housing associations either do not keep ethnic records at all, or fail to monitor the records which they have (Association of Metropolitan Authorities 1985, Dalton and Daghlian 1989). In order to see whether they are achieving their objectives, all housing organisations must monitor systematically the composition of their waiting lists and the social outcomes of their allocation process. This monitoring should not be confined to the race of their applicants and tenants, but should also be extended to include their incomes, socio-economic status and demographic characteristics. Not only will this help to ensure a proper understanding of the reasons for inequality of outcomes in the public sector allocation process but it will also provide an essential database for assessing the social implications of changes in allocation policy. Many local authorities and housing associations already collect household information as an ordinary part of the application for rehousing and an increasing number of organisations are adopting computerised systems for the administration of housing allocations. It would be a lost opportunity if this information and these systems were not designed and used for monitoring and planning purposes.

Local authorities have responsibilities which stretch further than the management of their own stock. With the growth in importance of other public landlords such as housing associations, and the disposal of their entire stock by some local authorities, these responsibilities assume considerable importance. At the very least, local authorities have to carry out their statutory duties to ensure that some homeless people receive permanent accommodation. We would argue the their responsibilities should be much more widely defined because they are best placed to be able to take an overall view of housing need in their area and to take appropriate action or encourage other agencies to do so. In order to achieve this, local housing authorities must have the ability to assess need in their area and to monitor the performance of other housing agencies. In addition, they need some mechanism for influencing the actions of these agencies through, for example, nomination or referral arrangements in which they can put forward tenants to other agencies.

Nomination agreements already exist between local authorities and many housing associations, but it seems that they are often not given the importance which they warrant. There is not much information on local authority nominations, but NFHA information suggests that in England 31 per cent of allocations came from this source (Stearn 1988). Niner and Karn (1985) suggested that housing associations varied markedly in their practice, with some taking no nominations at one extreme and, at the other, some only housing people from the local council's list. They also noted that often it was unclear whether local authorities played an active part in the letting process by seeking vacancies. Informal sources suggest that it is sometimes the case that local authorities do not nominate as many tenants as they are able to, and housing associations sometimes refuse to accept the nomination of people who do not meet their own allocation criteria. Stearn (1988) indicates that very few homeless people are rehoused by housing associations, but whether this is because of discrimination, a view that the homeless cannot afford the rents, or the unsuitability of associations' stock, is hard to say. There are also some administrative problems such as an inability or reluctance on the part of local authorities to provide housing associations with up-to-date and accurate lists of prospective tenants who want the kind of property and location that associations can offer. These failures almost certainly stem from the use of formalised points schemes geared to the characteristics of authority's own stock. It is worth noting that points schemes in general have been shown to create problems of administrative efficiency and high refusal rates for local authorities themselves. A precondition of progress in nomination agreements would perhaps be the creation of more discriminating and flexible systems for organising a waiting list by local authorities to better match the rehousing opportunities available.

Without the existence of effective nomination arrangements with other agencies, local authorities will find it increasingly difficult to fulfil their legal obligations towards homeless people and will also find themselves increasingly powerless to influence the future direction of the rented sector as a whole. The creation of effective nomination arrangements is the area of allocation policy which demands most attention in the next few years.

One important area to examine is the current power of local authorities to make nominations and to monitor the lettings policies of other agencies. The lettings policies of housing associations are monitored by the Housing Corporation (or by Scottish Homes or Housing for Wales) but these large centralised bodies can only have the knowledge to monitor policies against a general ideal. They cannot possibly have the knowledge of local housing needs to assess how well the policy meets those needs. Local authorities are in a better position to have this knowledge, but currently lack any effective means of ensuring that housing associations take this into account. If the stock available to local authorities to meet housing need declines further, then such powers may well be necessary to ensure that some needs are not ignored completely.

Conclusions

In the final analysis, the form of allocation policy and, by implication, the role of the public rented sector, will undoubtedly vary according to local politics and the character of local housing needs and resources. In practice, because local housing authorities have limited capital and revenue budgets and many lack managerial capacity, their ability to alter allocation schemes is likely to be restricted to marginal changes in the short run. Many authorities may see the three approaches discussed here not as immediately achievable alternatives, but as contrasting emphases or directions of policy which can be pursued and combined in different ways. From this perspective, change is likely to be incremental and slow. However, it is still essential to consider what sort of public housing sector is desirable if gradual change is not to be confused and contradictory.

At present, the emphasis in allocation policy, both as recommended and in practice, is on allocation according to need, and the role of public housing as a welfare sector is to the fore. With a sustained requirement for rented housing from people who cannot afford to buy, it is inevitable and desirable that allocation according to need should continue to be the predominant approach.

At the same time, the increased emphasis on decentralisation and tenant participation which is apparent in many housing organisations is likely to result in a growth in local lettings policies as the effects of centralised and standardised allocation schemes are understood by tenants. However, it is highly unlikely that many of these local schemes, if they apply to stock still owned by the local authority, will operate completely independently of the authority-wide system.

Any widespread movement towards market pricing as the principal operating principle for allocations policy in the public sector is unlikely. Fundamental changes in housing finance, in the output of public housing and in other aspects of the housing system would be needed to make it work. However, current changes in funding regimes, particularly with respect to the housing association sector, are introducing elements of market pricing which may overlap needs-based approaches. But, for mainstream public housing, as long as shortages persist, particularly of high quality dwellings, some kind of administrative rationing system will continue to be necessary.

References

Armstrong D (1983) (ed.) *Miles Better, Miles to Go* Glasgow: Housetalk
Association of Metropolitan Authorities (1985) *Housing and Race: Policy and Practice of Local Authorities* London: AMA.
Bradshaw J (1972) A taxonomy of social need in Maclachlan G (ed.) *Problems and Progress in Medical Care 7th Series* London: Oxford University Press.

Cantle E. (1986) The deteriorating of public sector housing in Malpass P. (ed.) *The Housing Crisis* Beckenham: Croom Helm.

Central Housing Advisory Committee (1969) *Council Housing: Purposes, Procedures and Priorities* London: HMSO.

Clapham D. and Kintrea K. (1984) Allocation systems and housing choice *Urban Studies* **21** 261–9.

Clapham D. and Kintrea K. (1986a) Rationing choice and constraint: the allocation of public sector housing in Glasgow *Journal of Social Policy* **15** 51–67.

Clapham D. and Kintrea K. (1986b) The social consequences of the allocation process: evidence from Glasgow *Housing Review* **35** 83–4.

Clapham D. and Kintrea K. and Munro M. (1987) Tenure choice: an empirical investigation *Area* **19** 11–18.

Cooper P. (1988) Access and the Market *Housing* 24(5) 16–18.

Dalton M. and Daghlian S. (1989) *Housing Associations and Ethnic Minorities in Glasgow* London: Commission for Racial Equality.

Donnison D. (1983) Urban policies: a new approach, *Fabian Tract 487* London: Fabian Society.

English J. (1982) Must council housing become welfare housing *Housing Review* **31** 154–7, 212–13.

Forrest R. and Murie A. (1983) Residualisation and council housing: aspects of the changing social relations of housing tenure *Journal of Social Policy* **12** 453–68.

Glasgow District Council (1984) *Annual Housing Review 1984* Glasgow: GDC.

Glasgow District Council (1986) *Annual Housing Review 1985* Glasgow GDC.

Glasgow District Council (1987) *Review of Allocations Consultative Paper* Glasgow: GDC.

Grey A. Hepworth N. and Odling-Smee J. (1981) *Housing Costs, Rents and Subsidies* (2nd edn) London: CIPFA.

Griffiths D. and Holmes C. (1985) A new housing policy for Labour *Fabian Tract* 505 London: Fabian Society.

Harrison P. (1983) *Inside the Inner City* Harmondsworth: Penguin.

Henderson J and Karn V. (1984) Race, class and the allocation of public housing in Britain *Urban Studies* **21** 115–28.

Henderson J. and Karn V. (1987) *Race, Class and State Housing: Inequality and the Allocation of Public Housing in Britain* Aldershot: Gower.

Housing Corporation (1988) *Setting Standards in Housing Management: Allocations* Edinburgh.

Karn V. (1982) Private housing at all costs: some lessons from America in English J. (ed.) *The Future of CouncilHousing* London: Croom Helm.

Kintrea K. and Clapham D. (1986) Housing choice and search strategies within an administered housing system *Environment and Planning A*, **18** 1281–96.

Labour Co-ordinating Committee (1984) *Go Local to Survive* London.

Labour Party (1981) *A Future for Public Housing:* The Labour Party.

Malpass P. (1983) Residualisation and the restructuring of housing tenure *Housing Review* **32** 44–45.

Merrett S. (1985) The right to rent: a feasibility study *GLC Housing Research and Policy Report* 2 London: Greater London Council.

Murie A. (1983) *Housing Inequality and Deprivation* London: Heinemann.

National Federation of Housing Association (1985) *Inquiry into British Housing* chaired by HRH Duke of Edinburgh: *Report* London.

Niner P. and Karn V. (1985) *Housing Association Allocation: Advancing Racial Equality* London: Runnymede Trust.

Nugent M. (1985) *Allocation, Policies and Lettings Procedures of the Twenty Three Community Based Housing Associations in Glasgow: A Survey Jan/Feb 1985* Glasgow: Shelter.

Power A. (1982) Priority Estates Project 1982. *Improving Council Estates: A Summary of Aims and Progress* London: DoE.

Power A. (1987) *Property Before People* London: Unwin Hyman.

Raynsford N. (1984) Allocating public housing in Labour Housing Group *Right to a Home* Nottingham: Spokesman.

Scottish Development Department (1987) *Scottish Homes: A New Agency for Housing in Scotland* Edinburgh:SDD.

Scottish Housing Advisory Committee (1980) *The Allocation and Transfer of Council Houses* Edinburgh: HMSO.

Shelter (Scotland) (1982) Council House Allocation in Scotland. Edinburgh: Shelter.

Spicker P (1983) *The Allocation of Council Housing* London: Shelter.

Stearn J. (1988) Who do they house? *Housing* **24**(5) 21–24.

Webster D. (1981) A Social Market answer on housing *New Society* **58** 269–72.

Wright A., Stewart J. and Deakin N. (1984) Socialism and Decentralisation *Fabian Tract* 496 London: Fabian Society.

Chapter 5
The administration of housing benefit

Introduction

Housing benefit is a means-tested payment which provides low income tenants, boarders and hostel dwellers with help with their rent. Community charge benefit is legally separate from housing benefit and gives income-related assistance to low income community charge or 'poll tax' payers. From an administrative viewpoint, both benefits are unusual in that, unlike the other social security benefits, they are administered by local authorities and not by the Department of Social Security (DSS). However, DSS does have administrative responsibility at central government level for the schemes.

The administration of housing and community charge benefits is without doubt a major responsibility of local authorities. For instance, in 1988–89, local authorities in Britain paid an estimated total of £5.2 bn in housing benefit[1] to over five million claimants, or one in every four households in Britain. The cost of administering these payments was £277 mn (National Audit Office 1989). Table 5.1 shows the numbers of recipients of housing benefit in 1987/88 and 1988/89.

Housing benefit in transition

Housing benefit has undergone considerable change in recent years. As these developments have had a significant effect upon the nature and scope of the scheme, it is important to recall what they were.

Table 5.1 Number of households in receipt of housing benefit in Britain in 1987/88 and 1988/89

Rent rebates		Rent allowances		Rate rebates	
1987/88	*1988/89*	*1987/88*	*1988/89*	*1987/88*	*1988/89*
3761	3435	1250	1050	7030	5840

Source: Hansard 5 June 1990

Housing benefit was first introduced in 1982/83. Prior to that, households on supplementary benefit (before 1966, national assistance) received help with their housing costs and rates from the Department of Health and Social Security (DHSS). For households not on supplementary benefit a national, mandatory rent rebate and allowance scheme was introduced in 1972. Before then, local authorities had a discretionary power (introduced in the Housing Act 1930) to grant rebates to their tenants, and a significant minority did so in various ways. Rate rebates became a mandatory function of local government in 1966 when a national scheme was introduced (DHSS 1985). Prior to this, rating authorities had only permissive powers to excuse payment of domestic rates on grounds of poverty, from 1925 in England and Wales and from 1947 in Scotland. At central government level, the department responsible for the rent rebate/allowance scheme and the rate rebate scheme was the Department of the Environment (DoE), while the DHSS was responsible for the supplementary benefit scheme.

In 1982/83, for reasons discussed elsewhere (Kemp 1984a), local authorities took over from DHSS local offices most of the administration of assistance with rent and rates for households on supplementary benefit. The two separate schemes were maintained in very much the same form as before, however, but were renamed certificated housing benefit for those on supplementary benefit and standard housing benefit for others (Kemp 1984a, 1987). DHSS local offices were still involved, though, in that they had to certify supplementary benefit recipients' eligibility for housing benefit. They also continued to administer, under the supplementary benefits scheme, help with mortgage interest payments for home owners and also payments to those living in hostels and board and lodging accommodation. At the same time, the DoE relinquished responsibility for rebates and allowances, leaving the DHSS solely responsible for housing benefit at central level.

Although the housing benefit scheme was intended to simplify administration, its introduction was accompanied by very considerable administrative difficulties. Indeed, one survey of a representative sample of 52 local authorities in 1984 found that all of them claimed to have experienced problems introducing the scheme (Kemp 1984a). The result of these difficulties was that many authorities quickly developed extensive backlogs (often running into several thousands) of claims waiting to be processed or paid, while errors in benefit assessments were common. These delays and errors led, in turn, to an increase in rent and rate arrears, particularly among housing association tenants whose claims were accorded less priority than other groups of applicants, and in a few cases it appears that tenants actually lost their homes (Kemp 1984a).

Because of the widespread public concern which attended both this administrative chaos and the cuts in housing benefit levels announced by the Chancellor in his 1983 Autumn Financial Statement, an independent inquiry was set up in February 1984, less than one year after the full start to the scheme. This review of housing benefit was later incorporated into the wider DHSS review of the social security system that was announced in April 1984 (Kemp 1984a).

The difficulties over the administration of the scheme were not all just 'teething problems'. Thus a survey carried out in the spring of 1984 found that, one year after the full start to the scheme, the majority of local authorities were still experiencing difficulties: 98 per cent of those contacted said housing benefit was more difficult to administer than the old system of rent rebates and allowances, and 94 per cent wished to see the housing benefit scheme changed to make administration easier; what was wanted was fundamental rather than piecemeal change. Surveys of housing benefit officers carried out by Walker in May 1984, December 1984, and July 1985, found that although improvements had been made in the administration of the scheme, difficulties remained (Walker 1985). The May 1984 survey found that while authorities varied in the degree to which they had administration under control, the general picture was of a system that had 'been close to breaking point'. In many authorities, the scheme was being run by under-staffed, under-trained, and overworked rebate sections. One result of this was that, in practice, the scheme lost much of the fine-tuning that was built into the regulations that govern it. Corners were being cut, often in an arbitrary and inequitable fashion. The emphasis was on coping (getting through the work) rather than on providing a good service. Many authorities were still reliant on overtime by staff in their attempt to keep up with the workload (Walker 1985).

Walker found that although there was a noticeable improvement between May and December 1984, by the latter date there were still considerable problems. Backlogs and delays were common, and there had been little change in the proportion of respondents who felt that the 'vast majority' of their claimants received a 'very good service'. Indeed, the general impression was that the scheme had not worked well to date and was not set to do so in the future.

By July 1985, a noticeable improvement had taken place in the administration of housing benefit. Almost three quarters of local authorities by that date claimed to be meeting the fourteen day period within which they were supposed to be processing claims. Most authorities had cleared their backlog of unprocessed claims and 60 per cent felt that they had administration 'pretty well under control'. Yet these improvements were in the speed with which claims were dealt with rather than in the *quality* of the service provided (Walker 1985).

Thus, by the time the government published its proposals for changing housing benefit in the summer of 1985, the scheme had to some extent 'settled down' in many authorities. Nevertheless, important problems remained, and in a very few cases the scheme could not even have been said to have settled down. For example, it was reported in September 1985 that one outer London borough council had a backlog of 14,000 cases waiting to be dealt with. A year later another London borough was reported as having backlog of over 37,000 outstanding claims for housing benefit, some of them stretching back to 1983 (*Inside Housing* 1986).

While many of the early problems in the administration of the scheme were implementation difficulties resulting from the way (particularly the speed with which) it was introduced, others were more enduring problems. These enduring problems were largely the result of structural deficiencies in the scheme (Kemp 1984a). The structural deficiencies were a product of the continued existence of two separate systems of benefit (certificated housing benefit for households on SB, standard housing benefit for others) overlapped by a third payment known as housing benefit supplement (see Kemp 1984a). Other problems related also to the means test basis of the scheme and, in particular, to its sensitivity to changes of circumstance. Finally, the fact that, in administering the scheme, local authorities had to rely on the involvement of DHSS local offices and, in the case of households receiving unemployment benefits, Department of Employment benefit offices, was also problematic. This was because, as one commentator noted at the time, it 'predicates a degree of inter-agency liaison between local authorities, DHSS local offices and unemployment benefit offices which does not exist, and may not be readily attainable (Walker 1985). To a greater or lesser extent, all three of these issues were tackled by the social security review, and it is to this that we now turn.

Whereas the 1982/83 reform was essentially an administrative one, the 1988 reform which followed from the social security and housing benefit reviews involved considerable change in the structure and the scope of the scheme (Kemp 1987). In particular, certificated and standard housing benefit were combined into a single scale of benefit, applicable to all low income tenants and rate payers, along the lines proposed by the London Housing Aid Centre (SHAC) in its evidence to the housing benefit review (Kemp 1984a,b) and as originally envisaged by David Donnison when he was Chairman of the Supplementary Benefits Commission (Donnison 1979).

An important aspect of the reformed housing benefit scheme was that it involved a common means test with the new income support and family credit schemes. For the first time, consequently, assistance with rent and rates was integrated into a coherent system of income-related benefits (Kemp 1985). A further change introduced at the same time was that rate rebates were restricted to a maximum of 80 per cent instead of the 100 per cent that had previously applied.

Local authorities were given more time to prepare for the implementation of the 1988 reform of housing benefit than they had for the 1982/83 introduction of the scheme. And it appears that, although there were significant problems, authorities largely managed to avoid the widespread chaos which accompanied the earlier reform. A survey carried out by National Audit Office in conjunction with CIPFA (National Audit Office 1989) found that 86 per cent of authorities responding to the questionnaire claimed to have been able to assess and pay benefit on time when the new scheme was introduced in April 1988. However, only 33 per cent claimed to have been able to implement the changes in full on time. In other words, although most authorities were able to make payments, in many cases these would not have been for the correct amount.

Since, on DHSS estimates, three quarters of housing benefit recipients suffered losses in benefit level or eligibility as a result of the 1988 changes (Kemp 1987), it is likely that many of the interim payments made in April 1988 were overpayments. In many cases these overpayments will have subsequently been reclaimed once the correct benefit entitlement had been worked out, with possible rent arrears implications. In any event, these cuts in benefit will have increased tenants' rent contribution just at the time of year when council rents are normally increased. It is notable that after a period of some stability, local authority rent arrears increased sharply in 1988–89 (Audit Commission 1989).

Further important changes were made to the housing benefit scheme in 1989. In April boarders living on income support payments ceased to be eligible for board and lodging payments from the DSS. Instead they became eligible for income support at the same rates as ordinary householders and could claim housing benefit for the 'rent' (but not the board) element of their accommodation charges. In October hostel residents were transferred over to housing benefit in the same way.

Also in 1989, domestic rates and rate rebates were abolished in Scotland and replaced by the community charge and community charge rebates respectively. In April the following year the community charge, and what was now termed community charge benefit (CCB), were likewise introduced in England and Wales. Unlike domestic rates, the community charge is not a tax on housing but rather is a personal tax. CCB, too, is legally separate from housing benefit and in several important respects is very different from it (Ward and Zebedee 1990).

The final point to note about how housing benefit has developed is that it has been cutback on no less than seven different occasions since 1982. These cuts are likely to have caused administrative disruption, not the least because computer programmes have to be altered, claims have to be reassessed, claimants informed of the outcome, enquiries about losses dealt with and any overpayments recovered. Together with the other changes discussed already, therefore, housing benefit since 1982 has not had time to 'settle down' from an administrative point of view. A further consequence of the successive cuts in housing benefit is that the scope as well as the generosity of the scheme has been significantly reduced compared with the rebate and allowance scheme that operated until 1982/83. Increasingly, the scheme has become confined to households on income support or those who have an income not far above the income support threshold. The circumstances, needs and resources of these claimants are likely to be very different from those that local authorities had to deal with under the old rebate and allowance scheme. And this, in turn, is likely to require a different and much more responsive service than used to be the case.

Issues in administration

There are a number of important issues in the administration of housing benefit which should be of concern to the housing service of the future. One such matter is that of which department should be responsible for administering the scheme within local government. Although there is a widely held view that local authorities, rather than the DSS or a separate agency, are the most appropriate organisations to administer the scheme because of their housing duties, many housing departments are not responsible for housing benefit. In a large number of authorities it is the finance department which has responsibility for administering housing benefit, while in many others responsibility is shared between the finance and housing departments (Kemp 1984a, Maclennan et al. 1989).

The large number of authorities where responsibility for housing benefit is divided between departments must be regarded as a matter of concern. Such division is likely to confuse and inconvenience claimants, who might not know from which office to claim or query their housing benefit. It is also likely to increase the possibility of administrative confusion and add to the volume of paper flow which is necessary to administer the scheme. Moreover, if a local authority is pursuing the goal of providing a 'comprehensive housing service', it may not be possible to achieve this effectively if private and housing association tenants receive their benefit from a different department from council tenants, and similar problems may arise if the scheme is solely administered by a department other than housing. In addition, where two departments within one authority are administering housing benefit, this can result in different policies and practices being pursued on the same aspect of the scheme by the different departments, as a survey carried out in 1984 found (Kemp 1984a).

As for *which* department within local authorities should be solely responsible for the scheme, the arguments are fairly evenly divided now that the community charge has been introduced and rate rebates have been replaced by CCB. Prior to the introduction of CCB, all rebates and allowances were *housing* benefits and there was, consequently, a good case for arguing that they should all be administered by a comprehensive housing department rather than by the finance department. Now that the community charge has been introduced, however, there is no particular reason why a housing department should have responsibility for the administration of the CCB. Giving CCB administration to the finance department and housing benefit to the housing department is not the answer, however, since tenants can receive both benefits and a 'single door' approach is preferable.

The answer may be that local authorities should set up a separate housing and community charge benefit department, perhaps incorporating welfare benefit advice as well. This could have the advantage of enhancing the status of housing benefit administration within local government. Housing benefit is, after all, an important duty involving billions of pounds of public money nationally. It has moved from being a largely backroom function under the 1972 rebate and allowance scheme to being very much a 'frontline' activity, and a separate department would reflect this new importance. Moreover, this would involve separating the charging (rent/local tax) and the benefit payment functions of local government, which may have the advantage of clarifying an important distinction.

Apart from the question of who should administer housing and community charge benefits, there is also the matter of how they should be (and are being) administered. Leaving aside the initial problems of implementation which were discussed in the previous section, it appears from the limited evidence which is available that significant problems exist in the way that the new housing benefit scheme is being administered. For example, the National Association of Citizens Advice Bureaux has argued, on the basis of the experience of their nation-wide network of local bureaux, that there is 'a widespread failure within very many authorities' to provide a satisfactory service to the public (National Association of Citizens Advice Bureaux 1989). The problems to which their report drew particular attention were: delays in processing claims; providing poor, and sometimes misleading, information to applicants about their claim or entitlement to benefit; overpayments of benefit due to failure to reassess claims following notification of change of circumstances; inadequate liaison between local authority housing benefit sections and local DSS offices; incorrect assessments resulting from computer software deficiencies; and widespread imposition of rent ceilings on private sector rents, in apparent disregard of the detailed regulations. If these findings are as widespread as the NACAB report claims they are, then it must be regarded as a matter of serious concern and should be addressed by the DSS as a matter of some urgency.

Given the large sums of public money spent on housing benefit payments and administration and the importance of ensuring that claimants receive on time the benefit to which they are entitled, it is important to ensure that the scheme is administered in an efficient and effective way. The housing benefit review made a number of proposals which, if implemented, could help to ensure that these two goals are more likely to be achieved (Housing Benefit Review Team 1985). These were that:

— There should be agreed arrangements for identifying and disseminating best practice in administration.
— There should be adequate monitoring within authorities, backed where necessary by external monitoring, to ascertain whether administration is efficient and effective.
— Management consultants should be commissioned to devise a set of key performance indicators, drawing on the needs of the service and the objectives which central government sets for the scheme.
— Local authorities should provide sufficient information to their electorate to show how they are administering the scheme.

Unfortunately, these recommendations have not been fully accepted or implemented by the DSS. The DSS did introduce, in April 1988, a Housing Benefit Information System, but this is largely concerned with the eligibility of local authority expenditure (on such matters as overpayments, high rents and backdated payments) for subsidy, though it does include information on the extent to which payments have been made within the statutory 14 day time limit. It does not, however, collect data on the quality of administration or on the accuracy of awards.

The DSS view is that it is only appropriate for them to monitor performance on the time taken to process claims since only here has a clear standard been imposed in law (National Audit Office 1989). The setting of standards and the monitoring of performance in other areas, the DSS argues, is a matter for local authorities themselves. The National Audit Office, however, has taken a different view. In a report published in 1989 it backed the recommendations of the housing benefit review. The NAO pointed out that the DSS has responsibility for ensuring overall that housing benefit is being administered efficiently and effectively and that it 'cannot adequately discharge this responsibility unless (it has) identified standards of acceptable performance on which to base their appraisal of achieved overall performance' (National Audit Office 1989). It argued that 'as a matter of urgency' the DSS should introduce formal monitoring arrangements covering the quality of service provided by local authorities and the economy and efficiency of their procedures in administering the scheme.

However, performance monitoring is not only an important way in which the DSS can discharge its duties. It can also help local authorities themselves to ensure that they are efficient and effective in their administration of housing benefit. Hence, in the absence of a lead from the DSS, authorities should themselves devise key performance indicators for housing benefit. Yet it would appear that most local authorities do not currently monitor their performance in the administration of housing benefit other than in respect of the 14 days time period for processing claims. Indeed, it is likely that many authorities do not have sufficient information to do such monitoring. Certainly, in July 1985 one half of local authorities were dissatisfied with the capacity of their computer system to provide adequate information for management purposes (Walker 1986).

Yet while monitoring performance is important, it is not easy or straightforward. The proportion of all applications processed within 14 days, for example, does not show whether the correct amount of benefit is being paid, nor does it give any indication at all about how well applicants are treated when they make their claim for benefit. Care will be needed, therefore, to devise a set of indicators that are informative for management purposes yet also sensitive to the different situations within which authorities process claims, for example, the proportion of claims that are from private tenants, which can affect performance. One problem with performance indicators that will need to be taken into account in monitoring is that their use tends to modify behaviour so that the indicators may be improved regardless of whether improvement in the indicator reflects actual improvement in the overall performance. For example, in its attempt to meet the 14 day target, an authority might cut corners in the interpretation of the regulations. While this behaviour adjustment problem is difficult to overcome, not least because the whole point of indicators is to change behaviour, managers and others responsible for monitoring must at least be aware of it. It suggests that a range of indicators is required rather than just one or two. Finally, monitoring of performance is not enough; it is only a means to an end, and that end is to improve performance. The results of monitoring — which should be a continuous rather than an occasional exercise — should be acted upon, otherwise it will have been a waste of time.

Another issue that needs to be addressed is the degree of central control versus local discretion. As with the 1972 rebate and allowance scheme, research has shown that there were important variations in the way the details of the 1982/83 housing benefit were administered. And it appears that considerable scope for discretionary behaviour has been carried over into the scheme introduced in 1988 (Kilcoyne 1989). One result of this has been that claimants in similar circumstances can receive different amounts of benefit depending upon which local authority area they live in. This is not good enough within what is part of the national income maintenance system. What is required is much better and much clearer guidance from the DSS to local authorities on how to interpret the regulations, and a closing off of the areas in which discretion is currently allowed, for example, in the backdating of claims or recovery of overpayments of benefit. Improved training in local authorities is also required to ensure that staff are sufficiently aware of what the regulations are. For their part, local authorities should recognise that they are administering housing and community charge benefits on an agency basis on behalf of the DSS and, therefore, that the regulations and guidance are there to be followed not ignored.

Where local authorities do have a positive role to play (apart, of course, from administering the scheme quickly, accurately, and sympathetically) is in ensuring, through local campaigns, that take-up of housing benefit is as high as possible. Given their role as housing and community charge authorities, this is something they are well placed to do. The introduction of income support and family credit in April 1988, especially the switch to a means test common with housing benefit, meant that authorities should be able to help improve the take-up of these benefits. And, of course, by improving benefit take-up, authorities will not only be helping to minimise their rent and community charge arrears problems, they will also be bringing money into their local economy.

Conclusion

We have seen that means tested help with rent and local taxes (domestic rates and the community charge) has undergone considerable change over the past decade and that the administration of housing benefits has been attended by considerable difficulties. The two are not unrelated, and benefit administration by local councils has not really had the opportunity to settle down.

Although the efficiency and effectiveness of service delivery is important in any scheme, the successive changes to housing benefit have made it particularly so. Prior to 1982/83, local authorities did not, for the most part, provide assistance with housing costs for supplementary benefit recipients. But with the transfer from DHSS of help with rent and rates for such claimants in 1982/83, local authorities were brought back into the mainstream of income maintenance for the first time since 1948 (Kemp 1984a). The changes resulting from the 1988 reform of housing benefit further integrated the scheme into the wider social security system in the sense that it was given a means test common with income support and family credit. At the same time, the 1988 reform also resulted in a substantial contraction in the number of non-income support households getting housing benefit. Consequently, the majority of households now getting help are almost wholly reliant upon the state to meet their essential living costs and have well below average incomes. The 1988 reform thus reduced the importance of housing benefit as an instrument of housing policy and further highlighted its role as an element of the social security system (Kemp 1985). The transfer of board and lodging residents and hostel dwellers to housing benefit in 1989 has emphasised still more the income maintenance aspect of housing benefit.

These changes have profound implications for the nature of the schemes that local authorities are administering and strengthen the argument for creating a separate department for them. Above all, it is necessary for some of the administrative issues discussed in the previous section to be addressed, namely, the efficiency and effectiveness with which claims are processed, the monitoring of performance against defined standards, and the appropriate extent of central control as against local discretion. It is only when these issues have been satisfactorily resolved that the housing authority of the future can be sure that it has proved itself to be the most appropriate agency to administer this part of the income maintenance system in Britain.

Notes

1 These figures are for rent rebates and allowances and for rate rebates; the latter has since been replaced by community charge benefit, which is expected to have more recipients than rate rebates.

References

Audit Commission (1989), *Survey of Local Authority Housing. Rent Arrears,*Information Paper No. 1. London: HMSO.
DHSS (1985) *Reform of Social Security, Vol. 2: Programme for Change* London: HMSO.
Donnison D (1979) Benefit of simplicity, *Roof.*
Housing Benefit Review Team (1985) *Housing Benefit Review. Report of the Review Team* London: HMSO.
Inside Housing 19 September 1986, p 4.
Kemp P. A. (1984a) *The Cost of Chaos: A Survey of the Housing Benefit Scheme* London: SHAC.
Kemp P. A. (1984b) *Housing Benefit : The Way Forward* London: SHAC.
Kemp P. A. (1985) *The Housing Benefit Review: An Evaluation* University of Glasgow, Centre for Housing Research Discussion Paper 6, Glasgow.
Kemp P. A. (1987) The reform of housing benefit *Social Policy and Administration* **21.**
Kilcoyne D. (1989) Central control and local discretion: the operation of the housing benefit scheme Paper presented to Department of Sociology Seminar, University of Salford.
Maclennan D. *et al.* (1989) *The Nature and Effectiveness of Housing Management in England* London: HMSO.
National Association of Citizens Advice Bureaux (1989) *System Overload: The Housing Benefit System in Crisis* London: NACAB.
National Audit Office (1989) *Department of Social Security: Housing Benefits* London: HMSO.
Walker R. (1985) *Housing Benefit: The Experience of Implementation* London: Housing Centre Trust.
Walker R. (1986) Aspects of administration in Kemp P. A. (e.d) *The Future of Housing Benefits,* Studies in Housing No. 1, University of Glasgow, Centre for Housing Research, Glasgow.
Ward M. and Zebedee J. (1990) *Guide to Housing Benefit and Community Charge Benefit: 1990–91* 4th ed. London: SHAC/Institute of Housing.

Chapter 6
Repairs and maintenance in the public sector

Introduction

The Local authorities in the UK own about 4.5mn houses and flats (including the Northern Ireland Housing Executive's stock). The repair and maintenance of that stock absorbs over 25 per cent of the total expenditure on the stock (53 per cent if interest charges and loan repayments are excluded) and can be estimated to provide over one hundred thousand jobs: in simple terms one job for every fifty dwellings. Maintenance is big business.

For many years the maintenance of council housing was not regarded as a major management issue. The housing stock was younger, resources were less constrained, the main emphasis was on new building. In current circumstances there is an increasing focus on the maintenance of the existing stock. It is expensive in material and social terms to undertake periodic clearance and rebuilding, resources are constrained, the stock is ageing and there has been a failure to invest in its modernisation, improvement and repair. All these factors and others have focused attention on the need to understand the maintenance function and carry it out effectively.

Repairs generate more enquiries by tenants than any other facet of housing management and are certainly the most frequent cause of complaint. A recent study of repairs (Stanforth, Malcom and McLennan 1986, DoE 1989) reported that the highest proportion of tenants saying they were satisfied with the service they received was 82.9 per cent and in two large authorities surveyed satisfaction was only around the 50 per cent level. Surveys seem consistently to indicate that large landlords provide lower performance levels in their repair services and that the quality of the repairs service is a major factor in determining their reputation as landlords.

There is little agreement about the financial input required for the proper maintenance of the stock, the needs of the building, the proper scope of service to tenants, the balance to be struck between response repairs and planned maintenance, or the most effective organisational models. Repair and maintenance is a misunderstood mess. These difficulties would be serious in isolation. Given that there is a consensus that it would take between £20bn and £30bn to put the public sector stock into reasonable repair, and that figure represents about seven to ten years total maintenance expenditure, it is reasonable to conclude that there is a major problem. The housing stock continues to age, and unless some urgent action is taken we will be faced with the inevitability of major replacement programmes with a decade.

The situation is not hopeless. The greater proportion of the stock is capable of restoration and has a potentially long future life. The financial requirement is not difficult to calculate for the stock as a whole though there are real difficulties in translating the overall financial requirement into allocations for individual estates. There are organisational models which are proving successful.

The maintenance functions

Buildings deteriorate with age, they are subject to damage in use and parts of them become obsolete. In order to address all these factors it is desirable that a regime of repair and maintenance exists which in a cost effective way will maintain the building for its designed use for the maximum length of time. The total operation may be conveniently divided into a number of separate parts. They are not clearly separate one from another, but have proved to be workable and understandable divisions based on various time intervals and the capacity to pre-plan.

Major repairs, replacement of structural elements and modernisation
Buildings are composed of separate structural elements which have different lifespans: roofs, walls, windows, heating systems etc. Different specifications for the same element will give rise to vastly different decay rates but for elements with the same specification in comparable locations the life span will usually be consistent and, within limits, predictable. Increasingly with modern structures there is an extra factor to consider which is the interaction of materials and elements. In assessing the comparability of location these special factors need to be considered. Provided that the main walls, floors and foundations are sound, or can be made sound at reasonable cost , it is always more cost effective to replace worn out or obsolete building elements than to renew the whole building.

Calculating the financial requirements and the points at which expenditure will be required is not a particularly difficult task. A building surveyor can easily divide a building structure into its major replacement components — roof covering, windows, electric supply, wiring etc. Knowing the specifications, it is not difficult to assess the probable life span of the element and knowing the age at the point of survey it is possible to predict when the replacement will need to be carried out.

Modernisation is not a separate area of work. Many elements will have their specification upgraded when they are replaced. There are however some elements of a dwelling that might become obsolete before they are worn-out. Predictions for the life of these elements are bound to be speculative but there is still value in making some prediction.

Example

Roof covering is plain clay tiles on battens. Estimated life-span is 50 years. Current cost of re-roofing is £2000. Age of roof is 30 years in 1989. Prediction: in 2009 the roof covering will need renewing at a cost of £2000 (or equivalent at 2009 values).

It is possible and useful to break the costs into an annual charge i.e. £2000, divided by a 50 year life-span gives an annual charge of £40 a year at current prices. If this breakdown is done for all elements over a wide range of stock it will provide an approximate average annual cost for the whole of this section of maintenance. This figure has been calculated and depending on regional cost variations produces a figure of between £10.50 and £13.00 per house or flat per week (1989 values). Such calculations will give landlords the average annual figure needed to keep their stock in good order and an estimate of when the spending will need to be made on individual houses — a forward prediction of expenditure (Audit Commission 1986).

The practice of capitalising these expenditures is wasteful and largely unnecessary. Capitalisation has a value in certain circumstances, for example to smooth out large variations in expenditure from year to year. It does not avoid the basic requirement to ensure that income is sufficient to cover the average total annual requirements for these repairs and replacements.

Faced with the task of making the assessment of the cost of major works and the predictions of when the expenditures will need to be incurred there has been some tendency by landlords to assume that the work requires very high level technical skills and will take up a great deal of time. Such an assessment usually results in the task being avoided. It is important that the surveyors are reasonably consistent in their assessments and know the limits of their skill but the task of carrying out the necessary sample surveys is generally not especially complex.

Example

The author and another surveyor independently carried out assessments of the Cloverhall Estate in Rochdale which is a management co-operative with about 250 properties of six different stock types. The author with one assistant took two days to complete the work. The variations between the two reports were unimportant.

It is important to note that the predictions are estimates not a fixed expenditure plan. Regular inspections are needed which, together with monitoring and use of day-to-day repair information, can define the optimum time at which individual expenditure should occur.

Cyclical repairs and preventative maintenance
Some elements of a building are so highly predictable in their rate of deterioration that confident future predictions can be made about their repair or renewal. The painting of external woodwork is an obvious example. Preventative maintenance may also be carried out on safety grounds — on gas boilers and lifts, for example — or because experience indicates that neglect will inevitably lead to problems — gutter clearing for example where they get clogged with leaves every year. Work which has to be done for safety reasons is obviously not controversial either in the requirement or in the carrying-out. Other types of work are not so obvious. External painting, and repairs made prior to painting are apparently the most obvious category of work, so obvious that hardly anyone questions that painting is good, more painting is better. It is in fact not so straightforward: good woodwork in sheltered locations may only need painting every seven years, poor woodwork in exposed locations every three or four years. More attention needs to be given to specification, the benefits of modern paint technology, decisions whether to repair or replace, and the question whether contracts should include other repair work which could be more economically carried out at the same time. For example, if scaffolding has to be erected to carry out the painting, is there other repair work need that could be done while the scaffolding is up? Different estates and different building types need their own regime, which reinforces the importance of keeping good maintenance data bases at estate level.

The cost of cyclical repairs is not easy to assess but there tends to be trade-off against the cost of response repairs because cyclical work reduces the need for response repairs, although different kinds of building have a different balance between cyclical and response repairs.
Example
Blocks of flats demand cyclical lift maintenance, but houses generate response repairs to stairs, handrails, etc. This is an over simplification but illustrates the differences in building types in their cyclical and response repair demands.

Day-to-day response repairs

Many elements of buildings large and small fail completely or partially in a completely unpredictable way — glass in windows is subject to breakage, and many other elements are subject to accidental damage: an odd roof tile may break, locks and hinges fail, gutter joints leak. These incidents cannot be predicted and therefore the repair operations cannot be pre-planned. Buildings are also subject to unpredictable damage from fires, subsidence, etc. Whilst some repairs, such as roof leaks, if neglected, would cause further damage or deteriotation, the vast majority do not. For this reason the most important consideration in deciding on the organisation of these repairs is the requirement of the tenants rather than the buildings. Dialogue between landlord and tenants on the scope of the service, cost, response times, etc. is essential.

Difficult-to-manage, unpopular estates almost always have a much higher than average damage for response repairs. Partly this is because unpopular estates are often composed of stock which is in poor physical condition, but the main reason seems to be that such estates generally contain proportionally more poor people, old people, large families, single parent families and young single persons — groups which on average are less aware of the need for repairs, or less able or inclined to do much of their own repair work. Some groups of tenants, larger families, for example, generate more need for repairs. Local authorities too often operate allocation systems which concentrate the most disadvantaged groups of tenants and/or the largest families in the worst stock and then fail to concentrate their repairs resources commensurately.

On average, throughout the UK public housing stock, each house or flat requires about 3 day-to-day repairs per year to be carried out by the landlord. The cost of these repairs varies widely but the average is about £65 per repair giving a per dwelling cost of about £195 per year. Taking response repair costs together with cyclical costs, a figure of about £275 unit per year is a reasonable average (1989 values).

Some of the misconceptions surrounding the day-to-day repairs operation must be eliminated before any effective service can be developed or operated.

— If landlords had proper planned and cyclical maintenance programmes the vast majority of day-to-day repairs would be eliminated. There are exceptional estates where a failure to programme repairs at the right time has brought a situation where the day-to-day service is having to try (usually ineffectively) to substitute for those programmes; however most day-to-day repairs have nothing to do with the basic structural condition of the buildings. The lack of good planned maintenance allows the stock to deteriorate but has only a marginal effect on the demand for day-to-day repairs, many of which deal with the equipment rather than the structure of the houses. For example, central heating systems require more maintenance than open fires.

— An increase in the provision of repairs, i.e. a faster and more certain response to requests for repairs, is widely believed to increase demand for them. Obvious though this seems, it does not always happen. In fact improvement in service very often produces a short term increase in demand followed by a reduction, leading to lower average unit repair costs. As yet this phenomenon, observed by a number of local authorities and measured in some instances, has not been satisfactorily explained.

— It should be possible to achieve economies of scale from a large workforce capable of carrying out all repairs. The reverse seems to be true for day-to-day repairs. In general, small housing co-operatives tend to provide better service at lower unit cost than housing associations which are better than small local authorities which are, in turn, better than large local authorities, but there are plenty of exceptions to this simple generalisation.

Summary
This Section has attempted to define the various elements of the maintenance requirement. It has also made estimates of the average costs:£10.50–£13.00

Major repairs, element replacement and modernisation	£10.50–£13.00 per unit per week
Cyclical and response repairs	£5.30 per unit per week
Total (1989 values)	£15.80–£18.30 per unit per week

This total represents an annual average per unit of £590. If this is compared with the average figure of £653 being spent by local authorities in England, Wales and Scotland (Audit Commission 1986) the difficulty of present circumstances can be judged. Average rents in England, Wales and Scotland £20.85 per week (Cipfa Housing Revenue Account Statistics, 1989-90 estimate). To finance the difference between the calculated annual maintenance requirement of £890 per year and the average expenditure of £653 per year from rent alone would require an average rent increase of £4.55 per week. In practice the calculation is not so simple because a proportion of the existing expenditure is funded from borrowing. A more realistic calculation would put all of the £890 per year on a revenue basis which would require an average rent increase of £8.58 per week. Projected across the whole UK stock the shortfall in current income is of the order of £2.1bn per year. Given in addition the acknowledge average backlog of repairs of over £4000 per dwelling, crisis is not too strong a word to describe the situation.

The organisation of repairs and maintenance

Repair and maintenance involves two separate demands — the building and the tenants. Three parties are involved in carrying out the work — the tenant, the landlord and a repair worker or team. The demands have been considered. The following sections deal with the various ways of getting the work done.

Major contracts

This section covers modernisation contracts, enveloping, re-roofing, re-wiring etc. — work in which a house or flat, or more usually a group of houses or flats, have the same or similar work carried out at the same time. Cyclical work such as external painting and prior-to-painting repairs may be done this way but there are alternatives. The building itself defines the need for this work but it is the landlord who should identify the need and is responsible for its planning and carrying out. How?

Council estates provide convenient groupings of dwellings and most rented housing is in definable estate groupings. Using estates as planning units has considerable logic. Almost all estates are large enough to provide sufficient scale for major contracts. They provide convenient groupings for other management tasks and are recognised by their residents as distinct areas.

— Using various tools, such as long term assessment of building element life-spans, regular sample condition surveys, and monitoring of repair requests, an estate database should be kept which will define approximately when the work is required. As the estimated date for work to be done comes closer the data gathered should become more comprehensive and detailed in order to define the optimum point at which the work should be carried out. Financial considerations may have to delay work beyond the most economical point of spend and the consequences of delay in increased day-to-day repair costs and affects on the lettability of the stock need to be considered.

— Once the decision to do the work has been reached, the fairly well understood professional processes of design, specification and tendering can proceed and a contract or contracts can be let.

So far we have not considered the tenants' role but this is fundamental. The tenants are the customers. Their participation is vital to success. The evidence gathered by the Priority Estates (Project Power 1987) which advises various local authorities in England and Wales is overwhelmingly that improvement and capital work carried out without effective tenant involvement and without careful consideration of the management issues will arise both during the carrying-out of the work and for its future management and maintenance all too often fails. In some cases the work is useless within weeks. There are too many examples of entry-phones which have never worked, fencing which is ripped down in days and heating systems which tenants cannot afford to use. Once the main programmes have been determined (and tenants should be told how and why these have been developed and be consulted before major decisions are taken) detailed discussion needs to take place involving building professionals and housing managers. Tenants will need to be involved in groups and as individuals and the discussions will have to cover.

— explanation of the need for the work;

—the benefit or improvement to be expected;
—participation in the design process;
—time scales and phasing;
—size of contracts;
—tenant liaison during the work;
—tenant education and training where appropriate, about operating heating systems, for example.

The process of involving tenants constructively requires that housing managers and technical professionals recognise that tenants individually and collectively are their customers (Glasgow District Council and the Northern Ireland Housing Executive are increasingly calling on their staff to refer to 'customers' rather than 'tenants'). Doing the job properly also requires time, effort and resources. Except for small programmes which may be integrated with response repairs there is only one reason for using a directly employed workforce to carry out major repairs: that they can consistently carry out the work at lower cost than private sector firms. No other argument is convincing.

Quality is a contractually enforceable requirement. The argument that an employed workforce protects against market price variations has little logic. Direct labour Organisations (DLOs) are as subject as any other contractor to pressures on wage levels, skill shortages and rising material costs, and as tempted to wield monopoly power.

Cyclical and preventive maintenance
It is possible to carry out some or all of the cyclical work, external repairs and painting contracts in the same way as other major contracts but there are alternatives. Day-to-day repair teams are subject to workload fluctuations and the integration of cyclical repairs of some kind with response. Again, there are other possibilities.

Example
The Cloverhall Co-operative in Rochdale employs its own painter who paints between one fifth and one quarter of the houses each year together with some internal decoration work on voids. This has some advantages.

—The whole estate does not look in need of painting at the same time.
—There is less pressure to carry on working when the weather is unsuitable.
—It is possible to organise work on each house to cause least inconvenience to the tenant.
—The painter knows he is going to be around after each job is finished and is going to have to do the painting next time round. Both these factors argue for making a 'good job'.
—The Co-operative knows it has the resources on hand to do an urgent redecoration job on a void. Also, and not unimportantly, there is expert advice for tenants doing decorating work themselves.

Carrying out day-to-day response repairs

This is the most difficult area of maintenance to organise for a number of reasons.

— Pre-planning is by definition not possible, the work consists of a multiplicity of small jobs.
— It is the part of the maintenance operation which is, or should be, most directly designed to serve the tenant.

Given the service emphasis, it is proper to start by defining the tenants' requirements. These will not necessarily be the same for groups of tenants as for individual tenants. A balance has to be struck. Part of the balance is consideration of the future value of the property: for example, if a particular tenant is prepared to sacrifice a bedroom for a larger and more lavish bathroom, what will be the effect of that choice if the tenant leaves and the property has to be re-let? Part of the balance is the amount of involvement which the tenants want, Figure 6.1 illustrates this.

Any situation short of owner-occupation of a single house requires some collective policy and there are scale economies to be gained by standardisation of performance standards and specifications.

Example

It will be cheaper to repair broken locks with one standard type rather than with a wide variety of different locks.

Despite these restrictions the contract between tenants and landlord regarding the scope and performance of the repairs service is a matter

Figure 6.1

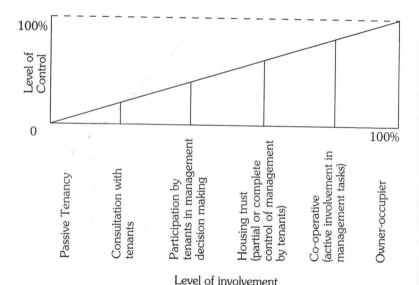

for legitimate negotiation between the parties. Such a contract is implicit in the tenancy agreement whether or not it is ever written down or published. Tenants as groups or individuals ought to have the following input and information:

— The right to know and agree the priority to be allocated to each sort of job.
— A convenient way of reporting or ordering work. It is probably not economical for a housing officer to visit for each repair. It is economically possible to provide a local housing office to which repair requests can be reported. Telephone reporting is generally not as effective as face-to-face communication. Experience has shown that taking repair reports properly is more dependent on the social and communication skills of the repair-taker than specialist technical knowledge.
— Tenants have a right to a receipt for repair orders which:

(a) states the repair ordered;
(b) confirms the access information given;
(c) states the latest date by which the work should be done.

(Some receipts can act as a quality check or 'satisfaction' note if they invite the tenant to comment on the work and return the receipt note after the work is completed.)

— Apart from the most urgent orders, appointments should be made for work to be done.
— Unlike owners, tenants do not require individual estimates or invoices because they pay a fixed charge in their rent. They must therefore have a right to well organised information about costs and service performance.

In order to fulfil the landlord's side of the contract the housing officers need the authority to ensure that the agreement is fulfilled in respect of the agreed service levels, quality and cost. Monitoring information in respect of these factors must be available to them and they should make it available to tenants.

Repairs have to be carried out by a range of operatives both skilled and unskilled. Those operatives may be self-employed, employed by private sector contractors or directly employed by the property landlords. The balance between the use of directly employed labour (DLO) and private contractors is a crucial factor in obtaining the best and most cost effective service and it is therefore worth discussing the various approaches.

(a) Predominantly private sector

Many small housing associations and co-operatives rely mainly on private contractors for repairs. Typically they invite tenders, usually on a daywork basis(a charge per hour for the various classes of operative plus the cost of materials, plant etc.). Contractors are selected on the basis of their rates plus knowledge of their service performance. Orders are rarely subject to any detailed pre-inspection. Control of cost and service is achieved by post-inspection, comparing different contractors' charges for similar work, examination of invoices and close consultation with tenants.

Crucially the system must demonstrate that the managers, acting for the tenants, can take their business elsewhere. The local and sensitive nature of management and control, plus perhaps the fact that the landlord has access to a diverse and numerically large number of contractors, usually achieves exceptional service at low unit cost. It should be noted though that even these small organisations usually have some directly employed maintenance staff; 100 per cent contracting-out is unusual.

(b)   Balanced response

There comes a point of scale at which the direct employment of repair workers can be justified. At one end of the scale are housing management units which employ an odd handyperson (or combine this role with a repairs organiser) and rely mainly on private contractors. At the other are organisations which directly employ labour for most general repairs and use private contractors only for specialist work. Depending on demand it requires between 75 and 150 houses or flats to support a single worker engaged in carrying out response repairs. Demarcation between trade skills means that to provide even the basic trades involves three persons — joiner, plumber and bricklayer/plasterer. This limitation means that under about 250–300 units it is difficult to justify directly employed labour without capacity to switch workers between separate trades. Large landlords obviously can use a DLO and many local authorities have very large directly employed workforces.

(c)   Predominantly directly employed labour

During the periods when major developments of public housing were under way, many local authorities built up substantial building organisations. There has been pressure on these organisations from government legislation (the 1980 Planning and Land Act, the 1988 Local Government Act) and from other sources, including tenants groups, to ensure that these organisations are more competitive and responsive. Despite these pressures, some local authorities still carry out almost all their response maintenance using direct labour. This often creates quite serious problems.

There is the, perhaps aprocryphal, story of the housing manager who required a road-roller to do a few hours work. At the year end he discovered his section had been charged £10,000 for two hours use of the machine. The explanation was that the road-roller cost £20,000 per year and as it had been used briefly on two occasions each user had therefore been charged a fair proportion of the costs.

Local authority landlords are faced with two major decisions. The first concerns the percentage of work and the types of work which are best carried out by directly employed labour. There is no reliable general formula. The decision will depend upon factors which will vary from authority to authority, and from time to time: the distribution and type of stock, the repair policy, the cost and availability of labour. However, monopolies of any kind are always apt to be costly to their customers: mixed strategies will usually serve best. The second decision which will concern any authority with a substantial DLO is how the organisation can best be structured to carry out its work. Three basic systems are in use:

— The central district depot for about 3000 dwellings and upwards. The arguments for this organisation involve economies of scale in materials held, transport, buildings, plant etc., plus flexibility of labour in responding to variable demands. The administration of these organisations is usually complex. They do not easily provide effective direct control. The evidence suggests they are generally poor at achieving target performance and that their unit costs are high. So much for economies of scale.

— The zoned system. This involves a multi-trade team moving round an area and perhaps covering two, three or more estates over cycle periods which vary from a few days to ten weeks or more. The operating experience is mixed. Those which serve small areas on short cycles tend to do better than those serving big areas on long cycles.

— Estate based repair teams. This organisation involves established repair teams and bases on estates which also have a local housing management office. The Priority Estates Project has encouraged this on estates in England and Wales. Experience has been that after an initial surge demand falls back towards or even below the previous levels, unit costs are reduced and service performance is improved. The key to improvement lies not only in the location of the repair team and factors such as reduced travelling time etc., but in a better relationship between the housing managers, repair workers and tenants. Relocation of the repair workers is not enough; clear authority for housing managers to act as client on behalf of tenants is equally important. To be an effective client the managers must 'own' comprehensive information at estate level. This approach is not new: it reaches back to the pioneering work of Octavia Hill in the integration of repairs and housing management (Hill 1933).

Speculation on future trends

There are a number of issues in housing management and local authority organisation which must impact in some way on the running of what is now local authority owned housing stock. There is nothing approaching a free market in housing provision. Public and private housing operates within a complex framework of subsidy and legislation. The future will be shaped more by government decision and action than by any inexorable economic 'laws'. Some current trends in action and thinking seem certain to have a considerable impact on housing provision and management.

De-centralisation
There is a growing trend for local authorities to de-centralise their organisation in some way. Analysis of the structures established and proposed shows a diversity of objectives and structures. At one end of the scale are attempts to produce genuine de-centralisation of the control of service provisions in both organisational and political terms. At the other extreme some de-centralisation proposals seem to offer little more than a dispersion of the points at which the public can contact the local authority (Hogget and Hambleton 1987). Deconcentration would be a better term for them. Most of the decentralisation initiatives are too new to make confident assertions about their potential for success, but those developments that involve genuine devolution of authority seem to show the most promise of being successful.

Diversity of ownership and management
There has been increasing debate over the last ten years regarding the suitability of local authorities as landlords. There have also been government initiatives to encourage changes in the management practices of local authorities: the encouragement of the Priority Estate Project and the activities of Estate Action (formerly the Urban Housing Renewal Unit) are examples. Government has also encouraged other forms of tenure — housing trusts such as Stockbridge Village and Thamesmead, ownership and management co-operatives, housing associations etc. There has been increasing talk and some initiative in areas such as index-linking of loans, co-ownership, equity sharing etc. Tenants' rights to pick an alternative landlord do not seem to have had any direct take-up but some local authorities have, or have tried to, transfer all or part of their stock to existing or specially created housing associations. How far these developments and proposals will take hold is still unclear. The provision of finance for various alternatives, and the strength of the motives of those seeking changes are key factors.

'Ring-fencing' of housing revenue accounts(HRA)
The Government's requirements, to end rates, or community charge subsidy of HRAs, to change the basis of central Government subsidy and to restrict further the use of capital receipts must increase the pressure on Local authority landlords.

The tenant factor
For all kinds of reasons more publicity and attention is being given to the complaints, views and opinions of tenants. Most tenants rent their houses from local authorities and it is therefore inevitable that criticism of the local authorities' landlord role has increasingly been highlighted. The repairs service has been the main focus of this adverse publicity. It is rare to find an edition of any local paper without a 'horror' story of some kind alleging gross neglect of any houses or flats by a local authority.

What effect is all this going to have on repairs and maintenance? More local authorities are beginning to address the problems of capital repairs and modernisation and there is a positive move towards more logical assessment of need, stock condition surveys, planning, consultation with tenants etc. This welcome trend is constrained by inadequate financial provision leading to much abrasive debate between government and local authorities about capital allocations, appropriate rent levels, income support for rent, etc. it is also made difficult by internal competition between areas within the local authority for the scarce resources available.

Local authorities are recognising the need to improve the quality of their responsive (day-to-day) repairs service to reduce the increasingly vociferous complaints of their tenants. But improvements in this area, when they have been achieved, have been hard won: DLOs are large, monolithic and difficult to change. The large public service trade unions view change with suspicion and managers are fearful of offending them and losing the tenuous control they have.

The outcome

The pace of change, particularly beneficial change, is slow, taking years rather than months to make an impact. Government initiatives show no sign of arresting the accelerating decline of much of the stock. Indeed the various financial incentives available or being canvassed to encourage tenure changes seem to be regarded more as a one-off 'price to be paid', rather than an attempt to resolve the continuing problem of chronic underfunding. They are accompanied by increasing financial restrictions on the housing stock left in local authority ownership, much of which is already in the worst physical condition.

The prospects are not encouraging:

— There is almost certainly going to be an increasing breakaway from the traditional local authority tenure. This will probably leave the local authorities with a large residual housing stock concentrated in buildings of the least desirable design, construction and condition, and housing the most disadvantaged sections of the population. American experience (Power 1976) shows how dangerous that can be.

— The 'new' landlords may find that new problems arise in providing response repairs. Their present smallness allows them a lot of choice in selecting from a large, diverse building industry. if they grow to become major clients their choice will be restricted.

— Investment in public housing shows no sign of increasing fast enough to stave off the need for a large replacement programme before the end of the century. The history of these programmes does not encourage the view 'that we'll get it right next time'. Re-housing for the poorest sections of the population has always started off with high standards and rapidly those standards have fallen as the emphasis shifts towards getting the job done quickly. We will almost certainly finish up again with poor housing for those with the least choice which will initiate the same depressing cycle again.

Perhaps more worrying than the cost and physical problems of redevelopment is the potential social cost. Rehousing always disturbs and fragments communities. Many of these communities are already weak. Some have never recovered from the last round of clearance and rebuilding. The potential cost of more disturbance in crime, vandalism, mental illness and welfare support is awful to contemplate. It is a price the people affected and society at large should not have to pay.

This pessimistic projection need not happen. Avoiding it requires that the state and the tenants recognise that the costs of providing housing are calculable and inevitable and that the providers of housing require an income which matches the cost. This would be a major step forward but it would not alone resolve the problems. The adequacy of financial provision does not guarantee the appropriate use of that finance. Continuous progressive investment in the maintenance and modernisation of existing housing stock is not a glamorous activity. Public or social housing is not a market in which real consumer choice is ever likely to exist. If it is to serve the needs of the consumer, structures must be created in which the consumers have control over the management. For all their problems, housing co-operatives have demonstrated the capacity of consumers to provide cost-effective and appropriate management and maintenance services. Some local authorities are attempting to establish locally based management providing the opportunity for real participation by tenants. Questions of tenure and ownership are intricately linked with the need to get the management structures right. Within all the facets of housing management the building is primary. If you don't look after the buildings you can't look after the tenants.

References

Audit Commission for Local Authorities in England and Wales (1986) *Improving Council House Maintenance,* London: HMSO.

Department of the Environment (1989) *The Nature and Effectiveness of Housing Management in England,* London: HMSO.

Hill O. (1933) *Extracts from Octavia Hill's Letters to Fellow Workers, 1868–1911, Compiled by her Niece, Eleanor Southwood Ouvry,* London: Adelphi Bookshop.

Hogget P. and Hambleton R. (1987) *Decentralisation and Democracy,* Bristol: University of Bristol, School for Advanced Urban Studies.

Power A. (1976) *Tenant Management Co-operatives in the US. Report for the North Islington Housing Rights Project* The Priority Estates Project.

Power A. (1987) *The Priority Estates Project Guide to Local Housing Management* The Priority Estates Project, The Department of the Environment (Estate Action), The Welsh Office.

Stanforth J. Malcolm J. and McLennan D. (1986) *The Delivery of Repair Services in Public Sector Housing in Scotland* The Scottish Office.

Chapter 7
Tenant and landlord relations

The relationship between a landlord and a tenant is bound to be ground for friction and contest. The fact that two parties have coincident use rights in the same parcel of property ensures that this is the case.

The underlying political contest that exists between landlord and tenant is clear from its long and sometimes bloody history. The medieval tenants' rights to graze cattle, gather wood or to rent with some security were whittled away by the landed gentry until they reached the nadir of the Scottish Highland Clearances of 1780 to 1860 in which thousands were forcibly evicted, their houses burned to the ground.

Since then there have been many dramatic occurrences which have served to bolster the folk image of the wicked landlord and the exploited tenant — be it the music hall figure in a top hat tying the poor damsel in distress to the railway line, or the cartoon Town Hall bureaucrat in the bowler breaking up the proletarian community with his evangelical desire to sweep away the old slums.

Given this colourful folk history what prospect is there of ensuring a mutually productive relationship between these two parties? If this cannot be achieved then do 'housing authorities' or indeed rented housing have any place in the future? In reality, of course, the existence of coincident use rights is not confined to the tenure of 'periodic tenancies' which is the particular form of tenancy with which we are most familiar in the public or social rented sector. Coincident rights exist also in the owner-occupied sector — that is between mortgagor and mortgagee — and in reality no English (or Scots) man can put such a moat around his domestic castle that he can avoid the influence of his neighbour's rights, or the duties of the local state to enforce planning and environmental legislation. So the conflicting interests that different parties may have in the same property will be with us no matter what the tenure. In any case there is clearly a future for rented housing in Britain and the debate in the late 1980s was about how to expand its quantity and improve and diversify its quality.

Nevertheless, the Government of this period wished to see the direct responsibility for housing provision taken away from local authorities as much as possible. If this trend is to be resisted it is essential that these public landlords improve the quality of their relationship with their tenants. This chapter describes a model which takes account of the various factors that determine the nature of that relationship and suggests how it can be improved. This model could be applied equally to the 'alternative' landlords that the Government is promoting and which, it expects, will supply an increasing proportion of rented housing in the future. It is, therefore, vital to the interests of local authorities that they establish the best relationship they can with their tenants in the face of this competition

The development of legal rights for public sector tenants

The politico-social push and pull between landlords and tenants is re-flected in the development of the law governing landlord–tenant rela-tions. There was a considerable strengthening of public sector tenants' rights in the 1980 legislation[1] which gave them security of tenure for the first time as well as an additional 'charter' of rights including the right-to-buy, the right (in England and Wales) to be consulted on changes in housing management practice and policy, the right to a tenancy agreement, the right to sublet and the right to succession. Since then a rather ineffective 'right to repair' has also been intro-duced for tenants in England and Wales[2] More recently there have been further changes which show that there is nothing inexorable about the movement to increase tenants' rights. The principle of a 'secure' tenancy has been disturbed by the introduction of an additio-nal ground for removal to 'suitable, alternative', accommodation when the public landlord wishes to sell the housing involved to an approved housing development agency[3]. The same legislation also allows tenants' associations to make proposals to the local authority for alternative forms of management such as management co-operatives. There has also been a marginal increase in actual and prospective tenants' rights of access to information held on computer due to the Data Protection Act.

The most fundamental underlying direction in legislation, however, is the encouragement of the breaking up of local authority housing in-to alternatives such as owner-occupation, housing associations, hous-ing trusts (such as those set up in Thamesmead and Stockbridge Village), private companies (either for profit or non-profit) and auto-nomous co-operatives. The local authority tenant now has the right to opt out of a local authority tenancy if an alternative and approved landlord can be found. This extension of choice is of course severely limited by virtue of being a one way, once and for all decision binding on all future tenants.

Clearly then, the development of tenants' rights is not a simple, collective strengthening of those rights to the benefit of all. The development of legislation interprets the experience of the past in a way which suits the dominant political pattern of the day.

Implementing the legislation

In practice the 'rights' of tenants or the 'duties' of landlords have to be interpreted and used. Take, for example, the rights of all public sector tenants to have a written tenancy agreement which, amongst other things, would make clear their rights on repairs etc. We will use the negotiation over the form of such an agreement in Glasgow in the mid 1980s as an illustration of the way in which local attitudes and organisation will influence the actual use which is made of legal rights and duties.

The idea of a legal right to such an agreement was welcomed by progressives within the housing movement, although many professionals grumbled that it was part of a Tenants' Charter which was not necessary because it was best professional practice anyway. In Glasgow the Council of Tenants' Associations (GCTA) had expressed an interest in negotiating a new agreement with the District Council back in 1978. The existing agreement of that time was typical of the narrow approach adopted in such documents in its lack of coverage on the respective obligations of landlord and tenant on key topics such as repairs and in its one sided emphasis on tenants' duties.

The process by which the GCTA and the Glasgow District Council came to negotiate together over the form and content of the new agreement was hailed by the Scottish Consumer Council at the time as the acme of progressive tenant–landlord relations. Certainly it improved on what was initially an entirely officer-drafted document which sought to reduce the Council's maintenance responsibilities from those existing ones which were loosely defined but with a wide coverage, to ones which entered heavily on major and external repairs. The improvements resulted from the willingness of a few key Labour councillors to sit down, without detailed guidance from their officers, and negotiate with the GCTA representatives and their advisors from the Castlemilk Law Centre, Shelter and Tenant Participation Advisory Service. The limitations of GCTA as a representative body were largely overcome by establishing links with all those local tenants' associations which were not affiliated to the federation via large consultative meetings at which the Federation's negotiators met representatives from local associations.

The resulting tenancy agreement agreed between the GCTA and the Labour Executive of the Council was, of course, a compromise. The tenants did not get legally binding commitment to fixed timescales for certain repairs, but the officers' objections to the inclusion of a strict 24 hour time limit on emergency repairs were overruled also.

One of the most novel aspects of the lease had never been controversial between councillors, tenants or officers. This was the setting up of a joint appeal tribunal to deal with voluntary referrals of disputes under the new lease. This was intended to act as a rapid, cheap and informal method of dealing with disputes which would avoid the necessity of going to court although still leaving such action as a possibility if the conciliation of the tribunal was not accepted. The tribunal consists of one councillor, one GCTA representative and one independent member from a relevant professional background[4].

After protracted delays and some discussion within the Council itself the document was finally agreed by both sides in early 1984 and was issued to all tenants for signature and witnessing later in that year. Despite an attempt to give a clear explanation of the procedure for filling in the tenancy agreement and returning it to the Housing Department, as well as the use of local radio and newspaper advertisements, only 70 per cent of tenants had returned their agreements by the middle of 1985.

Of those returned approximately 60 per cent were filled in correctly. This limited success rate was achieved despite the fact that the agreement extended the rights of the tenant beyond the statutory minimum on such matters as receiving compensation for improvements made by tenant, access to the independent tribunal and additional rights to succession of the tenancy. The GCTA itself did not have a great deal of influence in encouraging the take up of the new lease. The encouragement and interest shown by individual local associations varied greatly. The patchy response from tenants in taking up the rights within the new lease reveals the fragmented and individualistic nature of the public sector tenantry in big cities like Glasgow. It also shows the practical difficulties in 'giving' individuals additional rights. In practice they also have to 'take' them.

The effectiveness of the 1980 Act in giving tenants a right to a written tenancy agreement has been extremely disappointing from the viewpoint of the tenant activist. The only known Scottish case of a tenant legally challenging the contents of a new lease was in Hamilton. The tenant was supported by the local tenants' organisation. The result was an out-of-court settlement involving over twenty changes to the individual tenant's lease, but with no ensuing changes in the leases of the 20,000 other public sector tenants in Hamilton District.

The Scottish Consumer Council have reviewed the contents of tenancy agreements both before and after the legislation and after their own publicity about the one-sided, paternalistic and authoritarian nature of many tenancy agreements. They concluded that there was little reason to believe that tenancy conditions have become more relaxed than before the 1980 Act (Scottish Consumer Council 1983). Neither is there much encouragement of consultation with tenants — a state of affairs which has been further confirmed by a survey of tenant handbooks, leaflets and other information published for tenants by Scottish public landlords (Scottish Consumer Council 1986). The Housing Research Group at the City University have similarly concluded that 'the 1980 rights have had only a limited impact and that in general the rights have not been widely exercised' (Housing Research Group 1981).

All this says something not only about the attitude of the public landlord, but also about the attitude and organisation of the tenants. There was no outcry over the paltry take-up of the opportunities presented by the 1980 legislation. There has been virtually no use of the legal avenues that exist to challenge what has been done, or what has not been done, by housing authorities. If the landlords are authoritarian, then the tenants are politically weak; if authorities are individualistic in their approach, the tenants' movement is fragmented; if one group is paternalistic, the other is submissive. This is an unhealthy state of affairs both for the tenant and the landlord who claims to uphold and defend public or 'social' housing. It is partially a reflection of the much wider civic problem of having a submerged mass of uninfluential individuals in a large, centralised and hierarchical society. It is also a reflection of the hostile political and economic climate in which public housing has had to operate for the last decade. This can result in a defensive, self protective attitude from officials and councillors and in resignation amongst tenants.

Public sector housing in Britain is going through the most difficult stage so far in its development. It is a stage in its *development*, however. Despite the distant hopes of the privatisation lobby there is a clear need for a substantial subsidised rented sector. The success of the past must be defended and the massive inadequacies of the present must be corrected. A fundamental part of this correction will be the establishment of a new relationship between public landlord and tenant.

The relationship should not be based on an overly legalistic understanding of what makes a satisfactory landlord–tenant relationship. As Michael Harloe has written previously, 'the relationship between landlord and tenant in practice is socially constructed rather than legally determined. This does not mean that the law has no relevance but the law is only one factor in the relationship and it may not be the most important one' (Harloe 1985).

A model of a landlord–tenant relationship

Legal rights and duties
Figure 7.1 is a visual representation of the factors which go to determine the landlord-tenant relationship. We have already stressed the importance of the overall social, economic and political context from which the legal rights and duties on both sides of the landlord–tenant relationship crystallise.

There are some useful enhancements to these rights which could be added to the existing set of proposals:

Figure 7.1   Factors that determine landlord–tenant relationships: a model

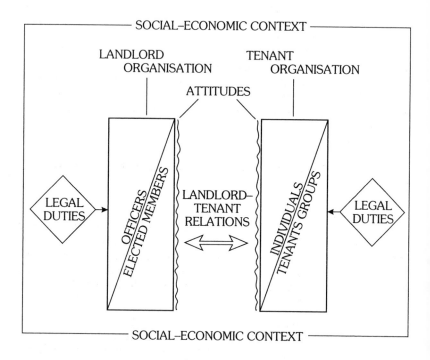

For individuals
— Rights of access to personal information held either on paper or on electronic file and rights to incorporate tenants' comments when they feel that this is needed (Basildon New Town have probably gone further in this direction than any other public authority).
— Right to a clear statement of the repairs service outlining method of reporting, a legally enforceable timescale for general types of repairs and the system for dealing with complaints. (This is a parallel to the current right to a statement on allocations policy).

For individuals and collectives
— Right of access to simple, speedy, informal housing tribunals for judgements on matters relating to interpretation of tenancy agreements between landlords and tenants and by this means the provision of an arbitration service which would not prejudice their rights to further court action or to approach the Local Government 'ombudsman'. (This type of tribunal already exists in the London Borough of Southwark.)

Collective rights
We would be sceptical of over-reliance on formal strategies of collective representation such as the proposal in the original Labour draft

legislation for England and Wales in the late 1970s that tenants should have the right to representation on the Housing Committee. Nevertheless this type of right could be useful if the inherent dangers of co-option and separation of representatives from their constituents are avoided by other means.

Move useful would be some amendment of legal procedures to make it easier for tenants' organisations to bring collective 'class' actions in which the judgement on an individual case can be applied to all other comparable cases. This would assist the tenants in their representation of those suffering from problems such as condensation, neglected fabric repairs etc.

Improving the organisation (on both sides of the fence)

Landlords
There is already a considerable amount of useful advice available to those local authorities that are taking a serious look at improving their organisation with an eye to improving the relationship they have with their tenants. We would refer them particularly to the work of the Housing Research Group at City University. It is clear that local authorities have not been good at:

1 Providing clear statements of mutual responsibilities
This includes, for example, making it clear what the landlord will do by way of repairs — allowing for a possible variation for different client groups such as the elderly or disabled — and what the tenant is expected to do by way of repairs, upkeep of common parts, gardens etc. These boundaries once set should be observed, which means enforcing them on *both* sides of the boundary. Just as means of enforcement must be provided for the tenants, so the landlord must take action in dealing with lack of tenant attention to stairs, gardens etc. The importance of this attention to detail is stressed by the Priority Estates approach publicised so effectively by Anne Power in her proclamation of 'neighbourhood' housing management (Power 1987).

2 Setting of objectives, targets and performance indicators
Management by objectives (MBO) may be old hat in management development circles but is has been little applied in local authority housing departments. Evidence from the research done for the Department of Environment by the Centre for Housing Research at Glasgow University supports the value of this approach in terms of its positive correlation with tenant satisfaction (Centre for Housing Research 1989). The established best practice of MBO must be followed; this includes the use of qualitative as well as quantitative indicators; staff participation in the setting of objectives and targets rather than imposition from above; public accountability and the monitoring of actual achievement against targets.

3 Efficient use of staff time

Internal studies of time management in housing departments have revealed considerable wastages in the use of staff time — particularly estate management staff who can, for example, spend as much as one third of their time pursuing repairs that have already been reported. One school of thought has argued for the development of more 'generic' working amongst housing staff, doing away with specialisms in allocations, rent arrears and estate management. The City University (Housing Research Group 1981) has proposed a model of 'Tenancy Officers' who would patrol the streets and police the provision of services while being supported by Administrative Assistants who would work in the same office and deal with the routine of rent collection and arrears and repairs ordering. Taking account of the potential for 'job enrichment' in some of these tasks it would seem that there is a role for the creation of more generic work for these administrative posts. It is time that housing organisations started to mesh together their organisational development with the development of individual employees' capacities. In the future we would expect regular staff surveys to measure the level of staff satisfaction and their perception of the efficiency of their own service. These could be set alongside measures of customer satisfaction and should precede and inform major structural reorganisation such as decentralisation or the development of patterns of generic working. This approach was first developed by the Northern Ireland Housing Executive (Housing and Planning Research Unit 1985).

4 Enforcement of the client role

A satisfactory housing management service depends on the successful co-ordination and direction of many services which are provided by other local authority departments and outside contractors. The Housing Department should be acting as a 'surrogate client' on behalf of the individual tenants who receive and pay for these services through their rent and rates. In practice this client role has been poorly observed by both the Housing Department and the service agencies. Little attention has been paid to the clear specification of service levels by the Housing Department (e.g. how often the grass is cut, how quickly the lift emergency is attended to), the enforcing of the required service level or monitoring of charges. Recent legislation on competitive tendering and the redefinition of the Housing Revenue Account on a more 'commercial' basis will assist the housing manager in ensuring more exact specification and enforcement of contracts with Departmental services such as back court cleansing, open space maintenance and stair lighting.

The Housing Department also has to establish productive relationship with 'colleague' departments which are not paid for their services to housing, e.g. public services such as the Police, Social Work, Education, Street Cleaning and Roads. These services still have a critical influence on the quality of life in the housing estates. Housing Departments must use their status as a colleague local authority service to develop the special relationship which will lead to effective joint planning and implementation at both strategic and neighbourhood levels.

Tenants' organisation
Past experience shows the lack of take-up by individual tenants of their legal rights and the failure of paternalistic housing managers to fill the gap. The collective organisation of tenants in Britain has always been weak in comparison to that of employees in the work place. This is but one manifestation of the weakness of consumers as opposed to workers in our economy. The arguments for 'industrial democracy' need to be parallelled by similar arguments for identifiable consumer groups such as tenants. There have been many local developments of tenant representation on Council Housing Committees, area committees and the like.

Some housing managers argue that the majority of tenants are more interested in informal, practical and local forms of involvement than in representation on the managing committees. Much can be achieved by such means but it is dangerous to rely on enlightened paternalism. We would wish to see the introduction of statutory rights for tenant representatives on the executive committees of all public sector housing authorities, be those local authorities, housing associations or quangos like Scottish Homes or New Town Corporations. The Labour Party had proposals of this type drafted in 1979 but withdrew them after receiving protests from their municipal wing. Many Labour councillors are still uneasy about working with other types of democratically elected 'community representatives'. This move will not have much effect on its own, but would provide a basic minimum against which best practice must be promoted by the professional bodies, pressure groups and federations of public sector landlords.

It is essential, however, to back this type of formal democracy with an infrastructure amongst tenants that can breathe life into the formal mechanisms and create a really effective representation of tenants' experience and views. Local tenants' associations' successes have usually been in relation to specific campaigns on issues such as modernisation or dampness. There has been little continuity in these campaigns at a local level and the experience gained is often lost and has to be learnt all over again in the next campaign. This has disadvantages for the public landlord wishing to enter into a dialogue with the tenants' movement because it is found to be fragmented and its experienced leaders few and overstretched. It would help to overcome these difficulties if a firm financial basis could be provided on which the tenants and their representatives could depend. Experience suggests that the independence and the terms of reference of any publicly funded 'community action' agency are likely to come under some challenge or stress sooner or later. The adversial aspect of the landlord–tenants relationship cannot be avoided, just as the underlying need for co-operation should not be denied.

What is required is a source of funding which does not depend on the landlord and does not fall prey to the control of a small and unrepresentative group within the tenants' movement. Temporary expedients such as urban aid may assist worthwhile projects on a temporary basis, but will not provide a basis for development over the long term which is required. Tenants in Sweden have a small proportion of their rent directed into the provision of independent administration and advisors to the tenants' movement, rather like the role of a fulltime union official. The Swedish experience also shows that, as with trade unionism, the administration can become centralised and divorced from the grass roots. It is essential, therefore, that these resources are used to support neighbourhood as well as federal organisation. Sheffield District Council introduced a small voluntary levy on tenants in order to fund an independent tenants' movement. Collection of this was greatly eased by the existence of a manual rent collection system in that city. One use for such funds would be to support a local federation of tenants' associations that could pool experience, fight joint campaigns and negotiate with the local authority on city wide issues. Public landlords can encourage such federations both by recognising and consulting them and also by encouraging other agencies which can provide them with independent legal and technical support.

Attitudes — a satisfactory service; a satisfying job

Staff attitudes

The 'paternalistic' attitude of local authority housing staff has been well documented in an anecdotal style by several observers (Gallagher 1982). The tone of many tenancy agreements and indeed, for some, the whole Octavia Hill tradition of housing management (Malpass 1984, Spicker 1985) has been taken as further evidence to support the image of the despotic bureaucrat. Any such tendency towards patronising attitudes is encouraged by a wider ideology which sees owneroccupation as morally or socially superior to renting. These same attitudes may also be used as a self-protective mental screen put up by staff who recognise the paucity of the services they offer and the desperate conditions that some of their tenants have to live in. Many of these conditions and some of the services are outwith the control of the staff who nevertheless appear to tenants to represent the authority of the local state. Once again there are issues here that are beyond the remit of this chapter. I will concentrate on what can be done *within* the organisational structure and culture of local authority Housing Departments to overcome any tendency towards a defensive or superior attitude to tenants.

Any such attitude amongst housing staff is encouraged by a lack of satisfaction amongst the staff themselves with the service they are offering. A mental barrier to someone on the other side of the counter can then act as personal protection against a feeling of impotence or even shame at what is being offered by ways of a housing service. Clearly then one of the most effective ways of improving the attitude of the staff is to improve the service itself. Thus many of the improvements in the organisation of the housing service will have this effect as a further by-product.

Training for housing staff has long been recognised as inadequate to the task. Much of the training must be in-house, work-team based rather than formal, out-of-work education. The better housing departments are now giving their staff customer awareness training, along with courses in stress management, dealing with the 'difficult' interviews and updating on the latest changes in legislation and procedures. The supervisors and managers are receiving training in counselling and communication to enable them to support their front-line staff.

The effectiveness of such training will be most apparent in those organisations that have a 'culture' which is compatible to it. Handy (1987) has described the 'role culture' which is typical and appropriate for a hierarchically organised organisation that produces a standard service in a steady-state environment, relatively well insulated from crises and sudden change. This type of organisational culture is not appropriate for the stressful and complex work of modern housing managers. The movement towards neighbourhood management, decentralisation and generic working makes a 'task orientated' team work approach to problem solving much more appropriate. Project teams and corporate management have been with us for long enough, 'quality circles' are starting to be used in the public housing service some thirty years after their advent in Japan. On their own, such techniques will achieve little, but used within the appropriate culture and structure they will help to encourage constructive attitudes towards the consumers of the public housing service and a supportive attitude between colleagues.

Tenants' attitudes

Just as with the staff, the most obvious way to improve the tenants' attitude is to provide a good service. Evidence has been collected in the comprehensive studies of housing management by the Centre for Housing Research at Glasgow University which shows that tenants' satisfaction is positively correlated to the standard of service they receive from their landlords and that there are significant variations in the levels of service and corresponding satisfaction between different local authority and housing association landlords.

Tenants' attitudes to their landlord will be affected by the content and style of the information they receive. There is a need for attractive, clearly written, leaflets, posters etc. Better still some authorities are using the local radio, television and newspapers to get across the short term messages that will be relevant to the majority of their tenants on the day they receive them. In the immediate future we must look at new computer-based technology to take the most up-to-date information into the community centre and the home. Individual tenants may not have the modems and other link-ups that will be required, but there is no reason why the tenants' co-operative, association or community hall should not be supplied with them. The tenancy officer who is doing home visits can be provided with on-line computerised information on the state of the rent account, the status of a repair order or the level of a welfare benefit.

In the late 1980s we finally started describing tenants as 'customers': a useful semantic trick initially, but one which rapidly loses its effect of making the staff think differently about the people they serve. The real trick is to make the tenants *feel* like customers and to do this they must be given choices. If they are not given choices while remaining a tenant then those who can will choose to stop being one. An unsympathetic Government won't help the process by its restrictive attitude to housing and welfare benefits but there will still be tenants who could be given the opportunity to choose whether they have a full or partial repairing lease, whether they have an integrated service charge for heating, stair and window cleaning, grass cutting, concierge service and decorating, or not, and whether they have fully furnished, partially furnished or unfurnished property.

Many local authorities will continue to provide direct services to a large number of tenants. The number of those who wish to continue to receive that service rather than opt for the various alternatives that will be open to them and the morale of those who supply the authorities' housing services is going to be critically effected by the local authorities' view of the relationship they have with their tenants. We believe that the comprehensive approach to landlord-tenant relations adopted in this chapter would greatly assist in making this relationship a good one.

Notes

1 Housing Act 1980 and Tenants Rights (Scotland) Act 1980 relevant parts of which have been codified in the Housing Act 1985 and the Housing (Scotland) Act 1987.
2 Housing Act 1985, Section 96; Housing (Scotland) Act 1987, Section 60.
3 Housing and Planning Act 1986.
4 A similar 'Arbitration Tribunal' has been in operation in Southwark since October 1983.

References

Centre for Housing Research, University of Glasgow (1989) *Housing Management in England* A Report to the Department of the Environment London: HMSO.
Gallagher P. (1982) Ideology and housing management in English J. (ed.) *The Future of Council Housing* London: Croom Helm.
Handy C.B. (1987) *Understanding Organisations,* London: Penguin.

Harloe M. (1985) Landlord/Tenant Relations in Europe and America — The Limits and Functions of the Legal Framework *Urban Law and Policy* (7) 359–83.

Housing and Planning Research Unit (1986) *Housing Executive Staff Attitude Survey* 1985 Northern Ireland Housing Executive, internal report.

Housing Research Group (1981) *Could Local Authorities be Better Landlords?* London: City University.

Malpass P. (1984) Octavia Hill *New Society,* 4 November 1982 Barker P. (ed.) *Founders of the Welfare State* London: Heinemann.

Power A. (1987) *Property Before People: The Management of Twentieth Century Council Housing* London: Allen & Unwin.

Scottish Consumer Council (1983) *Terms of Tenancy.*

Scottish Consumer Council (1986) *Telling the Tenants.*

Spiker P. (1985) Legacy of Octavia Hill *Housing* June pp. 39–40.

Chapter 8
Tenant participation

The housing authority of the future will encourage, enable and promote tenant participation — so it is frequently asserted. Few other aspects of housing management elicit such consensus. All the major political parties support the idea, as does the Institute of Housing and apparently most local housing authorities and tenants' organisations.

Such agreement prompts questions about how and why the idea of participation grew up; what the idea means in practice; and what the future prospects for tenant participation are.

Growing interest in tenant participation

Housing shares with some other areas of public policy and apparent growth of interest in the idea of lay participation from about 1960 onwards. The reasons for this are obscure but may derive from the growth of education and the mass media, the trend towards larger units of government, and growing scepticism about the traditional parties' approach to issues such as the environment and planning (Gyford 1984).

Little attention appears to have been paid to the nature and style of housing management — let alone ideas of tenant participation — by the early municipal landlords (Power 1987). But since 1945 party manifestos, government publications, tenants' groups and professional housing managers increasingly advocated various forms of tenant participation and ways of improving relations between tenants and landlords. Parallels can be drawn with developments in public education, town and country planning and the national health service. In these services new statutory requirements relating to lay participation were introduced in the early 1970s. Public housing followed in 1980, lagging behind perhaps because of the less powerful position of tenants — often seen as a sectional interest group dependent on state subsidy — unlike consumers in the fields of education, planning and health.

Between 1968 and 1973 several attempts were made to introduce Private Members' Bill proposing tenant representation on housing committees. Adopting a classic delaying tactic the Government in 1973 said the issue would be reviewed once more evidence had been gathered. The Association of London Housing Estates had already commissioned a report (Craddock 1975). Soon the Government itself commissioned research which reported that 11 per cent of English housing authorities had 'formal schemes' (including involvement in housing committees, sub-committees, advisory committees and regular discussion meetings) for tenant participation. If 'irregular discussion meetings' were included, the percentage rose to 42. Over half the formal schemes were to be found in London authorities (Richardson 1977). In 1974 interest by the new Labour housing minister in the idea of housing co-operatives led to the setting up of the Campbell Committee (reporting in 1975) to look into ways of encouraging them and to the enactment of provisions enabling local authorities to transfer management functions to co-operatives.

The Green Paper *Housing Policy* (Cmnd 6851) proposed in 1977 a tenants' charter to include: security of tenure, written tenancy agreements, the right to improve and be reimbursed, the right to sub-let and the encouragement of tenant participation and co-operatives. A consultation paper followed, elaborating these proposals (DoE 1977). Earlier reports by the National Consumer Council (1976) and the Housing Services Advisory Group (1977) on tenancy agreements appear to have been influential. A year later consultation paper *Involvement in Management* was circulated (DoE 1978) proposing a statutory tenants' committee. A wide range of issues, including changes in rent levels, were proposed for consultation. In March 1979 the Labour Government's Housing Bill was published, incorporating the proposal for a tenants' committee, with at least fifteen members broadly representatives of tenants, meeting at least twice a year and consulted over a wide range of issues — but it fell with the Government.

The new Conservative Government issued consultation papers proposing a major new right to buy, but replacing the idea of a tenants' committee with a more general statutory obligation for housing authorities and housing associations to consult individual tenants (DoE 1979). The subsequent Housing Bill limited the issues on which tenants had to be consulted to matters of housing management, including maintenance and management policy changes but excluding rent levels. The Tenants' Charter provisions (excluding the right to buy) received little parliamentary and public attention in contrast to the right to buy. Since 1980 individual tenants' rights have been marginally extended with a 'right to repair' which is very little exercised, and a right to be consulted over proposals to dispose of their homes to a private landlord which has become known as voluntary transfer. In 1988 the Government gave public sector tenants the right to choose a new landlord from the housing association, co-operative, or private landlord sectors. The controversial voting arrangements allow an application from a potential new landlord to proceed provided that 50 per cent or more of those entitled to vote have voted, *and* less than 50 per cent of the tenants entitled to vote have voted to stay with their present landlord. The 1988 Housing Act also provides that a majority vote of tenants against a proposed Housing Action Trust will prevent its establishment.

In Scotland, exhortations to provide tenants with an opportunity to have a say in housing appeared in official reports in the 1960s and 1970s. The Scottish Green Paper of 1977 (Cmnd 6852) reported 'signs that many tenants want more say in decisions about their living conditions', and supported 'alternatives to conventional tenancy arrangements which would give more responsibility to those tenants who seek it'. The idea of a statutory right to participation or consultation was dropped after the 1979 election, but the Tenants Rights etc. (Scotland) Act 1980 improved the rights to information of public sector tenants by requiring new tenancy agreements to be drawn up and allocation rules to be published. The tenants' choice provisions of the housing legislation of 1988 provide tenants with an individual right to accept or reject any proposed new landlord. The more commonly used voluntary transfer provisions are similar to those south of the border.

Public housing in Britain was therefore added to the number of public services which consumers could attempt to influence directly outside election periods and the normal conventions of relationships between councillors and constituents. Despite some resistance from local authorities (most effective for Scotland) there was all-party support at parliamentary level for the principle of tenant participation, although the reasons for this support may have differed — Conservative MPs were more likely to want to expose public service professionals to customers' criticism and to break Labour's hold on big city local government; Labour MPs were increasingly concerned about the image of the welfare state and how to give it a human face. But all parties then and since have been able to agree on the desirability of some form of participation. Since the mid-1980s, however, tenant participation has arguably been stimulated most by the Government's desire to demunicipalise public rented housing, coupled with the wish of housing authorities to retain their tenants. Tenant participation has been seen to play a crucial role in these developments (Hood 1990).

Tenants and participation

So far we have concentrated on the growth of political and professional interest in tenant participation. But before going on to examine in greater detail what is meant by the phrase 'tenant participation' it is worth considering whether there is any evidence of interest by tenants in the idea.

Tenants have traditionally organised to defend themselves against attacks on their housing conditions or costs, but only rarely have they explicitly sought a role in decision taking, and sometimes they have rejected it. The activity of tenants' groups, however, can often be seen as a clear expression of a desire to *influence* housing policy and practice even though not couched in such terms. For example, issues such as redevelopment and conditions in systems-built post-war housing have been the focus of much campaigning.

During the 1950s and 1960s, as the volume of council housing grew substantially, the formation of tenants' associations and federations proceeded gradually. In 1957 the London Council of Social Service was instrumental in establishing the London Standing Conference of Housing Estate Community Groups, soon named the Association of London Housing Estates (ALHE) and later called the London Tenants' Organisation. The number of tenants' associations grew, especially in London after the reorganisation of local government in 1963, and more generally and spectacularly as a result of rising rent levels from the late sixties onwards (Lowe 1986).

One of the most intensive periods of tenant organisation and activity followed the election of the Conservative Government in 1970. The Government's proposals for, and attempted implementation of, 'fair-rents' in the public sector doubled the membership of ALHE, for example (Laffin 1986).

A tenants' charter was produced in 1965 by the Liverpool Amalgamated Tenants' Associations Committee. It called for 'a proper tenancy contract, the control of rents, security of tenure and the right to be consulted on matters of housing management' (Laffin 1986). A similar charter was drafted in the same year by the National Association of Tenants' and Residents' Associations, which had been established in 1948 and survived until the mid-1970s. And in 1970 ALHE produced a five-point tenants' charter of demands, for example for security of tenure for public sector tenants, and for tenant representation on housing committees 'though this was seen as only one step towards the objective of estate control by the tenants themselves' (Laffin 1986).

After the 'high level' of tenant activity in the early 1970s, there were further demands for tenants' rights in the mid-1970s after the 'failure of the Labour Government elected in 1974 to grant the promised security of tenure or to review the overall system of housing finance' (Laffin 1986). In 1976, the National Consumer Council became concerned at the lack of an 'effective consumer movement' (Laffin 1986) and sponsored a conference (jointly with Shelter) at which the National Tenants' Standing Conference, later renamed the National Tenants' Organisation, was set up.

One of the first activities of the NTO was the drafting of a 'definitive' tenants' charter which was widely accepted as a model for local demands:

> The attraction of the phrase...led to its successive adoption by every political party each of which pillaged the original to produce their own saleable package
>
> (Moseley 1984).

The NTO, after a few years of activity involving lobbying and campaigning both locally and nationally, has declined and is now an inactive organisation apparently existing in little more than name alone. The Scottish Tenants' Organisation, set up in 1980, has survived, operating on very limited resources, and supporting the idea of tenant participation though not necessarily in all its possible forms. Federations of tenants' groups exist at city or borough level throughout much of urban Britain, representing a substantial increase in the level of tenant organisation and resources at a local level since 1980, and providing a sharp contrast with the weakness of tenant organisation at a national level.

Here to stay?

Several important points emerge from this brief review of the development of ideas about tenant participation.

Consumer involvement in the running of public housing has developed along with ideas about lay participation in other public services. This suggests a degree of continuity about the idea — it is unlikely to disappear quickly given the level of political, professional and consumer support for it in this and other areas of public policy.

Support for the notion of tenant participation is not universal though. Many tenant activists are suspicious or antagonistic towards particular forms of participation, fearing incorporation into a system in which freedom to speak and act on behalf of tenants would be too curtailed. Councillors too are sometimes suspicious or equivocal, fearing perhaps a threat to their traditional representative role, and suspecting tenants of taking at best a narrower view of the public interest than they would and at worst a racist or elitist one. Housing managers share this concern, while broadly seeking tenant co-operation in some of the difficult tasks of housing management.

These differences of attitude to participation perhaps explain why some issues rarely become the focus for participation while others frequently do. Modernisation appears to be the most popular topic for participation offered by housing authorities at the stage when a project is to take place. Tenants are less often asked to comment on the overall capital spending programme or the rent levels and infrequently on the allocations policy, although tenants and tenants groups are frequently vociferous in their views on these (Cairncross, Clapham and Goodlad 1989).

Where participation has developed it appears to rely on a combination of circumstances, including active and relatively assertive tenants' organisations and councillors, and housing managers who see a need and a place for participation of a type acceptable to tenants. Large Labour local authorities have apparently provided the best seed-beds, but it is not clear whether this is due to the community of interest and approach of tenant activists and councillors such as David Blunkett in Sheffield, or because these cities contain some of the worst housing conditions and the most desperate councillors and tenants, willing to try anything.

Housing managers in these areas have been crucial in assisting the difficult process of converting intentions into reality: traditional views of officer, tenant and councillor roles would otherwise be likely to stifle participation initiatives at birth.

Labour politicians have shown more interest in ideas of participation based on collective representation of tenants' association representatives on committee or in negotiations with the council. There are parallels here with trade union organisation and relationships with employers. Conservatives have shown more interest in extending individual tenants' rights.

Finally, support for participation stems from different motives. For example, tenants may want to use participation to improve their housing conditions while housing managers may want to use it to convince the tenants that government cuts prevent this. Conservative ministers may want to destroy Labour strongholds of municipal housing by giving individual tenants greater control, while Labour councillors may want to build support for public services through participation. These and other differences of motive and intention can lead to different views about appropriate forms and structures for participation. It is to these we now turn in attempting to establish what tenant participation means in practice.

Forms of tenant participation in practice

So far, I have used the phrase tenant participation without definition or explanation, as is commonly done whenever the issue is debated. This type of definition — tenant participation is whatever anyone believes it to be — is of limited help, and it is potentially confusing if different interest groups or individuals hold different views of what constitutes participation. Little is known systematically about the subjective, working definitions of participation held by councillors, tenants or housing managers but something can be deduced from the practice of tenant participation in Britain.

Three 'entirely different dimensions' have been distinguished in most definitions of tenant participation (Cairncross, Clapham and Goodlad 1989). These focus on methods, processes, and outcomes. Methods include use of the written word and face-to-face contact such as in tenant representation on advisory committees. Housing managers show understandable concern about whether public meeting or a household survey, for example, is the more appropriate method of participation in particular circumstances. The answer to such questions, however, usually depends on which process or form of participation is being sought — the second dimension. Processes such as providing information and consultation are common features of housing management and are arguably the least deserving of the title 'participation'. These 'indirect' forms of participation (Richardson 1983) together constitute probably the most common total experience of tenant participation for most public sector tenants. They often take the form of leaflets, tenants' handbooks, newsletters, invitations to write to the council, and occasionally postal surveys. Public meetings should also probably be seen as an example of information provision — despite the intentions of many housing managers that feedback be obtained.

Although these may not be 'true' participation they are important. They constitute an important aspect of more developed forms of participation, and in their own right they begin to influence the relationship between tenant and landlord. One study of the written information issued to Scottish public sector tenants by their landlords showed much scope for improvement and some evidence of it taking place (Goodlad 1986).

Less common are forms of participation such as dialogue, negotiation and joint management, although attempts at innovation with these have been a feature of housing management in the 1980s. Estate boards and budgets, and neighbourhood forums in decentralised authorities are intended to achieve such forms of direct, inter-active participation. Other examples are to be found in the authorities which co-opt tenant representatives onto housing committees, or sub-committees; or which set up liaison groups composed of tenants' representatives and various professionals to plan and monitor local capital projects. A final example of this type of participation is the experience of a few councils and tenants' representatives in negotiating the terms of a lease or tenancy agreement usually over a period of several months — as described in chapter 7.

These forms of participation usually involve tenants' representatives in influencing aspects of their own housing or its environment, as well as wider policy issues, at an estate or wider level, rather than individual tenants. These examples, therefore, involve collective action or representation of tenants — and the willingness of the councils concerned to accept the tenants as legitimate representatives. Areas lacking in organised tenants groups are unlikely to see such processes at work — but the existence of tenants' associations or similar structures does not guarantee that particular forms of participation take place.

Processes such as negotiation and joint management arguably illustrate the only correct use of the term participation — to take part in. They provide tenants with an opportunity to influence decisions *as they are made* — including sometimes the capacity to vote. But they do not guarantee that the tenants' views will prevail.

The third dimension of participation concentrates on its outcome, leading some commentators to suggest that participation is not 'real' unless it leads to the tenants' views prevailing. A concern with outcomes or achievements is associated with a view of the purpose of participation as being more than participation itself. Two types of possible outcome can be discerned. First, an instrumental view of the purpose of participation sees the outcome as being necessarily influenced by the participants. Tenants, for example, may see a well-conducted participation exercise as worthless if it does not result in a more satisfactory repairs service. Secondly, a developmental view of participation sees the purpose as educational or social, such as when housing managers use participation to achieve a better understanding of the financial constraints surrounding council housing, or when tenants get to know their neighbours and use participation as the means to a better community life.

Within this framework, housing co-operatives can be seen as a particular form of participation which involves tenants in directly controlling aspects of the management of their housing, and this attempts to guarantee that the outcome of decisions will reflect the views of participating tenants. Management co-operatives, in which ownership is retained by the council, are found in several conurbations of Britain but have been slow to develop despite government encouragement since 1975. This encouragement — extended also to ownership co-operatives — has been a strong feature of government policy since 1987, and is likely to lead to a significant growth in the number of co-operatives in formerly council-run housing, as has happened in Glasgow where several estates have been sold to tenant co-operatives established in areas of council housing requiring substantial renovation. More is said about this in Chapter 10. There are, of course, many co-operatives of the collective ownership type in housing never owned or managed by a council. A recent survey found 605 housing co-operatives in England and Wales of which almost two thirds were owned by their members, and one fifth were management co-operatives (McCafferty and Riley 1989).

Housing co-operatives impose special demands on the time and capacities of tenants, and are unlikely to develop spontaneously without the assistance and encouragement of appropriate professional helpers. Housing managers are not necessarily well equipped for this work and yet specialist housing co-operative development workers or agencies are few in number. The difficulties, delays and frustrations for tenants trying to set up co-operatives can test their endurance and commitment to the limit (Birchall 1988).

The practice of participation

How far is participation practised in Britain? The statutory requirements for consultation in England and Wales can be met by engaging in very limited forms of contact between landlord and tenant. Indeed, few councils have gone beyond seeking the views of individual tenants in writing, and some have made substantial changes in housing management without 'fully informing their tenants or seeking their views' (Key, Legg and Foot Undated). On the other hand a minority have gone beyond the terms of the Act to operate committees and other structures for participation which involve continuing opportunities for tenants to influence housing authorities, to share power, or to exercise control over certain aspects of housing as in co-operatives.

In a report on tenant participation in Scotland (Cochrane et al. 1986) 'progress towards' increased participation is said to be 'patchy'. The different legislative approach in Scotland has led to 42 per cent of authorities (containing well over half the public sector tenancies) adopting a 'policy' on tenant participation varying from one paragraph to a

12 page statement. The evidence suggests that participation is limited both in terms of form and content — most consult or inform tenants about modernisation projects, but do not involve them in discussions on allocations; most inform tenants about what is proposed for environmental improvements but few involve them directly in planning and carrying out repair policies. An increasingly common development is the employment of tenant liaison or community development staff within housing authorities to assist tenants' organisations and housing staff to develop participation.

The most systematic evidence available for England and Wales suggests that arrangements for participation have grown considerably since 1975. In that year only 12 per cent of housing authorities had a formal arrangement for tenant participation involving tenant representation on committees or regular discussion meetings. In 1986/87 44 per cent of housing authorities had such arrangements. If irregular discussion meetings are also included the growth is from 44 per cent in 1975 to 80 per cent in 1986/87 (Cairncross, Clapham and Goodlad 1990).

Participation is most developed in the larger urban areas of Britain. Several London boroughs, Sheffield and Glasgow tend to be quoted in discussions of tenant participation. It has continued to be promoted by all parties but has particularly featured at local level in attempts by some Labour local authorities to build support for public services in the face of cuts in public spending and pressure for council house sales and other measures of privatisation. Some divisions on the political left have emerged, however — for example, in the antagonism of left wing Liverpool councillors in the early 1980s to the housing co-operative movement in the city.

The future

Tenant participation is far from being an established feature of every day housing management. Whether it becomes one will depend upon a number of factors, including perceptions of the value of participation; the possession of appropriate skills, resources and knowledge; and developments more generally in housing policy.

The value of participation may be that it is seen as worthwhile in its own right, irrespective of outcome; seen both as a means to fuller citizenship or community development and the embodiment of that end. Or the value may be that it is perceived as bringing about a particular outcome — better housing, happier tenants, estates that are easier to manage or live in, for example. Tenants and landlords at times share sufficient of a common view to enable participation to proceed, but are unlikely always to do so. Tenants' interests may also conflict with those of the people on waiting lists, or the general body of poll tax payers. At times tenant participation will therefore be seen as more appropriate than others; councillors will not always welcome a challenge to their authority; tenants will not be inclined to devote time and effort to something they consider unimportant; housing managers will not make time for participation if more pressing considerations apply.

Participation itself may divide tenants, between activists and non-activists, and between winners and losers. Activists who offer their neighbours no more influence over events than the old systems of management did may give participation a bad name. So too may participation over issues such as modernisation or allocations in which one group of tenants wins what another group loses. So some tenants may see value in participation while others do not.

There is no reason to suppose that these conflicts or differences of value will diminish if participation grows: the opposite is more likely. But will participation grow? The history of the development of tenant participation suggests that it will — although not as far or as fast as its advocates sometimes suggest.

Some important practical features of the development of participation are the possession of skills, resources and knowledge. It cannot be assumed that housing managers or councillors know how to chair a meeting in a way that encourages participation; tenants cannot take part effectively if they cannot comprehend the jargon of housing; appropriate mechanisms for participation cannot be developed effectively by people ignorant of the range of possibilities. Specialist tenant liaison or community development staff can assist tenants and landlords here with information, advice, and training. But tenants are usually seriously disadvantaged by their lack of financial and other resources in contrast with landlords. Only three local authorities, Sheffield, Glasgow and Dumbarton, have assisted tenants to set up a scheme (of a kind familiar in Scandinavia) for a levy to fund the activities of tenants' organisations, including a federation. A few other local authorities are generous with grants and practical assistance in kind. But the development of an effective and independent tenants' movement requires greater resources.

Finally, tenant participation in future will be affected by trends and developments in housing policy. Current fashions in housing management coincide with government policy in supporting the notion that small is beautiful. Large, usually Labour controlled, local authorities have, since 1980, increasingly interpreted the maxim into proposals to decentralise the administration of housing services. Central government has sought to achieve smaller scale management through the tenants' right to pick a landlord, and through promoting decentralisation and tenant participation. It is likely, though, that the most significant changes that have arisen from the 1988 housing legislation are changes in attitudes towards housing management. Local authorities anxious to retain their tenants have been encouraged to develop new management tools, including the use of tenant satisfaction as a measure of performance (Centre For Housing Research 1989). The promotion of housing co-operatives and housing associations as alternatives to large municipal landlords is an important feature of policy.

There is some evidence though that smaller scale management does not in itself necessarily lead to enhanced tenant participation. The evidence of Richardson's study in the 1970s is of concentrations of participation in the larger urban authorities, and more recent evidence tends to confirm this (Cairncross, Clapham and Goodlad 1989). In addition, participation has proven to be one of the most problematic features of the efforts to decentralise housing services and to improve conditions in deprived or unpopular estates (Power 1987).

If broad consensus exists about the value of small scale housing management, the same cannot be said about the future role of local housing authorities. Central government supports the notion of housing authorities as enablers and strategic planners with a reduced role as direct providers. The view is opposed by many housing authorities which believe that the role of planner and enabler cannot be undertaken without greater policy levers or instruments as well as resources, and that a continuing need for substantial municipal ownership exists.

The reduction in the (absolute and relative) size of local authority housing stock is likely to continue. Two issues which arise are the effects of an increasingly residualised public sector on prospects for tenant participation; and secondly the relationship likely to develop between tenants and the new, smaller, landlords.

In relation to the first, the prospects for greater tenant participation are not enhanced in a sector containing poor and stigmatised tenants. The power of the sector — tenants and housing authorities together — to play an effective part on the wider stage of housing policy is reduced.

In relation to the second issue, housing co-operatives are the only form of smaller scale landlord which should *guarantee* greater opportunities for participation by tenants (Satsangi and Clapham 1990). Although co-operatives are notoriously difficult to promote and develop a recent review suggests that promotion of co-operatives by secondary co-operatives is the most successful form of development (McCafferty and Riley 1989). The stimulus, though, for most council tenants is the prospect of better quality housing at an affordable price, rather than participation *per se*.

The focus in tenant participation is likely to shift away from local authorities to smaller landlords. Little is known systematically about the participatory record of housing associations, but their practices appear to be as varied as those of local authorities (Platt, Piepe and Smyth 1987). Housing authorities could perhaps play a similar part in encouraging participation to the part they play in the lettings policies of housing associations. The idea of enforcing any general policy for tenant participation with 'traditional' private landlords has yet to be taken seriously by anyone.

Before leaving this review of trends in tenant participation, it is worth considering what tenants will be participating *about* with the public landlords of the future. Smaller scale management is likely to enhance the prospects for participation in the use of budgets, in discussing the impact of lettings or repairs policies on an area, and in issues such as neighbour disputes. But participation is less likely to have any impact on the *size* of budgets or on the delivery of non-housing services such as cleansing, public transport, recreation and policing which so often occupy the agenda at tenants' group meetings. Alternative channels for participation in these fields will be necessary.

References

Birchall J. (1988) *Building Communities: The Co-operative Way* London: Routledge & Kegan Paul.

Boaden N., Goldsmith M., Hampton W. and Stringer P. (1982) *Public Participation in Local Services* London: Longman.

Cairncross L., Clapham D. and Goodlad R. (1989) *Tenant Participation in Council Housing Management* Coventry and Salford: Institute of Housing and TPAS.

Cairncross L., Clapham D. and Goodlad, R. (1990) T*he Pattern of Tenant Participation in Council Housing Management Discussion Paper 31,* Glasgow: Centre for Housing Research, University of Glasgow.

Centre for Housing Research (1989) *The Nature and Effectiveness of Housing Management in England* London: HMSO.

Cmnd 6865 (1977) *Housing Policy - a consultative document* London: HMSO.

Cmnd 6852 (1977) *Scottish Housing - a consultative document* Edinburgh: HMSO.

Cochrane L., Downie A., Gillespie B. and Wilson, S. (eds.) (1986) *But Will it Fly, Mr. Wright* Community Development Housing Group, Glasgow: TPAS.

Craddock J. (1975) *Tenants' Participation in Housing Management* London: ALHE.

Department of the Environment (1975) *Report of the Working Party on Housing Co-operatives* (The Campbell Report), London: DoE.

Department of the Environment (1977) *Housing Policy Review: Housing Management — A Tenants' Charter: A Consultative Paper,* HPR/MAN (77) 2 London: DoE.

Department of the Environment (1978) T*enants' Rights: Involvement in Management* London: DoE.

Department of the Environment (1979) London: DoE.

Goodlad R. (1986) *Telling the Tenants,* Scottish Consumer Council, Glasgow.

Gyford J. (1984) *Local Politics in Britain* London: Croom Helm.

Hood M. (1990) Taking Notice of the Tenants *Housing Review,* 39, 3 May –June.

Housing Co-operatives Review Committee (1984) *Housing Co-operatives in Scotland,* Co-operative Union, Glasgow: TPAS.

Housing Services Advisory Group (1977) *Tenancy Agreements* London: DoE.

Kay A., Legg C. and Foot J. (Undated) *The 1980 Tenants' Rights inPractice* London: City University.

Laffin M. (1986) *Professionalism and Policy* Aldershot: Gower.

Lowe S. (1986) *Urban Social Movements* London: Macmillan.

McCafferty P. and Riley D. (1989) *A Study of Co-operative Housing,* London: HMSO.

Moseley R. (1984) Liberating the Public sector *Right to a Home,* Labour Housing Group, Nottingham: Spokesman.

National Consumer Council (1976) *Tenancy Agreements* London: NCC.

Platt S., Piepe R. and Smyth, J. (1987) *Heard or Ignored?* London: Natonal Federation of Housing Associations.

Power A. (1987) *Property before People* London: Allen & Unwin.

Richardson A. (1977) *Tenant Participation in Council House Management* Housing Development Directorate, Occasional Paper 2/77 London: DoE.

Richardson A. (1983) *Participation* London: Routledge & Kegan Paul.

Satsangi M. and Clapham D. (1990) *Management Performance in Housing Co-operatives* London: HMSO.

Chapter 9
Housing: a social service?

We started to write this chapter on holiday in Eire in a little village in Kerry. The village has a pub — The Mountain Dew Refreshment Bar. Outside there is a petrol pump and a telephone. Inside, the village children skip. The beer fridge is stacked with joints of the local lamb and sausages. And amongst the shelves crammed with fly catchers and cans of rice pudding there is a sign — 'hay for sale' it says. You can get most things you need there.

We propose that the housing authority of the future should in a comparable way cater for all needs, and especially the housing needs of disadvantaged groups.

Introduction

In this chapter we argue that the public housing service must work with its clients and other agencies to respond to the needs of the housing disadvantaged. Our approach is one recommended by Donnison and Ungerson a while ago, namely:

> The housing authority of the future will have a complex mixture of roles for which the old slogans will be a poor guide.
> Housing Committees and their staff have until now been public builders and landlords ... but the boundaries which once distinguished public housing from urban planning, from the regeneration of local economies and from community development are breaking down. 'Housers' will have to move into all these fields and acquire some of the outlook and skills of those who work in them.
> (Donnison and Ungerson 1982)

With this approach we want to look at the way in which housing authorities should deal with people who have 'special needs'. Often the main thing 'special' about these needs is that conventional housing policies have neglected them. So the term should always be escorted by quotation marks to remind us that the people whom it identifies may be more a product of traditional administrative practices and political priorities than a distinctive type of human being.

Housing authorities in the future must develop an understanding and appreciation of the wide range of people who want to use their services. The stereotype families of mother, father and two or three children are no longer the majority category of new applications for housing. In Glasgow 43 per cent of all new applications are single people. Soon the majority of applicants may be described as having 'special needs' which would clearly be absurd. Small 'special needs sections' in big housing departments will make little sense. The long-term aim must be that housing departments will deal with the full range of needs, recognising in a sensitive way how they will vary without stigmatising them as 'special'. That is still on the far horizon. Before we can reach that objective there will have to be a considerable change of view not just of housers but of politicians and the general public. This is the real challenge for housing managers, pressure groups and opinion leaders.

In the meantime the role of those concerned with 'special needs' will be to press within their agencies for changes in attitude and in practice. They will be catalysts of change. Sometimes this change will be brought about by argument and persuasion and by demonstrating the need and showing how it can be met by establishing examples of new kinds of services. This must be done working alongside others, widening their knowledge and raising their confidence so that they will be encouraged to expand on these developments. We hope that some of the examples we describe in this chapter can contribute to that process.

We start by looking at the kinds of people who may need special help. Their numbers, we shall show, cannot be precisely estimated, but the main groups currently calling for attention can be identified.

Next we look at strategies for housing some of these people, focusing particularly on the elderly living in poor housing, those coming out of hospitals for the mentally ill and mentally handicapped, homeless families with children, and single homeless people. We draw on the experience of Glasgow District Council, the authority for which we both worked.[1] Finally, we draw some conclusions from the chapter.

Housing — a social service?

For us, a major test of a housing authority's competence and humanity is its capacity to meet 'special needs' sensitively and imaginatively, giving them priority without any stigmatisation. It should be a 'social service' in the sense defined by the Barclay Report on Social Work;

that is, a client oriented service; a caring service which plans its social care in collaboration with other statutory and voluntary agencies and which takes account of the caring values of the community and uses its strengths (Barclay 1982).

Housing managers must be professional but also be 'political'. By 'professional' we do not mean that they have to polish up their text-book knowledge, refine techniques of administration or market a style. We are calling for a social awareness and a competence and commitment to work between professional and political power structures in order to serve the needs of our clients. Housing managers concerned with 'special needs' and priority groups also have an unavoidably political role because these clients and their needs have been previously neglected and changing that will provoke conflict.

Over the past few years this 'political element' has been recognised within Glasgow District and Strathclyde Regional Councils through the establishment of a number of very influential joint officer-member working groups which have dealt with a number of major, and often controversial, issues such as addiction, child care, disablement, travelling people, the social aspects of housing redevelopment, the management of hostels for single homeless people and, recently, a joint group to review the implementation of homelessness legislation in Glasgow. In several areas these working parties have also involved clients or 'outsiders' such as Shelter, Scottish Council for Single Homeless, Scottish Council for Civil Liberties and Glasgow Council of Tenants.

This method of working breaks with local government convention on at least three counts:

1 members, officers and others are working as equals in a task-oriented framework, each being assumed to have an expert and important contribution to make;
2 new policies are assumed to derive from a joint search and not only from professional or political authority and interest;
3 political commitment and leadership are assumed to play a vital part in posing questions and getting things done (Young 1977).

This method of working has an important role to play in the housing authority of the future and especially for 'special needs' groups whose needs are often the concern of more than one professional or political authority. Those needs cannot be fully met by any one agency working in isolation as will be seen as we identify some of the so-called 'special needs' or as we would prefer to put it 'priority groups' for housing. Nor can they be properly dealt with by a specialised housing approach which ignores the skills and values of other professions such as planning, social work etc.

So the housing authority of the future will have to broaden its recruitment and training programme to ensure the professionalism the future authority must have is not a narrow disabling one but is enriched by different backgrounds and skills and is client-oriented.

Priority groups

What can be done to improve the housing, care and support in the community for people whose needs are commonly categorised as 'special'? They include the frail elderly, the disabled, the mentally ill and handicapped, homeless families and single homeless people, ex-offenders, some groups of people addicted to alcohol and other drugs and various other groups, some of which overlap with each other. To look at all these 'special' needs together is not to imply that all the people concerned have similar needs, even within the different groups. Nor is it to imply that the needs of most of the people lumped together in this way are best described as 'special' — quite the opposite.

A large proportion of 'ordinary' people have these 'special' needs at some stages of their lives. At that time they still share ordinary needs with everyone else and their problems, if they are 'special', are often largely those of poverty, which may be both a cause and effect of homelessness, and exclusion from facilities like ordinary housing which are available to the rest of the population.

The needs and numbers

We cannot with any great confidence give estimates of the numbers of people in these priority groups. What is clear is that these groups are not insignificant minorities and that there is a quite disgraceful shortfall in the resources available to them. This can be seen by looking at the information available on just a few of these groups in Glasgow. Firstly, we should briefly describe the context of housing in Glasgow (Annual Housing Plan 1986).

The total population of Glasgow in 1989 was 696,577. The City's total stock of housing across all tenures in the same year was 308,808 and of this total 158,610 (51 per cent) were council houses. Glasgow clearly has a large public housing stock. Against this fact we need to set some significant other figures. In 1989 the vacancy rate (number of empty houses) in the public sector was 4.7 per cent (7260 houses) which is no higher than rates in other major cities. In 1989 17,953 lets were made (turnover rate of 11.3 per cent). Against this must be set the enormous demands on the available housing stock. In 1989 there were 34,000 people on the waiting list and 35,250 on the council's transfer list. In the same year 6711 applicants applied for housing as homeless and 2134 of them were permanently rehoused.

Right to buy sales are increasing the shortage of good council housing. At May 1989, 10965 council houses had been sold. At current rates of sales a further 23,000 (13.5 per cent) houses can be expected to be lost over the next years, seriously worsening the existing shortages.

The immensity of the demands on the available housing is further shown if we look more closely at some specific client groups in Glasgow. For example:

— Out of a total population of 696,577 there are approximately 150,000 over the age of 60 and over 70,000 over the age of 70. It is estimated that there is need for 11,720 units of sheltered housing. Currently there are only 3500 units.

— There are approximately 2500 single homeless people in Glasgow on any one night. By 'single homeless' we mean people who live in hostels, lodging houses, rough shelters or who sleep rough. We do not know how many single people become homeless in the year, but this figure might be many single people become homeless in the year, but this figure might be doubled or trebled over the year.

— There are over 1000 mentally handicapped adults in Glasgow living in hospitals. The Health Board plans to discharge 500 of these people into the community over the next five years. In addition, there are some 1500 people attending adult training centres and other day centres. This totals 2600 mentally handicapped people, many of whom could potentially be living relatively independently in various forms of supported accommodation in the community. There will be many more who are living with relatives and not known to welfare agencies.

— Within Glasgow there are 309 places for mentally handicapped people within hostels, sheltered housing schemes, group homes and group tenancies. At the most conservative estimates, this means that only 12 per cent of mentally handicapped adults in Glasgow have the opportunity to live independently in this way in the community. The bulk of these places (two thirds) are provided in hostels, increasingly acknowledged as not always the most suitable form of accommodation.

These are some of the groups we are concerned for. Other groups requiring priority attention include mentally ill people, travelling people, offenders released from prisons and other institutions and people who have problems with alcohol and other drugs. In addition, there are of course some ethnic minorities with 'special' needs — a problem only recently receiving attention in Glasgow.

For some of these groups the reasons for the lack of precise estimates are as revealing as the crude guesstimates of their numbers which some have offered. Research by the Department of the Environment on 'Housing for Mentally Ill and Mentally Handicapped People'(1983) quotes estimates that in England alone 15,000 mentally handicapped and up to 5000 people in hospital psychiatric care could be discharged immediately from hospitals if appropriate services in the community were available. In addition, the study claims that a substantial proportion of the 4000 mentally ill and 13,000 mentally handicapped people living in local authority homes and hostels in England could move to more independent accommodation provided they had the right preparation to do so. Many other mentally handicapped people live with their parents. For these, provision will have to be made some day when their parents can no longer care for them. But for mentally ill people living outside statutory provision, the need for suitable housing, they conclude, cannot be estimated.

Even as rough estimates these figures are alarming. But it is also important to understand why the authors consider estimates of the amount of housing provision for these two major 'special needs' groups are so difficult. They give three reasons for this 'each of which in itself has an effect on the flow of provision'. The most deep rooted difficulty, they claim, arises because of uncertainty about divisions of responsibility between health and social services and housing providers. The authors refer to their own estimates which show that many groups of people are capable of living outside hospitals and residential institutions, given appropriate rehabilitative and support resources, and they conclude:

> Thus what is the responsibility of the health authorities this year could be a social services responsibility next year and a housing need the year after that. From the point of view of people needing a community base, the source of provision is immaterial and it is clearly more useful to consider provision as a whole. From the point of view of funding and statutory responsibilities these demarcations assume greater significance.
>
> (DoE 1983)

Clearly, the balance between the contribution required of different services is a constantly changing one. The problems to be solved by a housing authority are often caused by the 'solutions' achieved by other services such as the discharged of patients from mental hospitals.

Where there is no such balance, thousands of 'hidden homeless 'people may be left behind in institutions or discharged into a community which cannot care adequately for their needs because no proper alternative accommodation is provided and because the different agencies involved have no co-operative plan.

The second difficulty identified by the authors arises because there are differing philosophies about the ability of people from these two groups to live in community-based housing. On the one hand there is a view that no-one needs to live permanently in a hospital. On the other hand, there are those who argue that however good community provision and primary care becomes, there are groups such as the profoundly handicapped who will always require long-term hospital care. Again, their conclusion is telling. Whichever way this question is viewed they argue:

> ...the extent to which people can move to live in the community will be determined by the amount and type of resources made available for them to do so. In other words, the need for housing could be radically changed as a result of changes in health and social services provision.
>
> (DoE 1983)

As the recent Audit Commission report (1986) has shockingly demonstrated, there is a reciprocal but badly managed relationship between the way in which health provision is being de-institutionalised and the lack of adequate housing and support in the community.

The third reason they give why estimates are difficult is because of the considerable variation in the extent to which individual health and social service authorities have attempted to review and assess the size of the problem. So, they conclude:

> If individual authorities do not review the needs of the population for whom they have responsibility, then it is difficult for sensible national estimates to be made.
>
> (Audit Commission 1986)

This third obstacle is not too difficult to surmount. The difficulties in making estimates of need are at the same time obstacles to the development of community care — which is one reason why hard pressed public authorities are often reluctant to make estimates of needs which they fear they cannot possible satisfy. But this is a short-sighted view because the resources required will never be available unless we have convincing evidence of the need for them.

Housing authorities should be statutorily obliged to resume annual estimates of all housing needs in their areas in the form of housing plans, (we say more about this in Chapter 11). Within these plans, housing authorities working with other agencies should estimate what amount and type of housing provision is required for the range of 'special needs' groups within their area. The pretext of shelving annual housing plans was that they had proved unduly burdensome to some authorities. In reality, as Robin Cook has argued (Cook 1983) 'it is the Government that has found the cost of meeting the need the plans revealed too burdensome'. If they are not statutorily required, it is still open to housing authorities to submit them. Glasgow District Council each year published a housing plan and a highly informative review. Such reports should, of course, not be seen as an end in themselves, but as a spring-board for action and the basis of the argument for the necessary resources.

However comprehensive our current estimates of needs may be, we must also be alert to respond to new needs as they emerge. A sudden influx of 'boat people' or other refugees (from Northern Ireland or Hong Kong perhaps?) or the development of new disabilities (owing to the spread of AIDS perhaps?) could precipitate an unnecessary crisis in the places most affected if neglected for too long.

The history of public responses to 'special needs' has often begun from a combination of economic and social changes (the growth of one-parent families coupled with the decline of privately rented housing and rooms let as lodgings, for example) to which the more innovative, but not always the best endowed, local authorities have developed creative responses. Their example has been quoted by pressure groups demanding more widespread action, and Parliament has ultimately passed legislation obliging the laggard authorities to adopt some, at least, of the policies already followed by the innovators. Sometimes there are setbacks: progress is not inevitable. But later, more legislation, extending the local authorities' obligations further, usually follows. For the groups dealt with in this chapter, we shall find provision is at various stages in this evolution.

The need for legislation

Housing needs become 'special' mainly because they are neglected by the conventional system. Vital, therefore, are measures like the Tenants Rights Act 1980 and the Housing (Scotland) Act 1987 which in Scotland included provisions preventing local authorities from discriminating against applications for housing on the basis of age, income or residential qualifications (measures which, absurdly, are not contained in the equivalent English Housing Acts). There is evidence (Alexander 1982) that some Scottish authorities are disregarding some of these obligations, but the legislation is, nevertheless, important because it sets down some basic rights to housing, or rather rights to apply for housing. It should be extended.

In the main, the Tenants' Rights Act was concerned with the rights of tenants and the local authorities' obligations to those they already house. Publicly acceptable ways must be found for giving higher priority, not just for those who are homeless but also for the range of priority groups who may not be 'roofless' but who can hardly be said to be living in their own homes — groups who may become roofless if nothing is done to prevent that.

Over the years there have been a number of attempts to provide local authorities with some guidance on how to adapt their allocation policies to take a comprehensive view of their housing responsibilities, most notably the Central Housing Advisory Committee and Scottish Housing Advisory Committee Reports (Scottish Housing Advisory Committee 1980, Housing Services Advisory Group 1978). In part, these reports merely repeated guidance which had been around for some time but they do provide a checklist for housing authorities to use in determining how best to respond to particular needs and they are also useful as statements of enlightened housing management principles. Where they fail is through the assumption that to define 'special needs' and to recommend action in themselves will somehow help these groups.

Both committees may have been reluctant to argue too vehemently for the expansion of housing responsibilities at a time when no increase in resources could be expected. But as Mary Brailey (1981) has argued:

> At a time of cuts it is all the more critical to acknowledge that acceptance of new responsibilities inevitably has effects upon old ones and that the question of priorities thus becomes all important ... The groups may have particular needs but they are still competing for the existing stock of housing.

Thus until new building again becomes possible, an essential response to the needs of these priority groups must lie in adjustments in allocation policies — adjustments which are bound to provoke controversy in places where housing is scarcest. For many years the Scottish Office has been promising firm guidance on how local authorities should try to integrate these new priorities into their allocation systems. In a recent report the Scottish Council for Single Homeless (1984) strongly recommend:

> that the Scottish Office should as a matter of urgency produce its long awaited circular translating the recommendations of the Scottish Housing Advisory Committee's 1980 report on the allocation and transfer of council houses into practical guidance to local housing agencies.

The Department of the Environment should do the same in England and the English legislation should be amended to specify the duties for local authorities in allocating houses set out in the Scottish legislation. Without such authoritative guidance, local authorities will continue to respond to political pressures which usually favour the existing priorities and discriminate against 'special needs groups'. This is not to say that letting regulations are the solution to the lack of suitable housing — they are only a method of fairly rationing what is available — but they must take into account the needs of the normally excluded priority groups listed above. We describe how later.

Housing authorities should also be required to review, assess the size of, and then respond to the needs of the many people in hospitals and other institutions who would not need to be there if appropriate housing and community services were available. Tragically, there are only vague statutory responsibilities in this important area. Since the 1959 Mental Health Act, which first gave formal recognition to a fundamental change of approach, away from segregation and towards community based care, there have been various consultative and policy documents which have re-stated the desirability and need for more community services. (DHSS 1977, 1980, Scottish Home and Health Department 1984). But still the responsibilities of housing and other authorities for these groups lack binding legislative direction.

What needs to be specified is a clear duty on housing authorities, together with social work and health authorities, to review and assess the size of the problem of unnecessary institutionalisation in their areas and to formulate strategies for the liberation of hospital patients into alternative and appropriate accommodation in the community. Housing authorities should have such duties not only in relation to ex-psychiatric patients but also for other groups, including the mentally handicapped, the disabled and the elderly, who remain unnecessarily and expensively incarcerated in hospitals and other institutions because of the lack of alternative accommodation in the community.

Given the obligation to take more positive action, housing authorities will find they need constant support from other services, statutory and voluntary, if they are to carry out their duties. Calls for improved local co-ordination of statutory services often evoke weary and cynical reactions. Many local authorities are fundamentally reluctant to develop services from their own funds for 'marginal groups'. Incentives and longer term assistance are, therefore, needed from central government budgets.

A good example of this kind of link up in Scotland is the legislation and excellent guidance (Scottish Development Department 1985, Secretary of State's Advisory Committee 1982) which required local authorities to provide sites for travelling people. This statutory requirement is backed by the availability of 100 per cent capital financing from central government for the provision of sites. On the basis of this subsidy arrangement, Strathclyde Regional Council are currently discussing with each of the 26 district councils within the region the possibility of a 'network' of good permanent and transit sites on the basis the each district authority contributes a per capita proportion to their running cost. That, if it works, will be a good example of effective collaboration.

We cannot expect the same kind of central funding for other projects, but there are good examples where a significant level of pump primping from the centre allows local agencies to work together to develop particular services. One of these is the Care and Repair movement which is developing service which local authorities working on their own seem to have been unable to provide.

Following several years effective experiences in England and Wales, a Care and Repair Initiative has been developed in Scotland. The Initiative, which is co-ordinated by Shelter (Scotland) in partnership with Age Concern Scotland and the Scottish Office has established eight Care and Repair projects throughout the country in urban, rural and island areas which will last until at least 1991.

The primary aim of Care and Repair is to enable elderly and disabled people on limited incomes in the private sector to maintain their homes to a comfortable standard of amenity and repair. As the stock of owner-occupied housing ages, so too do those who live in it. Elderly people now occupy a high proportion of properties lacking basic amenities and housing in a state of serious disrepair. 56,485 privately owned homes in Scotland are below 'tolerable standard' or unfit and this is thought to be a conservative estimate, as homes which suffer from condensation, dampness or which do not have a bath or shower are not considered to be below 'tolerable standard'.

Care and Repair projects offer elderly or disabled people a free, personal and professional service aimed at overcoming their fears and practical difficulties and getting necessary repairs and improvements done effectively. They enhance the ability of the elderly and disabled to live independently and to do so in greater comfort. They help to ensure better targeting of available resources to those in greatest housing and financial need, to groups which the Improvement and Repair Grant system has to a large extent found difficult to reach. In the long term, such projects help to improve our housing stock and to halt further decline, utilising a mix of public and private finance.

Their approach deals with more than the 'bricks and mortar' problems. They act as a social service linking the client into a local network of other services such as home helps, benefits advice, social activity etc. The £600,000 available for the project development, for four years from 1987 to 1991, is used primarily to meet the cost of employing full and part-time workers to develop and manage the schemes, together with associated start-up cost and overheads. The actual costs of carrying out work is met from other sources, e.g. through the Improvement and Repair Grant System, maturity loans from building societies and grants from DHSS. Already, the projects have, since 1987, assisted over 1000 clients with committed expenditure of £2.5m.

The Initiative aims to demonstrate to local authorities, financial institutions and the building industry the contribution that agency services can make in tackling repair and improvement of owner-occupied housing, particularly amongst elderly and disabled owners.

The Care and Repair Initiative will also give local authorities valuable information on the state of repair of the whole housing stock, and social work authorities and others further evidence of the needs of the elderly in their communities, encouraging co-ordinated approaches to meet the problems that the elderly often have to face alone. It has also generated some jobs.

In the vital area of community care projects for people who would otherwise be in psychiatric hospitals the link up between central government expectations and direct assistance is not so impressive. The Black Report recommended that 'the initiative of joint funding should be developed and encourage joint care programmes'(Townsend and Davidson 1982).

We would argue that, so far as central government is concerned, any review of community care needs to address the following points:

1 The Department of Social Security and the Scottish Home and Health Department should clarify in public documents the rationale of their policy on funding for local community care projects.

2 Joint financing should be developed in the way outlined in the DHSS document *Care in the Community* to allow more and longer lasting support from central budgets to community services. There should be no maximum period stipulated as a universal rule for joint financing of revenue costs of schemes.

3 The sums earmarked within National Health Service allocations for joint finance should be increased. (Otherwise many health authorities would probably not follow the guidance, preferring instead to spend money exclusively on existing services.)

4 The amended joint finance mechanism could also be used to make extra funds available earmarked in more detail for specific purposes, e.g. provision for drug addicts or problem drinkers.

5 Health authorities should be enabled to make lump sum or annual payments to local authorities and voluntary organisations, another of the options outlined in *Care in the Community.*

6 There should be a central fund specifically designed to promote innovation and diversity in the field of community care to complement other sources of funding. This fund would be applicable to preventative projects as well as those enabling transfers from institutions to the community.

7 There should be national and local advisory teams sponsored by the Government to promote care in the community and to develop good practice.

It is clear that all of these proposals cost money, but that was the unavoidable implication of long established government policies for community care which should also achieve savings as psychiatric hospitals are closed. Without adequate finance there is a serious danger that cheap and poorly co-ordinated schemes to discharge people into communities that do not or cannot care will discredit the valid notion of care in the community. This has been seen in other countries such as the USA and Italy. In America 'community care' has led to a dramatic increase in the number of people in night shelters, while in Italy the closure of psychiatric hospitals was pushed ahead at a rate which outpaced the development of adequate care facilities in the community and predictably threw the burden of care on families and especially on women.

We have concentrated so far on the need for legislation, central funding and the enormous problem of inadequate resources. We now turn to some practical examples, taken from Glasgow, which show how local authorities working within all the constraints and with little central funding can nevertheless move forward the frontiers of the housing services.

A comprehensive policy for homelessness

One of the main problems in tackling homeless was noted by Donnison and Ungerson (1982).

> Too many social service authorities have handed over their responsibilities for the homeless to housing authorities and washed their hands of the whole problem. Something may have to be done to keep them more constructively involved. Housing authorities too often assume that once they have provided the homeless with a house of some sort their task is over.

Because of the scale of deprivation and the severity of the city's housing problems, the incidence of homelessness in Glasgow is very high. In 1989 the city rehoused 2134 homeless applicants, nearly 20 per cent of the Scottish total, in council housing. Over the last 12 years, since the introduction of homelessness legislation in Scotland, Glasgow has tried to develop a more comprehensive approach to the problem which goes well beyond the limited provisions of the legislation. A more sensitive homeless allocation policy goes far to prevent the concentration of homeless applicants in particular places, and tries to find homes for them close to family or social support. The Housing Department works very closely with the region's Social Work Department because both recognise that their task is not simply to house the homeless but also to provide help and support to many people during this traumatic episode in their lives.

These responses were shaped following two critical decisions taken by the Regional Council in Strathclyde shortly after the introduction of the homeless legislation. Based on their reading of the enlightened Scottish Code of Guidance rather than the legislation itself, the Regional Council instructed its officers not to receive into care any children simply because they were homeless and later not to use discretionary payments under section 12 of the Social Work (Scotland) Act 1968 to assist persons to obtain or retain accommodation, i.e. to provide 'rent guarantees' or to pay off arrears.

Partly because of these fundamental stances, the Housing Department in Glasgow very rarely classifies any homeless applicant as 'intentionally homeless' because of rent arrears or 'anti-social' behaviour. Instead, the council has developed a preventive approach to rent arrears (last year from a total of 160,000 tenants less than one hundred were evicted for rent arrears). A multi-disciplinary approach to 'anti-social' behaviour has been devised which often solves the neighbour dispute underlying the problem by rehousing one of the parties, not 'down-market' but to like accommodation in another area. In comparison, it is striking that in Scotland as a whole (including Glasgow) in the first two years of the operation of the Act no less than 63 per cent of applicants who sought rehousing because they had lost secure accommodation had been council tenants. In other words, the public sector itself makes a disproportionate contribution to homelessness, much of which could have been avoided by more sensitive management.

Over 40 per cent of homelessness in Glasgow arises because of the breakdown of relationships. The Housing Department accepts the applicant's own statement of the breakdown as a condition which defines them as homeless or potentially homeless, whether or not violence has occurred or there is a physical or legal separation. Then the applicant, usually a woman and her children, is offered accommodation as near as possible equivalent to the family home they previously occupied. Because of this policy few women in Glasgow have used the provisions of the Matrimonial Homes Act which requires them to seek for themselves a judical order to remove their ex-partner from the home. The legal profession generally refer their clients to the Homeless Persons Unit rather than asking them to engage in the hassle of legal action — and the prospect of coming across the male prejudices frequently found in the courts.

The majority of the homeless families who apply to the Housing Department do so because they have to leave their parents' or friends' houses and have little priority on the waiting list. Glasgow, therefore, grants them additional priority to qualify them for a house, and has also built into assessment procedures a recognition of the applicant's wish to be rehoused near a relative or friend who may be able to provide some social support.

Families are referred to a special team of social workers if they are already clients of that Department or where Housing Department case workers feel that they require further counselling and assistance. In some cases the Social Work Department will offer the applicant a home-making course to prepare them for permanent housing. The Housing Department has also recruited welfare officers and a benefits advisory officer whose role is to support the homeless families while they are in temporary furnished accommodation and to help prepare them for permanent rehousing.

Glasgow, like other cities, has in the past placed homeless families in temporary accommodation in guest houses and cheap hotels. At any time in 1986, Glasgow's Housing Department would have had around 500 homeless families in such accommodation: poor quality accommodation, quite unsuitable and damaging to these families — very expensive too, to both the local authority and the DSS: all in all a very poor use of resources.

But all that has changed — by September 1987 there were no homeless families in bed and breakfast. This has been done by providing temporary accommodation within Glasgow's own housing stock. There are now approximately 500 furnished flats for homeless families with welfare support staff available to give housing advice when required. The furnishings and the staff are paid for through housing benefit and this is much cheaper than keeping people in bed and breakfast. Some £17 mn has been saved so far as result. In 1989 Glasgow District Council opened the Hamish Allan Centre in the city centre. Named to commemorate one of the authors of this chapter, the Centre, once an old fire station, now provides a 'one door' approach for all homeless people in Glasgow. Refurbished to a very high standard and at a cost of £3mn, the Centre is open for 24 hours a day to provide a comprehensive service for all homeless people and includes 35 furnished flats for emergency use by homeless people until they are moved into mainstream furnished flats and eventually permanent housing.

Single homeless people

The needs of single homeless people are in some respects different. Here too, Glasgow has given a lead. The Council has rehoused nearly 4000 men and women from hostels and lodging houses over the last few years. This has allowed the closure of most of the old Dickensian lodging houses in Glasgow. They were an embarassment to any civilised community, and hated by most of the homeless.

When rehousing hostel dwellers into mainstream council housing, the Housing Department works closely with another special team within the Social Work Department who offer help to the minority who ask for it, counselling them on emotional and other life problems. In some cases a team of homemakers are also employed to help in developing the practical skills necessary to run a house on their own — skills which may have never been learned or which have been destroyed because of long-term institutionalisation.

In making an allocation of a house, the Housing Department is again concerned to place people close to friends, relatives or the services they need. The aim is to help people to survive independently.

Because of this policy and because of the very close co-operation with social work, DSS and a number of voluntary organisations, the 'success rate' of rehousing has been very high. A 1985 study concluded: 'It is important to stress the overall success of the rehousing programme. Our report shows 90 per cent of those rehoused saying they were managing well or very well. They had regular contact with neighbours and get on well with them and 70 per cent liked the area they were rehoused in. Less than 2 per cent have returned to live in a hostel, while 70 per cent are still in their own home' (Duffy 1985).

Besides rehousing people from hostels, the district council also rehouses people who would otherwise become homeless when discharged from various institutions — mainly prisons and psychiatric hospitals. There are no elaborate tests of their vulnerability, it is simply accepted that they are homeless through no fault of their own — and the Housing Department tries to make a sensitive allocation and call on other agencies to offer further assistance and support when required.

Youth homeless

Studies of single homeless people (Drake, O'Brien and Biebuyck 1981, Scottish Council for Single Homeless 1981) show that if you look not at the 'stock' of those currently homeless who are mainly middle-aged and older men who have been homeless for many years, but at the 'flow' of those who became homeless in the course of a year, most of those who have this experience are young, and many are young women.

The number of groups becoming homeless is growing. Thus Glasgow District Council has extended its approach to homelessness to catch the increasing number of young single homeless people. The Council's policy is to offer permanent housing to young single people who are homeless, irrespective of other circumstances. Over the last eight years, over 2000 young people (aged 16 and 17) have been rehoused in independent accommodation (Kileen 1984). Again, the District Council works closely with the Region's Social Work Department who in all cases provide a full assessment report, advise the applicant in relation to benefits and ensure that any necessary practical support is provided.

In January 1987 the Glasgow Council for Single Homeless (GCSH) opened Stopover, its small emergency hostel for young homeless people. This is a good example of a number of different agencies working together to meet needs. For many years the need for such a service has been recognised but not one agency had been able to provide it. Eventually the District Council identified an empty tenement in need of repair which was given to the West of Scotland Housing Association who converted and repaired the building to a high standard with funds from the Housing Corporation. GCSH now manage the hostel with the staff being paid by Urban Aid funding. This is a small (14 spaces) hostel serving a large population. For it to work properly, there must be a rapid traffic through it so that there is capacity to receive new arrivals, i.e. exit points must be developed. This is beginning to happen with a range of independent and supported accommodation being provided by the Housing Department, Housing Associations and a number of voluntary organisations. Support is being provided when necessary by the Social Work Department and other agencies, though this needs to be much further developed: another good example of a number of agencies joining forces and pooling resources to provide a high quality service.

Glasgow is trying a comprehensive approach so that as a housing authority it becomes responsible for receiving, resettling and housing all homeless people. The Council is trying to do this without using arbitrary criteria of vulnerability or unworkable tests of priority need. To be homeless is in itself to be vulnerable to many forms of insecurity and hardship.

Glasgow's longer term objective is to build up a set of housing entitlements based on a person's need for a home rather than an arbitrarily defined measure of vulnerability. As Purkis and Hodson (1982) say:

> Housing entitlements must, in the long run, be the pre-condition for eliminating homelessness and building bridges in the community for many outsiders who have no home. This is not just a matter of abstract principle. If nobody is made clearly responsible for this it will not be done.

Homelessness can be a traumatic and devastating experience. To prevent it the Council has adopted an extensive approach. In the current housing crisis, the increasing number of re-lets going to the homeless causes resentment among those on the waiting list. A joint officer-member group meets to review the operation of the Act in Glasgow, and to explore ways of preventing homelessness. This group is considering changes in Glasgow's mainstream allocation policy to give more priority to circumstances of stress and insecurity and the need for family support and to particular household groups such as lone parents and the increasing number of single person households in our society.

Working together

In Glasgow there is a working relationship, often highly productive, between the statutory authorities, some of the voluntary organisations and the universities. This can be shown through the experience of the Glasgow Council for Single Homeless (GCSH).

GCSH was established in 1980 as a co-ordinating organisation for all the main agencies working with single homeless people in the city. Both Glasgow District Council and Strathclyde Regional Council are represented and the current convener is a senior councillor in the Strathclyde Region. Senior officers of the Housing and Social Work Department and the DSS are also present as are representatives of the Talbot Association and the Simon Community, to name just two of the voluntary organisations in Glasgow. There has also been representation from hostel residents.

An officer of the Housing Department was initially employed to act as Secretary to the organisation and much of the administrative costs were borne by the Housing Department. GCSH has now appointed a Director and support staff who have their own office base.

GCSH has many roles. It is a pressure group for improved services for single homeless people and seeks to defend their rights. It is a forum for discussion and strategic planning for the single homeless in Glasgow, and in 1984 drew up a strategy which was subsequently adopted by the District Council. The strategy proposed six 'targets' as being of prime importance ranging from 'better access to mainstream housing' for the single to 'the closure of rough shelter accommodation to be replaced by better quality housing'. In just three years many of these targets have been realised. GCSH is also a service provider, most notably through Stopover, its emergency accommodation for young homeless people, and has worked hard at improving knowledge about the needs of single homeless people. GCSH has also carried out a number of research projects in conjunction with Glasgow University, producing some very valuable reports (Glasgow Council for Single Homeless 1981, 1983, Duffy 1985).

Return to the community

Ideally, the definition of homelessness should be extended to include the many 'hidden homeless' people living in institutions which do not constitute a home who must stay there because no alternative accommodation in the community has been made available.

Glasgow's main response to this problem has been through the provision of group homes or tenancies. At present there are over one hundred known group tenancies in District Council or Housing Association family sized property catering for a range of client groups, including those recovering from mental illness, young people leaving care, the mentally handicapped, ex-offenders etc. But still the number of group tenancies in Glasgow constitutes a meagre 0.06 per cent of our total housing stock.

Group homes, hostels and other institutions often suffer from 'silting up' because of lack of opportunity for people to move on when they are ready to do so. The result is that those stuck in the group home no longer benefit from the type of care offered and in some cases suffer from it. In the meantime, other people are unable to gain access to the group home and the services from which they might benefit. In short, available resources are not being used to their full advantage. One of Glasgow's aims is to use its still quite inadequate resources as part of a network which will be considerably added to over the years ahead. To ensure that group homes are used to best advantage, we have introduced a points category called 'return to community'. This category is available to 'graduates' from group homes to add to any other points they may have to allow them to return to the community in independent housing.

While the Housing Department deals with individuals from the larger institutions who come their way as described above, there is not yet a proper strategy to liberate the many people who stay in institutions for no reason other than a lack of housing opportunities. In Glasgow and elsewhere there may be many hundreds of these 'hidden homeless' people. To extend the 'return to community' points to such people in big institutions would be a step in the right direction. But a piecemeal approach will not do — a discharge strategy is required. In Glasgow the Special Needs Strategy Group, which comprises representatives of the Housing Department, Housing Associations, Planning, Social Work and Health is reviewing the needs of these groups and planning such a strategy for the mentally ill, the mentally handicapped and others (Glasgow Housing Department 1986a, 1986b, 1987).

Equally or perhaps more important than a discharge strategy, is an admissions strategy. People may enter hospitals or other residential institutions unnecessarily when they might be able to remain in the community were appropriate resources made available. For example, a person suffering mental health problems might be able to remain in the community with a transfer of house, admission to a group home, or by staying in their present home with the help of a social worker or by respite care for the carers. It may be necessary to have an admissions policy which considers all these options before admitting a person who may then become a long-term patient with sometimes damaging consequences.

Some group tenancies have been for young people leaving care. They are part of a network similar to 'core and cluster' schemes — where there is a well supported 'core' centre with scattered, more independent, houses attached to it. The childrens'' home is the centre of the scheme with group tenancies, lodgings with a landlady and independent flats spreading out from it. The same staff can work in any of these different settings, according to the needs of the clients rather than the needs of a building. The policy on the level of support is 'as little as possible and as much as necessary'. Core and cluster schemes should be planned for other client groups too.

The provision of group homes for vulnerable people brings us yet again to the relations between housing and other helping services. That has not posed insurmountable problems in Glasgow because of the close liaison between agencies, but it has the potential to do so and it is important to be clear where the boundaries are and in which direction they are moving as social responsibilities evolve.

Conclusion

In this chapter we have tried to show that 'special needs' are not so very 'special'. Indeed, we may all have special housing needs at some stage in our lives. But housing provision and services to meet these needs must be specially developed. We have given examples in this chapter of how, with a different approach, provision which is both organised and sensitive can be developed to meet the housing needs of some of the disadvantaged in our society.

Our main argument has been that these services can be developed if housing authorities work with other agencies — statutory and voluntary — and go beyond their minimum legal duties jointly to plan housing policies and social services. This can only happen if they mix and share their skills and develop an outlook which is not narrowly professional.

Joint planning between the agencies involved in serving those with 'special needs' is, as David Hunter and Gerald Winslow (1987) say in their study of community care, 'remarkable for the virtual absence of any progress'. That is due in the main to the lack of a proper assessment of needs, limited legislation, the organisational fragmentation and confusion between a number of separately funded organisations who often fail to work together and totally inadequate finance for the development of community care.

These are major obstacles but we have tried to show with a few examples how housing authorities can develop a wider and more varied response to needs than they are obliged to do or have done in the past. In a small but significant way they are examples of how a housing authority can co-operate with others to provide housing in a caring way. Planned and provided in this way, housing is not, as the Griffiths Report on Community Care would have it, just the 'bricks and mortar'; it is the foundation of good care in the community.

Notes

1 In order to protect and develop Hamish's work, his family, friends and colleagues have established the Hamish Allan Trust. The main aim of the Trust is for promote good practice in the provision of services to those people anywhere who are homeless or otherwise disadvantaged in housing or social terms. Further information from Laurie Naumann, Scottish Council for Single Homeless, 9 Forest Road, Edinburgh.

References

Alexander D. (1982) *Council House Allocations in Scotland* Shelter (Scotland).

Annual Housing Plan (1986) Glasgow Housing Publications.

Audit Commission (1986) *Making a Reality of Community Care* London: HMSO.

Barclay P. (1982) *Social Workers — Their Role and Task* London: Bedford Square Press.

Brailey M. (1981) The Needs of Particular Groups in Centre for Urban and Regional Research, *Allocation and Transfer of Council Houses,* Discussion Paper No. 40 University of Glasgow, Centre for Urban and Regional research.

Cook R. (1983) in Brown G. and Cook R. (eds.) *Housing and Deprivation in Scotland: The Real Divide,* Mainstream Publishing, Edinburgh.

Department of the Environment (1983) *Housing for Mentally Ill and Mentally Handicapped People,* London: HMSO.

Department of Health and Social Security (1977) *The Way Forward* London: HMSO.

Department of Health and Social Security (1980) *Care in the Community,* London: HMSO.

Donnison D. and Ungerson C. (1982) *Housing Policy,* Harmondsworth: Penguin.

Drake M., O'Brien M. and Biebuyck (1981) *Single and Homeless,* London: HMSO.

Duffy J. (1985) *Rehousing Hostel Residents: The Experience in Glasgow,* Glasgow Council for Single Homeless.

Glasgow Council for Single Homeless (1981) *Homeless Men Speak for Themselves.*

Glasgow Council for Single Homeless (1983) *Homeless Women in Glasgow.*

Glasgow Housing Department (1986a) *Priority Areas for Housing Provision for the Elderly.*

Glasgow Housing Department (1986b) *Residential Respite Care for Mentally Handicapped People.*

Glasgow Housing Department (1987) *Accommodation for the Recovering Mentally Ill.*

Housing Services Advisory Group (1978) *Housing for People* , London: Department of the Environment.

Hunter D. and Wyston G. (1987) *Community Care in Britain: Variation on a Theme* London: King's Fund Centre.

Kileen D. (1984) *Homeless Young People in Glasgow,* Shelter (Scotland).

Purkiss A. and Hodson P. (1982) *Housing and Community Care,* London: Bedford Square Press.

Scottish Council for Single Homeless (1981) *Think Single: An Assessment of the Accommodation Experiences, Needs and Preferences of Single People,* Scottish Council for Single Homeless.

Scottish Council for Single Homeless (1984) *Opening Doors: A Report on Allocating housing to Single People.*

Scottish Development department (1985) *Scotland's Travelling people: Site Provision–District Pitch targets,* circular No. 13.

Scottish Home and Health Department (1984) *Mental Health in Focus,* London: HMSO.

Scottish Housing Advisory Committee (1980) *Allocation and Transfer of Council Houses,* London: HMSO.

Secretary of State's Advisory Committee (1982) *Third Report 1979–1982,* Secretary of State's Secretary of State's Advisory Committee on Scotland's Travelling People, London: HMSO.

Townsend P. and Davidson N. (1982) *Inequalities in Health —The Black Report,* Harmondsworth: Penguin Books.

Young R. (1977) *The Search for Democracy,* Heatherbank Press.

Chapter 10
Decentralised housing services
— back to the future?

Introduction

There has been tremendous interest in recent years in the decentralisation of local authority housing services. During a period when the image, management and resources of council housing have been under sustained attack, decentralisation has offered a glimmer of hope. Many local authorities have 'gone local', setting up a network of offices to serve estates or neighbourhoods and offering a more responsive and convenient service to the community. Decentralisation has been an attempt to transform a bureaucratic and paternalistic service and gain popular support for council housing. It is claimed that only radical measures such as decentralisation would restore the faith of tenants in the housing service, so they would rush to its defence just as surely as they would if local schools or health services were under threat. In consequence, decentralisation has become a central strategy to ensure the very survival of council housing in the 1990s.

In this chapter we will assess the experience of decentralisation over the last few years, and the extent to which these aims have been achieved. Let us start by considering the view of one major local authority, set out in its Annual Report:

> Although the scheme of decentralised housing management has only been in operation a matter of some months, there is already evidence that the establishment of Estate Management Offices is having a beneficial effect.

> All reports received indicate that the tenants are appreciative of the additional facilities which have been provided for their convenience and there is evidence that a closer relationship is being established between the Department and the tenants.

It is also of interest to report that whereas previously the staff was engaged on more specialised duties, under the present system, the staff is gaining a far wider knowledge of housing management.

Directly and indirectly, the Resident Housing Managers have already fostered a desire by the tenants on certain of the estates to create community centre associations, and every assistance is being given by the Department to encourage these efforts.

The above extract manages to embrace the key objectives of decentralisation — greater accessibility, the broadening of staff skills and knowledge and the spur to tenant participation. It is a fairly typical statement of the aims of decentralisation initiatives. And the year of this Annual Report? Not 1988 — but 1948 (Leeds City Council 1948).

More than forty years ago Leeds City Council established 22 neighbourhood offices in order to improve their housing service. Just like several recent initiatives, the programme was carried out under clear political direction — the idea sprang from the fertile mind of the redoubtable Reverend Charles Jenkinson, the Chairman of the Housing Committee and a committed municipal socialist. The Leeds scheme was launched in the immediate post-war period, when the Bevanite vision of universal public housing provision, serving all social classes and local needs, was at its zenith (Community Development Project 1976). In many ways, local authorities which have been decentralising their service in recent years are attempting to recapture this spirit, by providing a popular and comprehensive local service. Yet over the past forty years council housing has changed dramatically — its status, its funding, the tenants and the properties are all quite different. The legacy of poor management, inadequate maintenance, high-rise development, dwindling subsidies and confused and damaging government policies has placed a heavy burden on the capacity of decentralisation to revitalise council housing. Before considering these pressures, we need to outline the main factors which have prompted such renewed enthusiasm for the principle of decentralisation.

The trend towards decentralised services

The current wave of interest in decentralisation is generally linked to the decision by Walsall Metropolitan Council in 1980 to set up a network of 32 neighbourhood housing offices across the borough. Many of the ideas behind decentralisation, however, echo concepts raised in earlier debates about the organisation and delivery of local government services in general, and council housing services in particular (Hambleton 1978). In many respects, the recent enthusiasm for decentralised housing services has stemmed from a growing disenchantment with the larger units of local government created in the 1974 reorganisation. From the outset, it has been clearer to see what decentralisation is a reaction *against* than what it is a move *towards*.

The effects of local government reorganisation on council housing services were dramatic. In England and Wales, the average size of housing stock under the control of a local authority increased tenfold, from 1400 to 14,000 properties. At the time prevailing orthodoxy welcomed this transformation as a step towards more efficient services, as John Dearlove (1979) has shown:

> inefficiency was explained by pointing out that the overall structure of many small local authorities had failed to adjust to modern needs and changed circumstances. The existence of so many small authorities meant that men of calibre, economies of scale and the benefits of specialisation, all lay way beyond the capture of established practice at the same time as they were all seen as essential if efficiency were to be increased.

The career of this 'large is beautiful' ethic in local authority housing was short-lived. Soon tenants were becoming increasingly alienated from dealing with large, unresponsive bureaucracies (City University Housing Research Group 1981). Staff felt constrained by rigid structures, outmoded specialisms and paternalistic values in housing management (Gallagher 1982). Councillors were either mystified or frustrated by garbled messages of sub-technocratic jargon emanating from top-heavy corporate units in local authorities.

Decentralisation was, therefore, an antidote to the excesses of the large organisations running council housing after 1974. It offered both an administrative critique of the organisation and delivery of housing services and a political vision of community involvement and regeneration. It was an unstable distillation of ideas and impulses culled from diverse sources — the community action movement, priority estates projects, changing management theories, inner-city initiatives, new patterns of officer recruitment and councillor selection, and growing central–local government tensions. Decentralisation, then, addressed the administrative and political failings of council housing on several different levels, and it is necessary to distinguish between them.

The main thrust behind decentralisation is the attempt to tackle the problem of scale inherent in municipal landlordism. A centralised local authority cannot offer a responsive and personalised service to, say, 30,000 tenants. Any assumed economies of scale are dissipated by the diseconomies of poor service quality. The creation of a local network of offices serving one or more neighbourhoods makes for a more convenient and accessible service. The number of offices in the network and the size of areas served will in turn influence the scope of autonomy. Moving the service out of the Town Hall corridors and into local communities will reduce the social as well as geographical distance between consumers and housing officers in the local authority. The result, it is suggested, will be a more effective service, closely aligned to local needs, instead of the illusory efficiencies of large scale landlordism.

A second focus in many decentralisation initiatives is the problem of structure in centralised systems. Most housing departments still follow the dictates of 'classical' organisational theory, replete with finely graded hierarchies, clear chains of command, and a limited span of responsibility at each tier. The result has often been remote, inward-looking housing organisations. Decentralised housing services, on the other hand, require a more dispersed organisational structure. The structure provides more opportunities for neighbourhood-based staff to resolve problems directly, without central instruction or intervention. Tenants get a quicker response.

A third aspect of the administrative critique bears on the functional range of local housing departments. Despite constant exhortations from bodies such as the Cullingworth Committee (1969), the Department of the Environment (1983) and the Audit Commission (1986), many local authorities still fall far short of offering a comprehensive housing service, in which rent collection, allocation, repairs inspection, financial control, capital programming, housing renewal, homelessness and housing aid are all based in the same department. Reorganisation in 1974 changed the functional responsibilities of different tiers of local government and modified arrangements at the very top of the organisational structures — but it made little change to the ambit of responsibilities within departments. Housing functions often remained scattered in Treasurers', Planning, Environmental Health and Works Departments.

Neighbourhood–based provision makes it more difficult to resist pressures to broaden the scope of the housing service. Neat demarcations of departmental responsibility are more difficult to sustain when accessibility and responsiveness are the hallmarks of service delivery. Tenants may quickly become frustrated if only a partial service operates from the local office, and other housing problems are dealt with centrally. The logic of decentralisation, therefore, challenges the viability of selective provision and may make a formidable case for a more comprehensive housing service.

A further aspect of decentralisation concerns the effects on housing practice in the local authority. Decentralisation threatens the ideal of specialisation, writ large into many post-reorganisation housing departments. Specialisation and a detailed division of labour was originally seen as essential to enable the larger departments to deal with the growing complexity of housing problems. Localised systems, however, make specialisation both less tenable and less desirable.

On a practical level, it is simply difficult to retain existing specialisms while extending the number of service delivery points, without sharply increasing levels of staffing. Any system ostensibly organised around consumer needs rather than departmental requirements will place existing specialisms at risk. Front-line housing staff in neighbourhood offices will be expected by tenants to know about a wider range of housing problems without 'passing the buck' or deflecting enquiries. Many local authorities have made a virtue out of this necessity, and fostered the development of generic housing practice, following similar trends in social work (Barclay Report 1982).

Working methods may be affected as much as structures by the introduction of decentralised provision, transforming established patterns of communication. The physical relocation of the housing service will directly alter communication processes in obvious ways (staff no longer sharing the same vast open-plan office) and in more subtle ways (staff at all levels finding it easier to withhold information than before). Ideally, a two-way flow of information — passing *up* as well as *down* the structure — replaces the 'top-down' methods characteristic of centralised housing departments. On the front-line as well, a more open relationship is encouraged between housing staff and consumers. New technology can play an important role here, in providing residents and tenants with immediate information, as well as easing both vertical and lateral communication in a more dispersed structure.

Alongside this essentially managerial critique of the local authority housing service to be seen in the trend towards decentralisation runs a clear political impulse which challenges the dominant mode of decision-making in centralised systems. Despite the alluring rhetoric of reorganisation, local authorities in the mid-1970s were characterised by moribund political representation and consumer apathy (Gyford 1985). Hopes for decentralisation were therefore initially lodged within a broader strategy for political regeneration and community development as well as the revitalisation of services.

In many areas the ideals of representative democracy in local government were far removed from the realities of dynastic political leadership increasingly out of touch with grass roots pressures and excluding significant community interests. Rather than rely on local councillors, tenants were organising collectively to press their demands directly on the Housing Department. Staff also wanted their views to be heard in shaping the housing service. Opportunities for direct participation needed to be opened up. Housing services had to be reorganised around community needs rather than the prescriptions of a coterie of senior councillors and officers. A reduction in the power of centralised political and managerial decision-making structures would enable ward councillors, neighbourhood officers and consumers to influence the determination and implementation of local policies.

This move towards decentralisation was, however, taking place during a period of increasing bitterness and antagonism between central government and local authorities about the extent of control, levels of spending and priorities in service provision (Jones and Stewart 1985). These disagreements took a particularly sharp edge in debates about the future of council housing. For central government, local authority housing crystallised the failings of local councils, especially in Labour-controlled areas — impersonal, denying consumer choice, run by inefficient management, distorted by political dogma and lacking realistic financial appraisal (Henney 1985). For Labour councils, on the other hand, the decentralisation of housing provided a way of countering these criticisms and building up support for a hitherto discredited service (Blunkett and Green 1983). As the political heat of central–local relations grew fiercer, the hope that decentralisation could salvage council housing intensified.

Figure 10.1 Dimensions of decentralisation

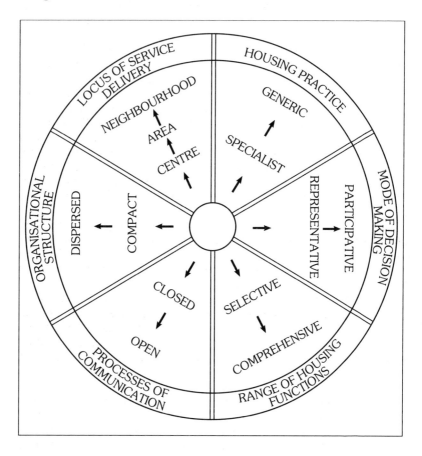

The experience of decentralisation

The different elements in the trend towards decentralisation are summarised in Figure 10.1. A centralised housing service is characterised by a large scale 'closed', hierarchical structure and sustained by a specialised division of labour and a formal commitment to representative forms of decision-making. In its place, a decentralised service is based in an 'open' dispersed organisational structure welded together by generic housing work and participative models of decision-making. We are not suggesting that decentralisation has an inexorable logic which forces all housing services down this path. The diagram is an ideal type, which seeks to uncover the centrifugal tendencies of decentralisation. It is not an exact representation of the changes brought about by any particular decentralisation strategy. In practice, a more selective approach has prevailed.

An evaluation of the impact of decentralisation is made difficult by the sheer lack of precision behind its objectives. The vagueness of its underlying principles makes the idea of decentralisation virtually immune to criticism. Who could demur from a strategy which seems to offer so much to tenants, officers and elected members? Rather than assess the concept of decentralisation on the basis of such elusive generalities or promises, therefore, it is more instructive to consider the actual experience of local authorities which have decentralised their services. Probably more than a hundred local authorities have decentralised their housing service to some degree since the Walsall initiative. Research undertaken by the Housing Decentralisation Research Project, for example, has uncovered a spate of plans, proposals and completed schemes among local authorities in the North of England. A majority of councils with a substantial housing stock (over 6000 properties) have decentralised their services since 1980 or are in the process of restructuring.

One of the most ambitious decentralisation programmes has been introduced by the London Borough of Islington. Twenty-four neighbourhood offices provide housing, social work and community development services and a network of neighbourhood committees is being developed alongside, as a mechanism for consumer participation (London Borough of Islington 1987). The devolution of council decision-making has been taken further in Tower Hamlets through the creation of eight multi-service area committees with considerable autonomy and independent budgets (Morphet 1987). Elsewhere, major housing authorities such as Bradford, Newcastle and Leeds have introduced or extended systems of housing management at the neighbourhood level.

It is, therefore, difficult to categorise the rich diversity of organisational structures and management arrangements introduced in decentralisation: some involve the creation of area offices on an experimental basis, while others involve the establishment of estate offices in areas of severe deprivation; some comprise multi-service reorganisation and in a few cases a full-blooded system of neighbourhood offices is planned. Most of these schemes are marked by a fairly pragmatic and piecemeal approach, propelled more by managerial priorities than political objectives.

Most initiatives have in practice reflected what Paul Hoggett terms the 'consumerist' aspects of decentralisation, emphasising service delivery and accessibility, rather than a 'collectivist' model, emphasising service democracy and participation (Hoggett 1987). A stronger role for tenant involvement is envisaged, but this takes second place to improving the public image and effectiveness of the housing service (Windle, Cole and Arnold 1988). Like many such strategies of organisational change, however, enthusiasm for decentralisation has rarely emerged from a rational review of policy options or detailed prior research — hope, intuition, desperation and political instinct have probably been stronger influences.

Elected members as well as officers appear to share a more chastened view now about the potential for decentralisation to regenerate local communities. Decentralisation might provide a better deal for tenants and an improved quality of service, but within existing systems of accountability and control (Cole, Windle and Arnold 1988). A number of earlier ambitious initiatives, such as Hackney's, have foundered owing to the immense difficulties of putting the original vision into practice (Shields and Webber 1986, Tomlinson 1986). Local authorities have increasingly adopted more modest proposals for action, in the hope of meeting a number of more limited objectives, rather than risk achieving none at all.

There is very little independent evidence about the effects — as opposed to the aims — of decentralising housing services, reflecting a more general neglect of impact and outcomes in policy analysis. Ideas about performance measurement or consumer feedback are at an early stage in most local housing authorities. Furthermore, the weak information base in many housing departments (Clinton, Groves and Williams 1986) makes any interpretation of impact extremely hazardous. For a strategy explicitly designed to provide a better housing service, attempts to monitor the nature or scale of any such improvement are rare indeed.

Our research into decentralised local authorities in the North of England has provided some grounds for optimism. In the view of chief housing officers, general indicators of housing management tend to look brighter after a dose of localisation. Decentralisation was thought to have decreased average letting times and reduced the number of long-term void properties in two thirds of the local authorities in our survey (Cole, Windle and Arnold 1988). These two aspects of a housng service seem particularly amenable to improvement as a result of a more convenient and accessible service. It was claimed that the average time taken to complete a repair was often less than before, and that levels of rent arrears either fell or remained unchanged after decentralisation. In many areas the level of take-up of welfare and housing benefits was also thought to have increased as a result of greater contact with local authority services (Cole, Windle and Arnold 1988).

Chief housing officers in the majority of decentralised authorities claimed that job satisfaction in their departments had improved after an initial period of disruption. In many cases, more generic forms of housing practice had been developed as a result of decentralisation, and this had broadened officers' knowledge of the housing service.

These results should be treated cautiously. The perceptions of senior officers and members may be far removed from realities on the ground. Key policy-makers will have invested a great deal in the success of a major decentralisation programme and this may blind them to subsequent failures or problems. One study has identified a 'hierarchy of commitment' to decentralisation in which the positive views of senior staff and middle managers contrast sharply with the more jaundiced outlook of front-line workers struggling with ever-increasing demand (Fitzpatrick 1988). The impact of decentralisation is also difficult to assess because so very few authorities have established precise methods to measure service effectiveness. It is impossible to isolate the extent to which any improvements are as a result specifically of decentralisation (localisation, accessibility, participatory structures) rather than ancillary factors (higher staffing levels, improved new technology systems etc.). Nevertheless, these research results are promising.

Over two thirds of chief housing officers in our research thought that decentralisation had increased tenant involvement in the service; 60 per cent felt that tenants were now more satisfied with housing management. Chairs of Housing in northern authorities were even more positive about the impact on tenant satisfaction and participation (Cole, Windle and Arnold 1988, Cole, Arnold and Windle 1988). Yet tenant perceptions of the housing service are not confined to those functions carried out in the Housing Department; more than anything else, they are influenced by housing repairs, usually carried out by the Works Department, and often on a centralised basis. Here the evidence is less encouraging. Less than one third of chief officers felt that decentralisation had increased tenant satisfaction with the repairs service.

Local people are likely to take an instrumental view of neighbourhood services. Our examination of the response of tenants' groups to decentralisation in one large, northern metropolitan authority suggested that consumers do recognise and welcome the benefits arising from the provision of a local housing office. Tenants commented on the value of increased accessibility, reduced travel costs, better relationships with local staff and direct, face-to-face communication in dealing with their enquiries. These improvements help to provide the quality of service which tenants expect to receive. Evident and tangible gains brought about by decentralising provision are generally supported; yet tenants may not necessarily leap to the defence of the principles of council housing as a result, or become politically active in their locality. This awkward fact was often overlooked in the heady days following the Walsall initiative, celebrated in style by Jeremy Seabrook as the renaissance of working-class culture and political consciousness (Seabrook 1984, Mainwaring 1988).

Instead, the experience of receiving a more responsive and personal housing service may lead to further demands for an equivalent change in the provision of other areas of community services. While a number of authorities (such as Islington and Tower Hamlets) have attempted to introduce multi-service decentralisation, most authorities have tended to concentrate on a single service — usually led by housing (Arnold et al. 1988). Our research evidence confirms the anecdotal view that consumers — appreciative of the benefits of localisation within housing — soon wish to see the process extended across a wider range of services. Consumers tend to evaluate service responsiveness in a holistic manner; individual or communal problems rarely fall into neatly identifiable departmental problems. When a local authority establishes a local housing office, to achieve objectives of customer responsiveness and greater community involvement, it inevitably becomes the focus for diverse local needs and issues. Many of these problems will fall outside the remit of the Housing Department, or even the local authority as a whole.

In our research, consumers identified a specific need for service integration — between social workers, the police, community and youth workers and race relations officers. All these activities lie outside the control or influence of the local housing officer.

The meeting of these demands, now encouraged and articulated by decentralisation, is often difficult. Organisational structures may be insufficiently flexible to respond. Hierarchical or departmental vested interest may inhibit change. As a consequence, front-line staff are placed under increasing pressure to respond to evident grass roots demands within inappropriate organisational structures still largely defined by service specialisms. The ability of the service to respond to such demands will influence the enthusiasm with which consumers continue to support decentralised provision of services. The single service model of decentralisation, therefore, runs the risk of frustrating consumer demands for more integrated and accessible service provision

Any more general discussion about the impact of decentralisation on local communities must remain speculative, in the absence of detailed research on consumer response. Several opinion surveys of residents and tenants in local areas have revealed considerable support for the provision of neighbourhood offices (MORI 1987, Prescott–Clarke 1983). Two thirds of residents in a survey based in Reading, for example, felt a local office would improve their dealings with the Council (Safe Neighbourhoods Unit 1987). This is perhaps scarcely surprising, if respondents see the prospect of a more convenient service as a cost-free option. More open to question is the capacity of decentralised housing services to meet these higher expectations when resources are restricted; and such constraints have tightened sharply in the past few years. This brings us to consider how the noble ideals of decentralisation have been translated into practice by local authorities adopting this new approach.

The difficulty of implementation

A more measured appreciation of the potential in decentralisation has emerged, as local authorities have confronted a range of problems in implementing their ideas. Decentralisation often requires major restructuring and the promotion of a new management culture in the organisation — a process which may be painful for those involved. New management practices require trade union recognition, especially when previously separate activities have been integrated and staffing profiles affected. Initial commitment to decentralisation has been tested in various industrial relations disputes over job determination, gradings and the lack of adequate training, or where vulnerable neighbourhood-based staff have demanded better support and physical protection. In some authorities, staff turnover has increased sharply during the process of decentralisation.

The management of organisational change through decentralisation is a delicate task. Careful thought has to be given to ways of enhancing job satisfaction, recruiting new officers without alienating existing staff, generating new skills and reviewing systems of communication. Management problems may intensify when the housing department is the only service in the local authority which is decentralising. Links between neighbourhood housing offices and other centralised departments may inflame inter-service tensions and compound problems of co-ordination, information and control.

Even those local authorities which have advanced a long way down the path of decentralising service provision have had to wrestle with awkward problems in the devolution of decision-making and control. It may be more difficult to observe overriding political priorities — such as the promotion of equal opportunities — in a decentralised setting. The hesitant moves towards neighbourhood participation have provoked further questions about ensuring an effective long-term dialogue between service providers and consumers, generating whole-hearted commitment and maintaining confidentiality with a more open style of service provision.

And the tenants? Well, at worst, they have seemed rather bewildered onlookers to the private grief of industrial disputes, political confusion and inter-departmental wrangling within the council, as the original aim of providing a better, more outward-looking service has been overshadowed by operational problems. Elsewhere, the impact of decentralisation has been more encouraging, although evaluation is difficult to come by. Once a neighbourhood housing service has been introduced, very few councils have then systematically explored tenant views through group discussions, analysis of complaints data, sample surveys or public meetings and fed this information back into the policy process (Cole 1987). Usually anecdote triumphs over analysis as a signal of the effectiveness of the new service. Yet decentralisation is not a once and for all exercise. Local authorities need to build on the closer relationship with tenants and the greater opportunities for participation to shape their priorities for the future — otherwise, the neighbourhood-based service may itself become ossified and unresponsive.

The pitfalls of decentralisation are considerable. Many of the strengths of the policy are also potential weaknesses. Greater accessibility is a case in point. By relocating the housing service in user-friendly neighbourhood offices, demands may increase sharply. In the past, tenants may have limited requests for repairs because they felt it was a time-consuming, complicated and demoralising process. They will be less constrained if it is a case of popping in to a nearby office where the staff are friendly, welcoming and informed. Expectations about the housing service may change dramatically. The pressure on staff to meet these requests will be greater if the service is locally based. It is simply more difficult to deflect, mislead or avoid angry or persistent tenants.

The pressure of new demands brings us to the issue identified in our research as the most predictable, but also most tenacious, obstacle to decentralisation — the lack of resources. Some writers have suggested that the introduction of estate-based housing services may not require additional expenditure, as the improved service results in lower voids levels and hence increased rental income (Building Use Studies 1987). Our experience shows that this process is only applicable to a very few difficult estates with a large number of empty properties. When applied across a local authority area, decentralisation costs money. It increases capital expenditure, because of the costs of building new offices or converting existing accommodation. It increases revenue spending because of additional staffing, repairs expenditure, computing and training requirements, staff regradings and even committee running costs. These costs cannot be calculated precisely in advance. If successful, the service will generate increased demands, placing a continuous additional pressure on existing resources.

Much of the initial proselytising about the virtues of decentralisation was conducted without reference to costs. This could not be sustained in the face of ever sharper reductions in housing investment, the imposition of tighter central government control over expenditure and the withdrawal of housing revenue subsidy. Many of the most exciting and progressive decentralisation initiatives, such as Manchester City Council's, have now been placed at risk for these reasons. The constraints on action have meant that the critical path to the goal of a local, responsive and accountable service has in practice been strewn with obstructions. This only serves to underline the genuine achievements of those local authorities which have managed to introduce an effective and popular neighbourhood housing service in such an unpropitious climate.

Decentralisation and the future of council housing

To the extent that decentralisation is a strategy to move away from large scale municipal landlordism it shares common ground with the housing policies of the Thatcher Government since 1979. Yet the thrust of the Government's programme has concerned the ownership, rather than control, of public sector housing. The Department of the Environment has introduced the Priority Estates Project and Estate Action to encourage more local housing management, but these initiatives pale into insignificance compared to the 'right to buy' programme. For central government, the solution to the problems of centralism in council housing has been to sell off the stock, rather than spend too much on localising it.

The re-election of the Thatcher Government for a third term signalled that the demise of local authority housing was at the heart of new housing policies. Legislation has been designed to encourage, or force, the transfer of council estates to housing associations, private companies, trusts or co-operatives. This raises the question whether those local authorities which have decentralised their service will be better placed to withstand pressures to transfer stock. Has decentralisation restored local confidence in the housing service to such an extent that tenants will wish to retain the council as landlord? Or has this strategy, designed to regenerate council housing, inadvertently contributed to a fragmentation of the service?

Certainly, decentralisation carries a risk of fragmentation which has often been overlooked. A network of neighbourhood offices threatens established systems of communication and control in local authorities, making them vulnerable to external pressure. The aim of community solidarity may dissolve into displays of parochial self-interest, exacerbating rivalries and social divisions between different neighbourhoods. Deakin (1984), for example, has pointed to the dangers of 'inter-area contests for funding, competition for access to decision takers and the manipulation of evidence to make special cases'.

Decentralisation may also fragment by the housing service provoking internal conflicts, between senior managers in different departments, between manual and non-manual staff, between front-line and back-line workers and between policy-orientated councillors and ward members of their parties. The scale of restructuring may place relationships, commitment and morale under strain. Ironically enough, decentralisation may help to overcome some of the operational difficulties involved in the transfer of council estates to other landlords. In a centralised service, the very intricacies of bureaucratic control, inter-departmental links, and aggregated financial and information systems may make it extremely difficult to slice off particular neighbourhoods to housing associations or private landlords. (The creation of Housing Action Trusts is in part a recognition of such difficulties. The role of the Trusts will be to parcel up council stock for different forms of ownership, making it attractive to new landlords.) In a decentralised service, on the other hand, the creation of neighbourhood 'cost centres' and the devolution of management and decision-making procedures to localised operation may make the selective transfer of council stock easier to achieve.

Decentralisation may, therefore, lay the groundwork for the gradual removal of the local authority's landlord, management and maintenance responsibilities. So have the apparent virtues of decentralisation back-fired on local councils? We think that this judgment would be too harsh, especially if the alternative is an adherence to a discredited, rigid and unwieldy centralised service. The impetus behind decentralisation will prevail, though with a stronger managerial orientation than in the days of the Walsall and Islington initiatives. The difficulties of coping with increasing expectations and demands and the principles of value for money and efficiency, for example, are likely to figure more strongly: but the move towards a more responsive service will intensify in the face of government proposals. A diversified rented sector, with neighbourhood provision undertaken by local authorities, 'social' landlords and tenant co-operatives, would keep the ideals of decentralisation alive even while the tenure pattern changes.

We have suggested that decentralisation has been used as an umbrella term for distinct processes — such as consumer involvement, generic working, accessibility. These trends are likely to continue. However, we suspect that the focus of organisational change in public housing will shift from a concern with structures, to a reappraisal of new processes. Much of the early discussion about decentralisation was dominated by an obsession with determining the right structure for the housing service — in terms of organisation charts, committee systems and neighbourhood boundaries. This has now been overtaken by critical evaluation of processes: the means by which the culture, image and operational priorities of a housing service can be changed. This shift in focus has been illustrated by a change in terminology — instead of 'decentralisation', now read 'customer orientation'. But the catchwords matter less than the continuing attempts to bring about improvements in the public housing service, and to strengthen its position in the new, competitive environment of rented housing.

Conclusion

Decentralisation is often seen as a passing fad, marking a short epoch in the history of council housing. We believe this view is mistaken. We began by showing how the ideas behind decentralisation were being discussed by local authorities forty years ago. We have ended by claiming that the aims will live on, albeit under different terminology. We would therefore emphasise the enduring rather than ephemeral nature of the decentralisation ideal in public sector housing.

In part, the commitment to decentralisation has stemmed from an attempt to retrieve some of the former strengths of council housing, such as localism, while also highlighting the failure of the corporate dream during the 1960s and 1970s. Yet it is not possible to turn back the clock. No strategy can wish away the impact of the intervening forty years on the nature of council housing itself. Decentralisation has tried to breathe new life into a service seriously weakened by long-term economic pressures, political pragmatism and managerial incompetence. Local authority housing is now a residual sector of the housing market, rather than the universal service Bevan hoped for. The social, economic and political constraints on the local housing management are enormous. As du Parcq (1987) has pointed out: 'decentralisation does not have the answer for. . . escalating problems of poverty, despair and homelessness'.

We need, therefore, to be aware of the limitations of organisational change, and to keep a sense of historical perspective before we can usefully assess the contribution of decentralisation to improving local authority housing services. Decentralisation has not produced nirvana at the neighbourhood level. It has, however, forced moribund organisations to be more effective. It has made housing officers, at all levels, listen to tenants. It has helped to break down artificial specialisms and rigid procedures. Above all, it has kept alive the principles of accessibility, responsiveness and participation in public housing. That is surely worth fighting for, especially in the face of pressures from the 'independent' landlords of the future. It is certainly a preferable strategy for local housing authorities than the alternative — unconditional surrender.

References

Arnold P., Cole I. and Windle K. (1988) *The Decentralisation of Housing–The Perceptions of Chief Executives Officers* House Decentralisation Research Project, School of Urban Studies, Sheffield City Polytechnic.

Audit Commission (1986) *Managing the Crisis in Council Housing* Audit Commission.

Barclay Report (1982) *Social Workers: Their Roles and Tasks* London Bedford Square Press.

Blunkett D. and Green G. (1983) *Building from the Bottom: The Sheffield Experience* Fabian Tract No. 491.

Building Use Studies Ltd (1987) *Monitoring the Cost of Local Housing Management* Royal Institute of Public Administration.

City University Housing Research Group (1981) *Can Local Authorities be Better Landlords?* City University, London.

Clinton A., Groves R. and Williams P. (1986) *Housing Information Research Project Final Report* Institute of Housing.

Cole I. (1987) The Delivery of Housing Services in Willmott P. (ed.) *Local Government Decentralisation and Community* Policy Studies Institute.

Cole I., Windle K. and Arnold P. (1988a) *The Impact of Decentralisation* Housing Decentralisation Research Project Working Paper 3, School of Urban Studies, Sheffield City Polytechnic.

Cole I., Arnold P. and Windle K. (1988b) *Decentralisation — The Views of Elected Members* Housing Decentralisation Research Project Working Paper 4, School of Urban Studies, Sheffield City Polytechnic.

Community Development Project (1976) *Whatever Happened to Council Housing?* Community Development Project.

Cullingworth Committee (1969) *Council Housing: Purposes, Procedures, Priorities* London: CHAC, HMSO 1969.

Deakin N. (1984) Decentralisation: panacea or blind alley *Local Government Policy-Making* July.

Dearlove J. (1979) *The Reorganisation of British Local Government* Cambridge, Cambridge University Press.

Department of Environment (1988) *The Organisation of Housing Management in English Local Authorities* London: HMSO.

du Parcq L. (1987) Neighbourhood services: the Islington experience in Willmott P. (ed.) *Local Government Decentralisation and Community* London Policy Studies Institute.

Fitzpatrick N. (1988) *Decentralisation: What do Staff Think?* B. A. Housing Studies Dissertation. Sheffield City Polytechnic.

Gallagher P. (1982) The Ideology of Housing Management in English J. (ed.) *The Future of Council Housing* London Croom Helm.

Gyford J. (1985) *The Politics of Local Socialism* London Allen & Unwin.

Hambleton R. (1978) *Policy Planning and Local Government* London Hutchinson.

Henney A. (1985) *Trust the Tenant: Devolving Municipal Housing* Centre for Policy Studies.

Hoggett P. (1987) Going beyond a rearrangement of the deckchairs: some practical hints for councillors and managers in Hoggett P. and Hambleton R. (eds.) *Decentralisation and Democracy: Localising Public Services* School for Advanced Urban Studies, University of Bristol.

Jones G. and Stewart J. (1985) *The Case for Local Government* London Allen & Unwin.

Leeds City Council (1948) *Housing Annual Report 1947–48* Leeds City Council.

London Borough of Islington (1987) *Going Local: Decentralisation in Practice* London: Islington Council Press.

Mainwaring R. (1988) I*The Walsall Experience* London: HMSO.

MORI (1987) *Council Tenants' Attitudes Towards Housing* Richmond upon Thames, Surrey.

Morphet J. (1987) Local authority decentralisation — Tower Hamlets *Policy and Politics* **15**, No. 2.

Prescott-Clarke P. (1983) *Decentralisation of Council Services in Hackney: A Survey of Residents* Social and Community Planning Research.

Safe Neighbourhoods Unit (1987) *Your Views for a Change* Reading Borough Council.

Seabrook J. (1984) *The Idea of Neighbourhood* London Pluto.

Shields R. and Webber J. (1986) Hackney Lurches Local *Community Development Journal* **21**, No. 2.

Tomlinson M. (1986) *Decentralisation — Learning the Lessons? The Radical Failure of Decentralisation in Hackney 1981–83* PCL Planning Study 18, Polytechnic of Central London.

Windle K., Cole I. and Arnold P. (1988) *Decentralisation of Housing: Structure and Process* Housing Decentralisation Research Project Working Paper 2, School of Urban Studies, Sheffield City Polytechnic.

Part 3
Looking ahead

Chapter 11
What price? Social housing

Rent matters

Rent setting ignorance
This chapter is concerned with rent setting in British social housing. After seven decades of public housing there is still little knowledge of how property rents are related to characteristics of dwellings, either for a single landlord or across different providers. Policy debate has focussed on comparisons of average rent levels across tenures or time periods and more recently on 'affordable rents'. Much less attention has been paid to the intra-organisational patterns of rents in relation to housing type and area, that is, the rent structures.

There was, and is, little justification for this neglect of detailed pricing policies. Price structures have both 'fairness' and 'efficiency' characteristics. For those concerned with 'fairness' issues there should have been a concern to establish the detailed distribution of subsidies, which are best defined as the gap between the value of specific dwelling services received and rents paid, by tenants. Without such knowledge there is no basis for the belief that large council subsidies will benefit poorer households. 'Efficiency' consequences may be equally important. The free market critique of social housing has stressed the resource allocation inefficiencies which arise from poor pricing, but there has been a muted response from the defenders of public housing. 'Free market' advocates argue that in 'social' systems poorly judged prices may result in empty houses, unduly long waiting lists, false investment signals, mismatches of households by house size etc. It is not necessary to adopt a 'New Right' view on rents to believe that the failure of central and local governments to recognise, let alone address, the broader consequences of rent setting has meant that the negative consequences of poor pricing have become more apparent as the social system matured. Similar concerns have been expressed regarding the Fair Rent (rent regulation) system as applied to private rental housing in Britain (Maclennan 1982) and to housing association tenancies (Maclennan et al. 1989).

Rent Setting, A New Importance
The Duke of Edinburgh's Inquiry of 1985 elevated 'consistent pricing' to the centre stage of the policy debate. And this debate, in a piecemeal and partial fashion, had a major influence on ideas about reviving private rented investment in housing.

Whilst academics, see for instance Hills (1988) and Ermisch (1984) have advocated a more rational rental pricing system, it is not these proponents who have created the pressures for change but changes in the housing and local government legislation of the late 1980s. These Acts were aimed at curtailing council provision, pluralising social housing and reviving private investment in rented housing. Many of the specific, operational details of policy are still unclear but it is apparent that there are pressures to change rent levels and rent structures in each of the three main rental tenure sectors. Indeed, we argue below that present proposals are piecemeal in nature and do not constitute a 'level playing field' for pricing and investment policies (see also Maclennan et al 1991).

The 1988 Housing Acts abandoned the 'fair rent' system for the pricing of new housing investment in the independent rented sector (private lets and housing associations). Housing associations are now confronted with the task of setting their own rents (on new lettings) for the first time since 1974. This change has been complicated by conflicting advice from central government. Associations are being encouraged to develop rational pricing schemes which reflect property quality and costs but at the same time ensure that rents are, in the Government's ill-defined phrase, 'affordable'. Rent-setting is now a crucial area of housing association business.

In contrast to associations, councils have been left (apart from short periods in 1919 and 1972–74) to devise their own rent schemes. However they are now also subject to pressures for change. During the 1970s flat rate rent increase limits, as part of counter-inflation strategy, distorted pre-existing differentials and this process continued in the 1980s as the majority of councils implemented flat rate or percentage rent rises in accordance with central government rent guidelines. Many councils have now recognised the long term consequences of these changes. Another pressure for change has arisen as local authority Housing Revenue Accounts (HRA) were 'ring fenced' in England and Wales from 1990. That is there are to be no transfers from or payments to other accounts within a local authority. Council housing finance is to stand alone. Further, 'reckonable' income for housing subsidy purposes is to be assessed upon a multiple of capital values within the council sector. In a similar vein, rent officers have been given (in the 1988 Act) the new task of checking housing benefit payments for rents against a 'value-for-money' standard (related to capital values) and this is likely to force some uniformity of criteria upon councils.

British housing policy is therefore entering a period in which local rent setting will become a more crucial issue for all social sector landlords. Although central government has developed neither a national rent scheme nor a national rent strategy, important policy issues will arise in relation to the equity and efficiency aspects of rent setting across the main rental tenure groups.

This chapter is essentially forward looking, and our emphasis is upon the merits and demerits of likely rent schemes. The next section sets out the key features of market pricing systems and major implications of departures from them. There then follows a brief review of UK experience with administered pricing systems and their consequences. The final substantive section examines in detail proposed pricing systems and sets out the pros and cons of the main rent scheme types available to social sector landlords.

Are market prices right?

British housing is often described as being a mixed (public–private) system. The label 'confused', may be more apposite. Early proponents of public housing who advocated a departure from market provision had little conception of what the alternative structure of housing rents ought to be. It was enough for them that rents were not market determined. This is not to suggest that there is any *a priori* 'correct' theoretical price. Rather, if price is defined as the terms on which purchasing opportunities are made available and accepted, then it is clear that different, rational and coherent pricing systems may exist as long as they are designed to attain objectives over and above those which would prevail in a market system. That is, the 'correctness' of a price has to be assessed against both the objectives of housing (and related) policies and the means available to government to intervene by price and non-price measures.

The 'correctness' of competitive market prices is restricted to instances where there are accepted ethical judgments that individuals are best at judging their own well-being, that the distribution of income which underpins consumer spending is fair and that spillover effects, or externalities, do not matter. This view also assumes that the market works without frictions or monopolies. Thus, the present debate about housing pricing in the UK is little more than a latter day return of the classic debates between the pro-marketeers and the pro-planning economists (see, for instance, Nath 1969).

In many respects, this debate left the issue of pricing of housing untouched, with most rent schemes shaped by pre-debate positions. In the housing context it is, therefore, still pertinent to lay out and emphasise the advantages and disadvantages of market and planned prices. For whilst few associations and councils will set market prices, some quasi-market pricing schemes are possible.

Market prices

In textbook economic analysis market prices emerge from the smooth workings of a competitive market. The market, if not already in equilibrium, is always assumed to be moving swiftly, and automatically, towards a competitive equilibrium. Prices are assumed to reflect the relative scarcities of resources and consumers' preferences and incomes.

In a given market context, prices will ration out the existing stock of goods. In the short-term, if there is a shortage of goods, prices will rise and commodities will then pass to households most willing and able to pay the ruling price. In the housing market, for example, rising rents per unit of space will encourage households under-using their dwellings (a problem in the British public sector) to economise on space use, perhaps by taking in a lodger or by moving to a smaller unit. It is arguable, for instance, that the observation that 25 per cent of council tenants live in houses which they regard as too large for them (Maclennan et al. 1989) would not occur in a market allocation system. Unfortunately, the same rise in rents will invariably ration poorer households into more overcrowded, lower quality or less accessible, housing. Thus, even a single direction of price change may have effects regarded as being both beneficial (a better use of stock) and harmful (pressurising the low paid).

A short run price rise, with its generally greater adverse consequences for low income groups, is the dark side of the market system. Pro-marketeers would argue, however, that market rents provide a set of clear signals to which producers will respond. Prices of unpopular housing will fall, developers' profits will be reduced, and resources will be transferred to more popular sectors. Or, in a new location with expanding employment, demand will rise, prices will rise and new investment, using efficient techniques and with the correct mix of land and capital, will flow forth with, perhaps, prices returning towards their initial level. Again, in the context of the council sector, it could be argued that the poor design and location choices so characteristic of the 1960s would have been less likely to arise if 'price signals' had driven investment.

In the new financial regime for housing associations, some capital is to be raised in the financial markets. Investment returns earned will signal to private investors the associations which take appropriate risks and safely manage investors' capital. In time, the price mechanism will favour, arguably, more efficient associations with lower risk premia and, therefore, lower capital costs. But, does the housing market work in this simple and efficient fashion?

Elsewhere (Maclennan 1982) it is argued that the housing system is not best viewed as being a simple competitive market. At the very best, in structural terms, the private housing market may be characterised as combining elements of monopoly and competition. Further, since housing is a complex commodity, shortage of housing in a given location may raise prices there but at the same time it is likely to lead to some households trading to other submarkets or even dropping out of existence as a separate household unit (e.g. young married couples living with parents). Thus, quantity adjustments or queues occur as well as price signals and it is often quantity rather than price signals that a builder, let alone a social investor, requires. In the absence of such signals, then, suppliers may tend to systematically under-supply the market. Even if housing shortages were to be reflected in a clear overall price signal the large number of potential local respondents may mean that an overall price response is not a clear signal for individual action — again estimates of probable quantity requirements will also be preferable for risk averse suppliers (Richardson 1959).

It is not at all clear, then, that price can be relied upon to organise the housing system within any moderately acceptable period of adjustment. The diffusion of price signals due to commodity range and complexity, the lag in supply response, and the importance of quantity information are all key considerations in the housing system. It is hardly surprising that proponents of reform, such as the Duke of Edinburgh's Inquiry (1985), focus upon reasonable rates of return on long term capital values, but without much guidance as to how we are to identify them.

Pricing issues for the social sector
The above comments have been directed at housing markets in general. Additional problems arise in the context of public sector pricing. First, a local authority may often be a dominant monopolist in the local rented housing market. In British cities exceeding half a million in population, council housing still provides more than 50 per cent of all housing. At the more local scale concentration of municipal ownership is often greater, for example in the public estates on the edge of British cities where 3000–10,000 council houses may exist in isolation from other tenures. Second, these authorities are discriminating monopolists, in the sense that they can vary the relationship between price, quantity and quality as they wish for particular groups of consumers or houses (as long as rents fall below market levels). Finally, even if a monopolistic authority chose to replicate prices and invest in line with consumer signals central government restrictions on capital spending are likely to preclude such rational investment. It cannot be assumed that, in their present centralised form, UK housing authorities would create efficient social markets for housing. As Robinson noted, decades ago, regarding market signalling, 'the whole beauty of the system is lost if the seller can manipulate the price'(Robinson 1962, p 265). It is not inconceivable that in some localities housing associations will also have local monopoly power.

The above paragraphs have raised the problems associated with generating housing market responses, but there may well also be concerns with housing outcomes, even if the system were to respond smoothly to price signals. A government concerned with housing, aside from wishing to minimise the short term costs of price adjustment while achieving long run adjustment, may also wish to intervene in the housing market if prices fail to reflect social concerns on a number of counts. Indeed, as in the post-1919 development of council housing, intervention leading to price distortion could reflect an inability to redistribute income via the tax or benefit system. This problem also now lies at the heart of the confused notion of 'affordable rents' which permeates discussion of the association sector. If housing policies are to pursue multiple objectives then it may be naive to assume that a single policy instrument (income related subsidies) will achieve all ends.

In many respects then, the case for departing from market prices (and by implication, income related subsidies) in housing will tend to be greater when:

— bad housing conditions produce serious side-effects, or externalities;

— society demands a decent minimum standard of housing for all;

— these standards are not likely to be attained even with some redistribution of income;

— income related subsidies are not technically feasible or are limited by government spending decisions (such as the limits now imposed on the Housing Benefit system);

— incomes are low and housing is essentially concerned with shelter;

— shortages of adequate housing are severe.

This list of considerations is, in effect, a statement of the *raison d'etre* of social housing in Britain. Recent research in Scotland and England makes it clear that extensive groups of people cannot be housed decently without the assistance of considerable subsidies (Maclennan et al 1990 and 1991). Further, research in Glasgow indicates that there are major spillover benefits from rehabilitation activity (Maclennan 1990). There is no reason why tenants alone should pay for the production of these benefits; this is an obligation for the whole of society. Indeed, the Glasgow study noted that if given the equivalent of Housing Association Grant (HAG) as an income increase tenants would spend less than half of it on housing, and those that did would move away from rehabilitation areas.

If such considerations are to influence policy, then various pricing systems can be adopted to achieve social and economic objectives. These systems will probably differ for a rapidly urbanising low income economy, a relatively mature economy emerging from a prolonged war, and an advanced economy with relatively high incomes, complex housing demands, computerised information systems and a broad balance between households and houses.

Economic progress and improvement in national housing conditions in postwar Europe has, correctly, been associated with a progressive shift from 'bricks and mortar' to 'income related' housing subsidies. But few governments have abolished 'bricks and mortar' subsidies and the key problem now may be that government has misconceived the extent of progress in the British housing economy. For there is a widespread assumption that social housing investment is primarily about removing shortages for low income households. This view may be pertinent in Southern Britain. In the North, however, the key issues relate to renewal, modernisation and reinvestment, and in general, these tasks may require different pricing criteria, as indeed may strategies to solve homelessness in London.

We must consider how a single housing association or housing authority ought to price its housing. The solution will depend on the nature of the housing system within a local area and government objectives. Both these critical concerns may vary over space and time.

Administrative rent fixing

The general experience of rent setting in the UK can be contrasted with the above 'in-principle' discussion of the role of rents in housing systems. The association and council sectors are examined separately.

Housing Association rent setting
Prior to 1974 housing associations set their own rents, usually covering project costs net of subsidised loans. The 1965 Rent Act introduced, for the private rental sector, the concept of rent regulation through the application of so-called 'fair rents'. The 'fair rent' system was extended to housing associations in 1974 (and briefly to councils under the 1972 Housing Finance Act).

The concept of regulation was fundamentally different from earlier policies of strict rent control. The essential aim of the system was to establish greater equity between landlords and tenants, in an attempt to both protect tenants from excessive rents and to enable landlords to obtain an acceptable return on investment. The Act laid down a formula for fixing fair rents on the basis of individual dwelling characteristics, particularly the age, character, locality and state of repair of the dwelling.

The system also made provision for periodic rent reviews (every two years in England and three years in Scotland) and rent officers could make an allowance for expected inflation in setting rents. When reviewed, rents were therefore adjusted either upwards or downwards, though after 1974 a restriction in the form of rent phasing was applied to rent increases. The fair rent system has often been criticised for producing inconsistent patterns of rent in relation to property quality and location, and for failing to halt a continuing decline in the private rental sector. The criticisms stem from two main factors. Firstly, the fair rent system sought to determine a rent which would apply in market equilibrium by setting an allowance for scarcity (excess demand) against assessed reasonable pre-tax rate of return. The mechanism for determining this 'scarcity factor' was far from clear, though it did specifically exclude personal circumstances and thus willingness and ability to pay.

This procedure which may be described as a means of establishing a non-scarcity market rent, has been described by Maclennan (1982) as 'an economic nonsense'. Similarly Hills (1988) noted that since price is usually determined by the interaction of supply and demand, the fair rent setting mechanism is 'almost without economic meaning'. It is also interesting to note that the (1971) Francis Committee report into the workings of the 1965 Rent Act suggested that rent officers had difficulty in quantifying scarcity and therefore did not discount for it.

It is likely that fair rents were based on the concept of housing need, so that rents would be set at the level which the marginal household is able to pay. As a consequence of the scarcity factor, fair rents, especially in areas of excess demand, will be below likely equilibrium market levels acting as a disincentive to investment in rented housing. Therefore the scarcity factor, by specifically excluding consideration of shortage or surplus, ensured that fair rents were not market rents, and thus prevented the rental sector from ever reaching long-run equilibrium and undoubtedly served to distort inter-sectoral tenure choices.

Determination of an appropriate rate of return presented a second problem. Difficulties in the process of assessing and comparing capital values (in relation to market prices ruling in the owner-occupied sector) were compounded by the effects of house price inflation and anticipated capital gains. For example, some landlords may have been prepared to let at relatively low rents in anticipation of high capital gains whilst others sought premia to compensate for tenant security of tenure. These difficulties in determining appropriate rates of return, in conjunction with the 'scarcity factor' problem, led to inconsistencies in fair rents.

The setting of fair rents, in practice, was a more perfunctory exercise. Reference was made to comparable properties and recently set rent levels. Inconsistency in approach was revealed by the Department of the Environment's 'Beacons' exercise which showed wide variations in the percentages of both gross and net rent against capital value, with net rent ranging from less than 1 per cent of capital value in parts of inner and outer London to between 3 and 4 per cent in Northumberland, West Yorkshire and Avon. Returns were quite different for other property types in the same areas.

The Duke of Edinburgh's Inquiry (1985) also noted that on average fair rents appeared to give a gross (pre-tax) return on capital value of about 3–4 per cent in England and Wales, although there was considerable variation, with areas of high capital value tending to produce lower returns. There is, however, evidence of much higher returns being obtained where lettings operate outwith Rent Act control, effectively already in a deregulated market. In contrast, fair rents in other more depressed areas may already be equivalent to market rents (see Maclennan et al, 1991).

It is clear that the fair rent system, does not lead to an efficient or rational rent setting process. By suppressing market forces, it led in many areas to rents which were well below market levels and which bore little relationship to the capital or revenue costs of housing provision. The critical point for housing associations, was that they had little direct financial interest in the level of rent set on subsidised (HAG) properties, since the fair rent determined either the initial grant rate or the extent of subsequent grant redemption fund (GRF) contributions. Different rent levels would have left the financial position of the association largely unaffected. And this is now the crux of why associations find rent setting such a crucial issue, with grant rates prefixed by government (at least for the foreseeable future). It should also be noted that for the next few years associations face the further difficulty that the fair rent status of tenancies will remain until a change of tenant occurs. Thus associations will not be free to set rents on many of their properties.

Rent setting in the council sector
There have been few studies of how councils in Britain actually set relative rents. A brief review in the late 1970s was followed by a sample study in 1983 of 48 English authorities (Maclennan and Wood 1984), a sample of 44 Scottish councils (Cochrane 1985) and a more widespread English summary in 1986 (Maclennan 1986).

The 1983 study showed that around half of councils set rents in relation to a multiple (differing from place to place) of assessed annual value for rating purposes (GAV/RV). Most of the rest used points based schemes relating to property characteristics. Large authorities had a higher proportion of points schemes as opposed to GAV/RV measures. Past reliance on such schemes means that rent schemes based on a shift to assessed capital values will call for little change of approach for many councils.

Around three quarters of the councils which had points schemes used only three or four criteria to determine relative property values. Dwelling age, type and size were the most widely used and important factors. These schemes were crude and problematic. Large authorities such as Sheffield and Manchester developed much more sophisticated points schemes relating rents to 10–15 dwelling characteristics, including locational and neighbourhood attributes as well as internal dwelling features.

Impacts
It has to be noted at the outset that rent pooling and cost pooling, the use of historic cost concepts in accounts and the nature of the housing benefit system all act to reduce the efficacy of the allocative and signalling role of rents. For instance, in the 1988 Act, the Government were rather naive in assuming that passing rent setting powers to associations would solve consumer 'signalling' problems. Generous producer subsidies (on average 75 per cent in England in 1989) coupled with having two thirds of tenants on housing benefit, immediately frustrated that aim. However, if rent schemes are not related to dwelling quality or value these problems are exacerbated and problems of fairness are generated.

We have already noted, in a general fashion, how poorly structured rent schemes encouraged poor investment decisions and exacerbated a mismatch between housing sizes and household size. In addition, inefficiencies in service provision decisions should not be disregarded. A recent report on housing management in England (Maclennan et al 1989) indicated that almost 40 per cent of council tenants and a third of association tenants felt that they were being provided with the wrong mix of services. Further, one third of tenants indicated that they would be prepared to pay on average an additional £1.50 per week for better services. Such inefficiencies are not small.

These problems may be tolerated as long as the degree of subsidy is high for all tenants. But if subsidy is reduced, then the impacts of un- fairness and inefficiency may become more apparent. Some groups, disadvantaged by the rent scheme, may choose to leave the sector by purchasing their dwellings or by opting en masse to transfer to another landlord. These issues will become important in the housing associa- tion and council sectors over the next few years.

Local mismatches in the relationship between rents and quality have probably grown over time. The original pricing schemes may have been quite appropriate for the initial phases of public sector development. With the passage of time, however, simple schemes are affected by two sets of forces. Growth of the public sector has involved the development of new locations and house types and public housing has come to encompass a range of housing possibilities not envisaged in the original scheme. At the same time, ageing of the existing stock occurs at different rates for different houses. Identical housing units in equivalent locations built at the same time mature in different ways; some neighbourhoods may improve over time whereas others suffer an inexorable decline. Council pricing schemes seldom allow for this divergent dynamic, and it is doubtful whether rent officers allowed for such influences in setting fair rents in the association sector.

Variations in the quality of stock associated with perverse rental patterns may attract attention on grounds of fairness, but often it is the pattern of vacancies and the emergence of unpopular areas that first cause concern. Thus many authorities may now wish to use revised rent schemes to assist in solving their 'difficult-to-let' problems. If housing association rents rise rapidly this issue may well confront them as well in the 1990s. These concerns may be reinforced as 'social' landlords recognise the need to cater for housing preferences and as pervasive excess demand no longer prevails.

Until the 1970s two broad operational assumptions shaped the pricing policies of housing authorities. First, a simple conception of housing needs, based upon a limited view of the range of household services or activities, guided policy and this was reflected in rent patt- erns. The importance of locational, environmental and other amenities in determining housing values, and, therefore, rent/quality relations were widely disregarded. Real household incomes have grown marked- ly in the postwar period and people have, in the market sector at least, tried to secure housing related services (amenity, comfort, accessibility, status) extending beyond basic shelter. This poses problems of pricing and allocation for authorities. Whilst physical 'shelter' needs may be fairly easily defined and measured for most households in a relatively uniform fashion, environmental and accessibility requirements are most complex and vary from one household to another. This raises the critical question as to whether, for a large and diverse stock of housing, with different preferences for different customers, administrative pricing remains efficient, or even feasible. The second major assumption was that 'deep' council subsidies would prevail in a context of excess demand for dwellings. Clearly, such assumptions are no longer valid.

The advantages and disadvantages of different approaches are examined in the next section and, finally, some conclusions are offered.

The menu of pricing schemes

There is a large set of possible pricing schemes available to councils and associations, not all of which are likely to be efficient in achieving landlords' objectives, let alone national housing policy goals. And of course, we recall our earlier caveat that the continuance of the fair rent system for existing tenancies constrains choices for housing associations. The schemes examined here fall under two broad headings, first rent structures which reflect various concepts of dwelling characteristics, cost and value. Secondly, and this issue has only gained currency with discussion of the new financial regime for associations, there are pricing schemes related to tenant characteristics rather than dwelling attributes. These may be loosely termed 'affordability' rent setting schemes.

Characteristics
Such schemes essentially relate relative dwelling rents to the characteristics of the units involved. As such they are often labelled as 'comparability' schemes. Comparability rent schemes take two broad forms which, for most purposes, can be regarded as equivalent. In the principle form dwellings are allocated points on the basis of a selected set of characteristics and this generates a total of property points for each property and, in aggregate, for the landlord's total stock. Where the rental revenue to be raised is already known then total rent divided by total property points yields a rent-per-point figure which can then be applied to each dwelling. A second variation is to identify the required average rent per dwelling and then to adjust the rent for each individual dwelling upwards or downwards depending on its characteristics. Adjustments may be in proportional or percentage terms (when they apply to all embracing attributes such as size, etc.) or they may be of a fixed absolute amount (for instance for the presence or absence of some discrete attribute, such as a garage, etc.). The broad outcomes are similar.

Gavin Wood, has clearly summarised the main features of comparability schemes, and the following paragraphs are based on his work (Maclennan and Wood 1984).

Two basic principles are observed by such a scheme:

1 Gross rents and rent differentials will relate solely to the physical attributes of properties and their environment and location.
2 The basis upon which rents are computed is open to public scrutiny. This enables the components of the scheme to be the subject of tenant consultation. Furthermore, the accuracy of individual rents can be independently checked by tenants.

There are then important distinctions to be drawn between such comparability schemes and those based upon market principles. The former take no cognisance of changes in those demographic and economic factors which help to determine the composition and level of demand. They will not, therefore, explicitly use rent as a rationing device, to mould choice by reference to the ability of individual tenants to pay for housing (although the overall multiplier value may take account of such considerations for the tenantry taken as a whole).

This reflects a particular analytical perspective concerning the operation of housing markets, both public and private. Important influences upon this perspective are the nature of housing demand and supply. Households' structure of demand can be specific in nature. Older households tend to prefer ground floor dwellings not readily substitutable for others. For people seeking work, vacant dwellings in a town with little or no employment opportunities, are not close substitutes for dwellings located near employment centres. These examples serve to demonstrate the segmentation of demand that can occur, and which will weaken the linkages between areas and different house types. In such circumstances, the housing stock can become segmented into quasi-autonomous submarkets, in which housing demand will be insensitive to rent differentials in neighbouring submarkets.

Allowing rents to reflect mismatches between demand and supply which arise from changing demographic and economic factors can seriously exacerbate the financial barriers to choice for low income groups. Furthermore, the fluctuations in rent patterns can, by the very nature of their cause, increase the rate of loss, via sales, of those dwellings which are the subject of excess demand. Rising rents may then signal not the production of more housing of the most popular kinds, but its loss through sales to sitting tenants. This impact will damage the landlords' capacity to meet the housing aspirations of waiting list and transfer applicants.

The half of British councils which do not use annual value pricing schemes could be deemed to be using 'comparability' schemes. When a comparability points scheme is selected as the basis for pricing, the landlord faces two critical questions. First, which dwelling and neighbourhood attributes should be included? Second, and perhaps more difficult, what weight of points score should be attached to each item? There are essentially two (potentially overlapping) processes which can be used to resolve these issues. Committees, officers and tenants may produce schemes by a process of consultation and negotiation. This process is of course open to manipulation and dispute as the gainers and losers will quickly identify which schemes are most advantageous for them. At the national level such a plethora of 'politically' determined schemes could result in quite different schemes and rents for properties of adjacent landlords. This would undermine the credibility of all schemes and create problems in assessing value for money in housing benefit payment. Neighbouring housing associations developing identical units but with different rent schemes could conceivably secure different levels of subsidy for their developments.

A second approach would be to consider, from valuers' experience and statistical analysis, the way in which property characteristics influence market rents and prices. Academic research on the determination of property prices has much to offer in this regard. There are literally hundreds of studies of the impact of property and neighbourhood characteristics on house prices (see Maclennan 1982).

These 'hedonic' studies do reveal the broad structure of price determinants in the market sector and they could form a baseline for the political process. The use of weights derived from hedonic index studies would have the advantage of aligning the points used in calculating rents to the weightings observed in market (or capital) value based approaches. However, the application of market-based valuations to the social sector poses problems which arise from the fact that the physical characteristics and resident profiles of market and social sectors differ. A key point is that if social sector residents were forced to find shelter in the existing private stock then market rents and values could be lowered, as incomes drive demand and demand, in turn, influences prices. This effect is, however, likely to be more important in relation to rent levels rather than rent structures.

Two further observations are pertinent. First, local housing associations may be able to drop a broad range of neighbourhood influences from their schemes because in small areas these factors may be taken as a constant. Secondly, reflecting the way in which housing is developed, house type, size and location, tend to be correlated. That is to say, a few indicators may, via multicollinearity, explain much of the variation in property prices. Where such 'complex' indicators exist they may allow schemes with relatively few items to be quite accurate in determining relative property values.

The problem for landlords is that they cannot predict in advance which indicators will perform such a function for their stock. Consistent rent setting will require consistent data. Systematic, computerised property information lies at the heart of comparability rent setting, and government may have to give appropriate guidance to councils and associations.

Gavin Wood continues: 'Caution should be expressed with regard to two aspects of property information collection. Firstly, where such information has been collected in the past there is inevitably an incentive to tailor schemes to fit the already existing information. The purpose for which the information has been obtained could be quite different from that of introducing a new rent scheme (repairs and maintenance for instance), and may not be wholly suitable as a basis for setting rents. Secondly, unlike dwelling characteristics, there tends to be considerable ambiguity concerning measures of relevant aspects of the environment. For instance, the Northern Ireland Housing Executive scheme issued for consultation intended to incorporate access to shopping facilities, public transport and leisure facilities as components of the environment grading. Robust measures of access are difficult to arrive at, partly because what is accessible for say a young person, differs significantly from what would be considered proximate by an old age pensioner and in consequence such inconvenient measures often disappear from pricing schemes' (Maclennan and Wood 1984).

Arriving at an appropriate listing and measurement of attributes is the first stage of construction. The second involves the choice of points weightings. The procedure observed in Northern Ireland was that of dividing the list of attributes into the five broad categories: house type, house size, internal and related amenities, age and environment. Within each category, attributes were ranked by reference to what was judged to reflect tenants' preference orderings. Thus, for example, within the same house type category the ordering was detached, semi-detached, terraced, low rise flats and maisonettes and, finally, high rise flats and maisonettes. Decisions were also made on the relative importance of each of the broad categories. This took the form of ascribing a percentage value for the proportion of the average points score of the stock which each category should account for. A programming exercise was used to choose points values which satisfied both the rankings within categories and the constraints placed upon the relative importance of the broad categories.

Subjective judgements are of course susceptible to error. A public consultation exercise can serve as a crosscheck. Consultation exercises, however, have not been widely used in this area. There are, therefore, no well established methods of effectively eliciting tenants' views. The consultation exercise in Northern Ireland attracted some criticism concerning its nature.

Once a computerised property record scheme is developed officials can develop a range of weighting schemes and, importantly, assess how they will impact particular properties. The pattern of increases and decreases from prevailing rents can then be determined. If suitable household information is also available then the impacts of rent changes by socio-economic, income and benefit groups may be ascertained.

Rents based on costs and values

Quality related schemes of the kind noted above essentially 'impute' rents or values to dwellings without reference to external price or cost considerations. However, there are a number of pricing schemes, increasing in importance, where 'social' landlords attempt to relate rent structures to costs and prices. This section considers such schemes.

As noted in our introduction the setting of rents requires absolute as well as relative considerations. Here, as above, we are focusing upon how cost and value criteria are used to determine the relative rents of dwellings, whereas the setting of absolute levels requires a consideration of costs to be covered and the rate of return which is to be earned upon housing capital. We first consider rents related to costs and then to values

Historic cost
No coherent argument exists for scaling rents by historic cost or, in related form, allowing age to dominate a pricing scheme. Clearly if prices are set in relation to historic costs, with older properties being charged less, then pricing inequities and inefficiencies may rise. New properties may depreciate more rapidly than old, so age and overall housing quality are not clearly correlated. Older housing associations and housing authorities which have been building for a long time would have an asset base which is greater and rents which are therefore in general lower than newer associations and authorities which began building more recently.

Central government must now address this issue with some urgency. The Housing Corporation has decided that associations can pool (to a limited extent) the rents and costs of new developments with those of historically developed projects, the latter having lower historic costs. In the past, critics of council rent schemes, (see Hepworth et al 1981) and indeed Conservative central governments have been concerned about the extent to which local authorities were able to pursue either low rent or large surplus policies as a consequence of pooling. Prior to the 1988 Act central government extracted from housing associations surpluses arising from historic cost accounting via the Grant Redemption Fund. The new financial regime allows associations to accumulate these gains (in pre-1988 HAG funded schemes) via the Rent Surplus Fund (RSF), although the application of these funds is restricted in the main to provision for future major repairs and renewals. However, the RSF could become the vehicle for explicit subsidisation of new (high cost) schemes by old (low cost) houses as under present arrangements English associations have been permitted to utilise up to 15 per cent of the RSF for this purpose.

In the council sector, ring fencing of housing revenue accounts and new (capital value based) approaches to assessing reckonable income for housing subsidy purposes are likely to reduce the actual impacts of historic cost accounting. The two main social sectors are, therefore, being reformed in an inconsistent fashion.

A more sophisticated alternative to crude historic costs pricing would be to index costs by using an index showing changes in building costs over time. But again this proposal has inadequacies. What if there has been poor, high cost decision taking in the past, so that indexing overstates their present worth to tenants? Rates of return are more correctly assessed in relation to current real property values and not indexed historic costs.

'Economic' cost and rents

The term 'economic rents' has several meanings. Here we employ the term to connote rents which are set to cover costs of management and maintenance, the cost of capital and provision for replacement of the asset. It is arguable (see Hills 1988) that a properly constructed cost of capital measure would include depreciation, asset value gains and tax concessions and would exclude the repayment of principal. We would concur with this strict economic definition of the user cost of capital but note that in UK housing practice 'economic cost' is usually applied to loan and interest repayments plus current management and maintenance costs. Different concepts of 'economic cost' are used in each of the main rental tenures and the Housing Corporation has recently promoted use of the concept in the housing association sector.

This recent debate has illustrated the problems of agreeing upon the relevant cost of capital measure. For all investors the cost of capital is effectively the opportunity cost (revenue or benefits foregone) by not investing capital elsewhere. Clearly the foregone interest or interest paid on a loan to finance the investment is a critical influence on such costs. But there are other considerations. Inflation in asset values reduces the real opportunity cost of capital. And tax concessions on housing loan interest would have a similar effect. Conversely, the recognition that houses do not last forever requires some form of replacement provision. In theory the investor could ensure replacement by current expenditure on maintenance, by an intermittent injection of major repairs or by including an element in charges to enable loan debt to be repaid.

Hills (1988) notes that only one of these options has to be charged in the economic rent to leave the landlord's financial position unchanged, since if the rent covered both a provision for major repairs and modernisation, and loan repayment, the rent would in effect purchase the property for the landlord. However, Hills then suggests that in practice a major repairs or depreciation allowance would not be sufficient to produce an everlasting house and that a combination of both depreciation and loan repayment should be charged, but not at the full rate.

In the British council housing system such concepts have never underpinned the housing revenue account. Rents and subsidies cover costs which include the repayment of principal and major rehabilitation but which generally exclude any allowance for depreciation. In the context of the new financial regime for housing associations, the concepts are most pertinent since associations are now required to make provision for major repairs and renewals. While Hills' 'economic rent' model may be correct in theory, practical cash flow difficulties may arise in practice since most loan structures require repayment of principal. Associations would therefore require to recoup this cost through rents as well as ensure adequate major repairs provision. At the end of the loan period, however, associations' costs will be considerably reduced and without a corresponding reduction in rent the revenue surpluses generated could finance the construction of a new dwelling (although it is unusual in public finance to require present generations to pay for future provision). These observations illustrate the difficulties for policy makers in devising a subsidy system which copes equitably and efficiently with falling real debt values under conventional borrowing mechanisms.

Even if agreement could be reached in practice on which economic cost concept to utilise it is difficult to envisage how one moves down from the level of the landlord's stock as a whole to specific units. The key problem arises in allocating management and maintenance costs to particular dwellings or estates. Arguably councils and associations should be required to develop estate based management and accounting systems which could reveal such costs on a localised basis. However, recent research (Maclennan et al 1989) suggests that neither councils nor associations are capable of such disaggregation at present. We conclude, therefore, that cost based pricing schemes are not feasible for existing individual units.

Assessed and market capital value rents
The economic cost rent concept, as set out above, requires an understanding of specific property management and depreciation costs as well as an assessment of capital values. As noted earlier, many local authorities, and not a few reformers, have utilised capital value rent relativities as a means of rent setting.

It was noted above that almost half of housing authorities, use rents based upon a multiple of net annual value (NAV) or assessed capital value (ACV). Both these measures are approximations to impute the market price for a dwelling. In principle, NAV should bear a close relation to the market rent which the dwelling would attract if rented on the open market. Capital value (CV) can be defined as a measure of the market price which the dwelling would attract if purchased in the open housing market. Assuming that valuers accurately assess market values then either NAV or ACV can be used as the basis for a rent setting scheme.

The fundamental assumption of NAV and ACV schemes is that assessors make an accurate assessment of 'reasonable' annual rent, as evaluated with reference to quality and size. But it is also assumed that demand is both evenly spread across the public housing stock and matches the pattern of that stock. This is, of course, tantamount to assuming that long-run equilibrium prevails. This assumption will rarely, if ever, be satisfied and thus one of the chief advantages (improved short run stock utilisation due to price signals) of introducing such a rent setting scheme is negated. In contrast ACVs based upon observed market prices (which may be difficult to observe for stock equivalent in size, location etc. to social sector stock) have the disadvantage that they may embody short-run, even ephemeral, fluctuations in market prices.

Assessors' valuations, as in the fair rent system, may contain anomalies in pricing. For instance, flats may be viewed by assessors as intrinsically less valuable than houses, thus reflecting their use of the private rented sector as a reference point in assessment. Secondly, there may be overlapping ranges of rents between distinct property types and sizes, to an extent which makes anomalies between major property sub-divisions a likely feature. Lastly, there is likely to be a general absence of any clear link between rent differentials and area demand. Thus research cautions us against the blind acceptance of valuers' conclusions. The traditional secrecy of valuers about their methods merely conceals these anomalies and a more open approach, subject to external critical scrutiny, is required if these schemes are to be widely applied.

We believe that there are eight key points which must be borne in mind in using NAV/ACV approaches.

1 Anomalies can appear as a consequence of the need to use the private housing sector as a reference point from which to assess NAVs and CVs. Their significance will depend on the extent to which the private sector is characterised by property types and locations which are considerably different from those provided in the public sector. Even within the private sector prices and rateable values are not very closely related.

2 Restrictions upon access to council housing through the allocation process can produce distortions to market values in private housing for some households looking for shelter. These may be transmitted back into 'social' rented housing via the valuation process. Those households who are treated as low priority cases on waiting lists, for example, will rely heavily upon private sector provision. The properties they inhabit may then be used as a reference point for the valuation of similar properties in the public sector. In turn, these valuations will come to reflect the ability and willingness to pay for the excluded households, and may bear little relevence to those expressed by the occupants of similar properties in the public sector, e.g. pensioners.

3 Market capital values for owned housing in general will reflect the capitalisation of tax subsidies to owners. Such subsidies are not proportionate throughout the price distribution and are probably less important in the upper and lower tails of the price distribution.

4 The influence of public sector subsidies upon the rent structure is such that the rent differentials produced by applying NAV multipliers will not entirely resolve the mismatch between demand and supply. This is because equality of demand with supply requires that not only rent differentials be 'correct', but also that the absolute level of rents be allowed to rise in order to clear the market.

5 In order for the rent scheme to reflect changing conditions accurately, regular revaluations would be necessary and thus the rent structure will also change regularly. With the advent of the community charge there was some doubt as to whether all regions would retain systematic, computerised valuation roll data and figures, but a revised valuation register will be required for the operation of the new 'Council tax'.

6 Rent differentials would be largely outwith the control of public authorities (though some may view this as advantageous). Further, such schemes are not particularly amenable to public scrutiny as the use of secret weights on NAV and CV deliberately 'mystify' the procedure as viewed by tenants. There is no reason to believe that public authority tenants are well informed about the procedures used by valuers in arriving at NAVs and CVs.

7 If market rent differentials reflect environmental features within the control of tenants, tenants in 'well kept' estates may well be penalised. The public authority can be viewed as the perpetrator of this penalty, as the gain from environmental improvement is appropriated in the form of higher rents. This can be viewed as inequitable treatment when compared to the position of the owner occupier who gains on resale from the market value appreciation.

8 To the extent to which current rent differentials diverge from market rent differentials any revision of the rent scheme along market lines will lead to changes in rents and distribution of subsidy. An important implication for the authorities and associations is that council house sales could receive a boost in more popular sites. This is because market related rent schemes will raise rents in some areas thus rendering renting a less attractive proposition.

In many respects a consistently applied, if flawed NAV/CV scheme may be preferable to ad hoc pricing schemes or comparability points schemes based on only a few variables. However, the above objections are grounds for believing that comprehensive analysis of comparability may be preferable in some instances. The application of NAV rent setting procedures will depend upon the manner in which the public authority wished to spread its central government subsidy across dwellings. The simplest means will be by equi-proportionate or flat-rate reductions, so that, in the former case, a fixed value multiplier would be applied to the NAV of all properties. With regard to capital values a target rate of return would be applied to the CVs. The rent figure arrived at would be modified in accordance with the manner in which central government grant is distributed.

The Duke of Edinburgh's Inquiry into British Housing (1985) adopted capital value rents, with a real return of three to four per cent, as the basis of its proposed rental sector reform (assuming there would also be a new housing allowance to help tenants). Subsequent research by Whitehead and Kleinman (1986) has suggested that a 3 to 4 per cent real rate of return would imply 10 to 11 per cent nominal rates to allow for inflation and that in the private sector (especially in Southern Britain) the rent increase effects would be unsustainable under the present housing benefit system. Hills (1988) has a similar view in relation to housing association activity but suggests that capital values with a lower rate of return might constitute the basis of a long run rent setting system. In this regard a well constructed points scheme and a capital value basis for rent-setting may be little different in practice.

Recent developments in England would suggest that the Government is moving closer to the Inquiry's thinking in relation to rent setting.

Two part pricing
Comparability schemes, whether based upon points, GAVs, ACVs etc. have all assumed that, in some broad fashion, rents should be proportional to dwelling quality. However, with deep capital subsidies, management and response maintenance costs may absorb 50–70 per cent of rental revenues.

Recent debates on the structure and effectiveness of housing management have stressed the possible role of rents as a signal in relation to service quality. Better services may require higher rents and, arguably, tenants within an authority should be free to choose, and pay for, higher levels of service provision. Some authorities already implement such policies.

Variation in service delivered, within a landlord's stock, does not change the comparability pricing arguments in principle. But they do require rent for the property component and rent for management and maintenance services to be identified, and billed, separately. This will require landlords to have precise service accounts for small areas or sectors of their stock and this will represent a major challenge for landlords in the future.

Affordable rents
During the last two years the concept of affordable rents (the numerator of an affordability ratio with net disposable income as a denominator) has come into prominence in discussions of pricing for housing associations and the NFHA utilise ratios to develop indicator rents. We have explored and criticised this concept elsewhere and refer to it only in passing here (Maclennan, Gibb and More 1990).

Empirical analysis for around 10,000 households across six British regions has produced a number of damaging results for the credibility of rent/income ratios as measures of affordability. Measured ratios fall sharply as incomes rise from low to moderate levels. The standard errors estimated are much larger for lower income groups. Ratios observed are influenced by age, households' size, gender and race and by housing conditions secured. Simple ratios are no guide to what is 'affordable'.

A more appropriate approach is to examine the disposable income left to households after paying rent for housing which is judged, socially, to be adequate for their needs. Income compensation, moderated by household type could then be paid. This approach confronts two problems, however. First, the benefit system levels of payment would have to be revised. Secondly, the benefit system would require restructuring to minimise poverty trap effects.

As benefit reform is not currently taking place, associations have to balance capital subsidies against indirect housing benefit receipts. However, this does not make a case for setting specific property rents in relation to the incomes of particular tenants. This would generate quite grave allocative inefficiencies with little incentive for the efficient use of stock.

Whilst associations, like councils in the past, may be wise to check their general level of rents against the incomes of their tenants (and not by using ratios), relative rents should still reflect property characteristics.

Conclusion

This chapter has set out the different approaches that can be used for rent setting in social housing. There is little doubt that the unsystematic nature of central government policy towards social sector rent setting will allow a range of approaches to be adopted. Diversity is often to be welcomed in housing policy, but this may not be the case in relation to social sector rent setting. Unified approaches to HAG and housing benefit make little sense if landlords are to set the rents on identical houses in different ways. Competition, through the right to transfer and capital allocations related to rent policies may force some long-term uniformity.

Our concluding remark is that British housing would be better served if there were to be a unitary strategy for pricing social houses with landlords free to vary service provision levels in relation to an unsubsidised standard payment for management, maintenance and other services. This would only be possible, however, if there were an associated reform of the housing benefit system. The rental sector revolution promised in the 1988 Housing Act may never happen if unrealistic rent levels and chaotic pricing schemes proliferate. The experiment needs to be redesigned, and quickly.

References

Cochrane E (1985) *Rent Schemes in Scottish Local Authorities* Diploma Dissertation, University of Glasgow (unpublished).

Ermisch J. (1984) *Housing Finance: Who Gains?* Policy Studies Institute, London.

Hepworth N P, Grey A and Odling–Smee J (1981) Housing Rents, Cost and Subsidies London: Chartered Institute of Public Finance and Accountancy.

Hills J (1988) *Twenty-First Century Housing Subsidies: Durable Rent-Fixing and Subsidy Arrangements* Welfare State Programme Discussion Paper No. 33 London: London School of Economics.

Maclennan D (1982) *Housing Economics* London: Longmans.

Maclennan D (1986) The Rents of Public Housing in Britain, in Best R (ed) Papers for the Duke of Edinburgh's Inquiry into British Housing London: National Federation of Housing Associations.

Maclennan D (1990) *Urban Change Through Environmental Investments, in Urban Challenges* Stockholm: Swedish Government Publications.

Maclennan D et al (1989) *The Nature and Effectiveness of Housing Management in England* London: HMSO.

Maclennan D, Gibb K and More A (1990) *Paying for Britain's Housing* York: Joseph Rowntree Foundation.

Maclennan D, Gibb K and More A (1991) Fairer Subsidies, Faster Growth: Housing Government and the Economy. York: Joseph Rowntree Foundation.

Maclennan D and Wood G A (1984) *Rent Schemes in British Public Housing* CURR Discussion Paper No. 18, University of Glasgow.

Nath S K (1969) *A Reappraisal of Welfare Economics* London: Routledge and Kegan Paul.

Report of the Inquiry into British Housing (1985) London: National Federation of Housing Associations.

Richardson G B (1959) Information and Investment, Oxford University Press.

Robinson E A G (1962) The Structure of Competitive Industry, University of Chicago Press.

Whitehead, C M E and Kleinman J (1986) Private Rented Housing in the 1980's and 1990's, Occasional Paper 17, Department of Land Economy, University of Cambridge: Granta Editions.

Chapter 12
Extending the strategic role

Introduction

For almost a decade central government has been committed to reducing the share of social housing in the national tenure structure. The ownership growth imperative has, with the recognition that social housing was likely to remain as a significant presence in particular regions and urban areas, been supplemented with a concern to demunicipalise social housing provision. At first this was accomplished by placing less rigid restrictions on new investment by housing associations and co-operatives than on investment by local authorities. The 1988 Housing Act and subsequent ring-fencing measures have sharpened this process by introducing, for council tenants, a right-to-transfer to a range of landlords (including privately financed concerns with a 'social' intend) and upward pressures on council rents. That is, the monopoly powers of council providers have apparently been reduced.

Central government's moves against municipal housing, have been based upon the view that local authorities, in many instances, have been ineffective in managing and financing local social housing. Now central government wishes local authorities to reduce their role as direct provider and to focus instead upon the strategic and enabling housing functions which they undertake. These views have been reinforced by a number of independent inquiries, for instance the Duke of Edinburgh's Inquiry (1985), The Audit Commission Review (1987) and the Grieve report on housing in Glasgow (1987). Academic commentators have also reviewed new local authority roles (Brook 1990, Rao 1990).

The proposed change in role may have a prima facie rationale. However, it fails to consider two key lines of argument. First, have local authorities fallen into disrepute because they were poor managers in a practical sense, or do present problems reflect strategic failures? Have local authorities had an adequate strategy for their own stock, let alone the wider provision of housing within their jurisdictions? Is there a clear base of well-informed strategy formulation on which authorities can now build? Second, even if such experience exists, does the new competitive order for the provision of social housing introduce real conflicts of interest which will make it impossible for a municipality both to compete effectively and plan honestly?

This chapter seeks to explore these and related questions. The conclusion is that central government must give greater thought to strategic housing planning in Britain and that it is not at all obvious that local authorities will always be the appropriate enabler.

Decisions, strategies and housing systems

As a prelude to the discussion it is important to consider what is meant by strategic and strategic housing role. These terms are not without important ambiguities. The kinds of decisions confronted by managers can be classified as being operational, administrative and strategic (see Ansoff 1987).

Operational decisions are concerned with producing goods and services taking products, production processes, resources and administrative systems as given and fixed. Administrative decisions focus upon selecting reward, incentive and control systems and structures to ensure that the firm or organisation achieves its given objectives as effectively as possible. Operational and administrative decisions share some common features. They both tend to be inward looking with the organisation as their focus and they have a concern with the present rather than the future. To a large extent, they can both be implemented using the internal authority structures of the organisation.

Strategic decisions, by way of contrast, are about coping with or creating change. They are concerned with the identification of new products and new processes of production. And these changes may be initiated within the organisation but more normally will be triggered by a changing external environment. Thus strategy involves the identification of ends as well as means, the external environment is of paramount importance and the long period and uncertainty are key considerations in the decision process. Uncertainty arises not solely from the consideration of a longer term period, but because the organisation can no longer rely upon internal, authority-based control mechanisms, but must now compete or co-operate with other investors or agencies.

In this context strategic decisions by one organisation are designed to achieve objectives in part by influencing the behaviour and strategy of other investors. As Schelling (1960) notes a strategic action is one which 'influences the other person's choice, in a manner favourable to one's self, by affecting the other person's expectations of how one's self will behave'. And these expectations may be influenced by pricing and investment decisions indicating competition or by signals of a more co-operative nature. Threat signals may be a dominant feature of competitive strategies.

Strategic decisions or behaviour as implied in the above paragraphs are a feature of at least some housing market investors, public or private. The Northern Ireland Housing Executive has a well-developed corporate strategy, the Housing Corporation, Scottish Homes and Tai Cymru all have investment strategies, so do Barrats, Wimpeys, Quality Street and Woolwich Homes. Housing associations in Scotland now have a formal requirement to prepare business investment plans and some English associations are developing similar documents. Housing authorities also have their own investment strategies and plans but it is difficult to separate such actions from a wider general understanding of local authority housing planning and strategy. British local authorities have a statutory duty to provide local housing plans which are intended to form a framework not only for their own activities but to indicate activity areas for other investors.

Local housing plans
The importance of having some co-ordinated local housing plan (LHP) makes sense given the inherent complexities of housing markets and systems. For simplicity of illustration of the LHP concept consider initially a system in which the state was not a housing investor or subsidiser and where housing investment had no externality (spillover) effects. In this pure market system for housing provision the nature of the housing market is likely to generate market failures (see Maclennan 1982). Market based strategies are, to a large extent, driven by price and profit signals. The housing market is composed of a large number of buyers and sellers and prices and price change vary across neighbourhoods and product groups. Hence investors will be concerned not just with generalised market information, but price data which refers to, at least, location an property type. An additional complication is that shortages and surpluses are not always fully reflected in price signals, because reduced household formation, sharing, longer commuting etc., are all 'non-price' adjustments to housing shortages.

There is then a clear case for a co-ordinated provision of market information, although there is no reason why local authorities should provide it. Further, market monitoring evolves into market planning as investors realise that house purchase decisions will be influenced by consumer expectations regarding future property prices. Hence the lags involved in the supply process as well as consumer expectations will force the building industry to look forward.

However even the provision of good monitoring and accurate market forecasting does not remove key developer uncertainties. It is not enough for individual firms that they are aware that some quantity of dwellings is required in a given region over some time period. Even in these contexts firms' assessments of their relative competitive position may lead to either over or under-investment. In effect, co-ordination and planning may be required to transform a generalised profit opportunity for the housing industry into specific competitive provision by particular firms in an orderly fashion.

Housing investment does not continually provide identical types of dwellings in repetitively similar neighbourhoods. From time to time important structural change may be required. For instance, in recent years the provision of sheltered housing and rebuilding on 'brownfield' sites have been important structural changes in the output of the building industry in Britain. However structural change, in effect new product provision, creates periods of particular uncertainty for investors. A major problem in the housing industry is that the high costs to consumers of shortage mean that they may accept less than 'ideal homes'. That is, housing investors are seldom penalised for failing to take risks, but their customers too often are.

The increased provision of new housing units on 'brownfield' sites in some British cities in the 1980s has often only followed intense local and central government action to create investor confidence in older urban areas. Often subsidies and persuasive strategic planning by authorities were required to create this important market bandwagon. In Glasgow some 80 per cent of new construction now takes place on sites ignored until a decade ago, and the equivalent figure for London is almost 50 per cent. Much of this investor confidence stemmed from strategic governmental advice. There is then clearly a planning role for some independent local agency given the inability of individual builders to assess how market demands can evolve. Other market failures may also generate planning demands. Housing production not only uses land, but the quality and style of units, and indeed the users of buildings, may have important impacts upon the quality of the surrounding neighbourhood and the well being of its residents. That is, in economists' jargon, housing creates important 'externalities'. Markets cannot, generally, resolve the problem of externalities. Land and building use controls are inevitably required and their use requires some public agency or level of government charged with balancing the interests of different groups and considering the future as well as the present. In the UK such control powers have generally rested with local authorities and they still do (subject to central government scrutiny).

The role of state action in shaping housing provision moves well beyond information, strategic advice and land and building controls when non-market approaches to housing output and pricing are adopted. If government were merely to restrict assistance with housing costs to housing vouchers or allowances the minimalist strategic role outlined above could be implemented. However where the state provides housing directly through non-price systems or allocates subsidies and public investment permissions differently to different investors then LHP takes on a more complex form. Where the state invests directly it has to plan its own investment strategy. Where it subsidises other investors then it has to consider which investors or partnerships it will inform, co-ordinate and favour through finance and planning enablement.

But this is not the end of complexity. The local level of government may focus on programmes which are local in incidence but central in origin, that is the local authority acts as agent for central government. Indeed, it could be argued that such a relationship governed the two major post war investment programmes in Britain, namely investment in council housing from 1950 to 1975 and rehabilitation of pre-1919 housing since 1974. A second, co-operative, mixed approach can exist when central government allows local authorities to use their own resources, or the block grants they get for housing, to pursue local investment preferences at the same time as other agencies locally provide some of central government's policy requirements. This mode of operation, which generates co-operative partnerships, is illustrated by the supplementary role of the SSHA (Scottish Special Housing Association) in Scotland from 1936 onwards, or more generally by housing association investment in Britain in the 1970s. This was the housing planning context envisaged in the 1977 Green Papers, from which the present housing planning systems originated.

The key question, to which we return below, is the extent to which this co-operative partnership approach is to prevail in the future. Clearly government wishes to replace public with private investment, and to displace municipal landlords by other providers. Central government cannot, and does not, then expect municipalities to behave as if roles were being created *de novo*. 'Competing' and 'co-ordinating' roles may be in conflict. Before addressing these questions we have to first consider the extent to which local housing planning is in fact conducted satisfactorily. Or did state failures merely compound market failures in the housing planning process?

The adequacy of local housing strategies

Is strategy important?
It is not always the case that good strategy development determines the effectiveness of organisational behaviour. There may be long periods when strategy can remain relatively fixed while operational and administrative decisions determine competitive performance. This point is well illustrated by Ansoff with reference to the 'corporate economy' (Ansoff 1987). From 1800 to 1900, strategy was all important as new production processes created a turbulent environment. However, from 1900 to 1930, when innovation waves were less pronounced good administration and operational decisions determined corporate success. After 1930 growing incomes underpinning consumerism and new social obligations required of private corporations began a new, and as yet unended, era of change. Indeed as early as 1950, Drucker had labelled this 'the age of discontinuity'. Ansoff also notes, and this may now be pertinent for social housing providers, that this change was often unrecognised or resisted 'because it introduces new uncertainties, threatens a loss of power by the entrenched managers, requires new perceptions and skills'. 'Firms are generally very

slow in recognising when the operating problem must give way to a concern with the strategic. Usually when such conditions occur, operating problems neither cease nor slacken. On the contrary, they appear to intensify'.

Does this diagnosis and outcome have any relevance to the context of municipal housing provision in Britain? From the early 1950s into the mid-1970s housing officials within local authorities had no great need to examine either organisational or area-wide strategy. In the era of mass social housing product, the product was clearly (if inadequately) defined, and the processes were driven by local town planning officials (zoning land for new development, identifying clearance areas) and heavily subsidised social housing construction. In this period no attention was given to alternative (market or social) providers, state control and commitment removed uncertainties and there was minimal involvement with consumers. In an organisational sense this period of major activity was not turbulent nor uncertain and did not call forth new strategies for mixed housing systems.

These old certainties really began to crumble in the early 1970s. The sustained growth of home ownership began to force authorities to take a wider view of local housing plans, and this was reinforced by new agencies (housing associations in particular) taking on new tasks. Since 1980, British housing policy has entered an era of sharp discontinuity, perhaps even disorientation. At the same time as central government has reduced local financial discretion, local choices for the means of strategies have expanded. Indeed, much of recent innovation in British housing policy has stemmed from municipal entrepreneurship creating new approaches. Managers may be slow to recognise environmental 'sea changes' as such. In 1977 the introduction of Housing Plans in Scotland and HIPs (housing investment plans) in England and Wales, with associated state-of-the-art advice on plan preparation, should have initiated a more purposive approach to housing strategy. The unfortunate fact is that, although there are now more strategic housing planners than a decade ago, there are few authorities in the country which now prepare an adequate local housing strategy.

This demise of housing planning, in an era which demanded strategic thinking, has its origins in a number of factors. First, after 1980 central government downgraded the importance of local housing plans by seeking less copious plans more infrequently. A review of Scottish housing plans in 1985 indicated that the majority were short, ill-researched and were no basis for strategic action. Two of the most sophisticated strategic housing plans in the UK are prepared by Glasgow District Council and the Northern Ireland Housing Executive. And this partly reflects their statutory obligation to produce an annually updated plan to justify their large expenditures. A second consideration is that after 1980, at least in England, there was a widespread view that housing plans had little impact upon the distribution of expenditure which was largely formula based. Finally, since 1980 there has been minimal advice to local authorities regarding plan preparation, not least because central government has had little recent experience in improving estimates of housing needs and demands. Both the Audit Commission and the National Economic Development Office have been critical of the central government's expenditure planning system in which government embodies its strategic view on housing. Its programmes were set out only for a year at a time.

One wonders, how many authorities would now bother to prepare a local housing plan if it was not a statutory obligation? And even when it is prepared, who uses it? Confronted with a major decision, do officers consider the consistency of their actions with the plan? Do officials, residents, tenants and investors know what the local housing plan contains? If they do not, what purpose can such a document have?

Is planning well concerned?

Although central government actions and municipal pre-occupation with the short term may have reduced the importance of plans, the real difficulty may be that housing planning as set out in the mid-1970s may now lack credibility and have the wrong emphases. In the advice about housing planning of a decade ago there was a presumption that the local authority was in control (the authority was more important than the market), that needs estimates could be made convincingly, that co-operative strategies prevailed, and that fixed plans would hold over a number of years until they require revision some time in the future. The 'plan' emphasised a set of figures, clear investor roles and read as if change and uncertainty were minor considerations.

In the outline below of a local housing planning process, it is emphasised that, for the foreseeable future, strategic planning is a difficult and continuing process surrounded by uncertainty. Alan Massie, novelist, recognises this clearly with these words which he attributes to Augustus Caesar (Massie 1986):

> The value of planning [a rigid strategy, my insert] diminishes in accordance with the complexity of the state of affairs. It may seem paradoxical. You may think that the more complicated a situation is, the more necessary a plan to deal with it. I shall grant you the theory. But practice is different. No plan can be equal to the complexities and casualties of political life. Hence, adherence to a plan deprives you of the flexibility which you need if you are to ride the course of events; for a moment's reflection should enable you to see that it is impossible (even with the help of the wisest soothsayers and mathematicians) to predict what will happen; and it is folly to pretend that you can control the actions of other men with certainty. Therefore a plan is only suitable for the simple operations of life; you can plan a journey to your country house, but you cannot plan a battle or a political campaign in any detail. You must have a goal ... but to achieve it, nothing is more important than that you retain fluidity of thought.

There is much wisdom in this imperial aphorism. However in the current age of microcomputers and University trained soothsayers, there is no reason why we should restrict our planning to an optimistic disembowelling of sheep in the top floors of housing departments. For if there are clear objectives, an assessment of the best opening strategic moves and a continuing capacity to observe and react to change, then organisations, with bounded rationality, may best cope with the unfolding future. The next section sets out a list of desiderata, and current practices by way of contrast, for local housing plan formation.

Housing planning as a process

Objectives
The housing planning process, in a formal sense, can be said to start with the identification of objectives. For municipalities key housing politicians and senior officers, at the least, must establish a set of objectives which have empirical content rather than expressing some vacuous, if noble, social aspiration. Many housing plans contain only the latter, thus rendering them non-operational for use within the authority and immune from external evaluation.

In the process of setting local social objectives for the housing system, planners must also take cognisance of the objectives of other investors including central government. If objectives conflict then we have to attach higher levels of uncertainty to the outcomes implied by the strategy forecast.

Strategy formation
It is unlikely that objectives will be formed at the outset of the process without some prior understanding of the nature of the local housing system and its changes over time. However objectives may be revised in a sequential fashion when more detailed analysis and planning are undertaken.

In some authorities, especially smaller rural councils, there may be no officer with a continuing involvement in housing planning. In others, the plan may be prepared as an annual chore by a group of officers drawn from other duties. Plan preparation is likely to be more satisfactory or innovative where key officers have planning defined as their most important duty. That is, where their capability as a public servant is judged by the adequacy of their plans.

Ideally the plan should be prepared by a team. Where, as in larger authorities, teams exist they may often be seen as the organisation's 'research' team. However in the current context planning teams require more than post graduate degrees (perhaps in housing and soothsaying). Analytical skills have to be reinforced by practical experience (to understand reactions internal to the organisation), evaluation skills, liaison, communication, team building and, where the enabling role is also involved, bargaining, negotiation and entrepreneurial skills. Teams, in contrast with perhaps half of authorities at present, are best located in housing departments.

In the absence of a national survey of housing planning practice, the views expressed here are based on smaller, selective studies and personal experience. Few authorities possess teams with the requisite skills and the housing profession provides little training for such jobs. Indeed, most housing managers with their Institute's professional qualification or equivalent are trained at a stage when they had no strategic tasks to perform.

Information and analysis
Notwithstanding the importance of this wide range of team skills required to prepare a plan, good information and analysis are central to the preparation of an action plan and the revision of objectives. This section deals at some length with the kinds of information potentially available to authorities, much of which is currently scorned in favour of guesstimates.

The present approach to local housing planning in Scotland has been systematically reviewed and analysis of a more limited number of English cases reveals an essentially similar approach. The housing plan is demographically led. Population forecasts plus a net migration estimate are transformed into future household numbers (usually four or five years ahead). Planners then establish a shortfall of total housing units and units for 'special needs' groups. The latter are usually estimated by applying constant fractions (devised in the 1970s) to total populations of households.

The planners then usually emphasise their estimate of required municipal investment and the likely contributions to output by other social investors, such as housing associations. Rehabilitation and modernisation needs are similarly assessed. None of the Scottish plans make any estimate of future investment by private landlords and forecasts of owner-occupier demand (see Maclennan 1987) are made either by linear extrapolation of past performance or by assuming that developers will close the gap between total households and needs. These calculations generally ignore changing household headship rates (i.e. the proportion of people in particular groups who are heads of households), they provide no rationale for tenure split and make no concessions to the role of income growth (as opposed to population change) in shaping future needs and demands. It is hardly surprising that such analyses are not credible to researchers, politicians, or central government. A new approach based upon monitoring and constant plan revision has to be based on locally gathered information and databases. It is salutary that it was only in 1987 that the Institute established a working group to look at local databases. Looking to the future, new monitoring systems based on already existing data have to be developed.

Improving local monitoring and information

Describing the system
It was implied above that local housing systems are complex. A housing system consists of a series of dwelling units, which usually form well-defined neighbourhoods in which cost, price or availability of dwellings in a particular small area is connected to movements of

similar phenomena in other parts of the system. This interrelationship arises because similar areas compete for households or because there are systematic flows of households from one part of the system to another. Connectedness and inter-dependence are the key identifiers of system interaction. A local housing authority, since it will have its domain of action limited by municipal boundaries, may only have sovereignty over a sub-part of the system. This may create difficulties in the overall co-ordination of policy if poorer central city residents vote for more publicly oriented programmes of action than more affluent suburbs — tenure differences between municipal cores and the suburban municipalities are often important in Britain. On the other hand a municipality may have within its space relatively unconnected systems and this is most obvious in large rural authorities.

Leaving aside these difficulties, how should an authority begin to describe and classify the housing system within its region? Let us first focus on a description of the static structure of the system. Housing as a complex commodity, as indicated earlier, contains an important range of attributes. Hedonic house price studies indicate that house prices are influenced by dwelling style, size, internal amenity, accessibility to services and shops, distance from the centre of town or the urban edge and the social mix of the area. Studies of public sector estate popularity indicate that similar dwelling and neighbourhood amenity factors may influence popularity there. It would seem an obvious step for an authority to identify the range of product groups existing within its area and undoubtedly housing tenure will be an important influence on structuring product groups.

It will also be important to identify where demolition is depleting product groups and where new construction and rehabilitation are adding to existing types or creating new product lines. At first sight this may appear to be a very theoretical approach but why do housing authorities not undertake such a task? Using decennial census data supplemented by the valuation roll — information which is kept in every British local authority — each housing department could replicate the product group analysis conducted for Glasgow (see Maclennan, Wood and Munro 1987). But at present, how many local authorities can even accurately describe, from property record files, their own housing stock? In Northern Ireland, for instance, this can be done precisely and is an essential component of the rent scheme, but fewer than 20 per cent of English authorities provide such an analysis.

The condition of the existing housing stock is of course a central concern of local strategy. In England and Wales there is a national house condition survey undertaken quinquennially. But the samples are small and of little use for local planning. In Northern Ireland a sample survey of condition generates critical planning information and Glasgow which has reached the limits of manipulating inadequate data has now completed a 7 per cent sample survey of the local housing stock.

In a city which has spent more than £100 mn per annum on improving housing conditions over the last decade such monitoring of present condition and past policy impact was long overdue. Some other large authorities have conducted similar surveys but the present nationwide database for designing policies to tackle problems of housing condition is inadequate. In 1988 government in Scotland has prepared a manual of advice for authorities regarding the conduct of local house condition surveys, but to date only 7 from 56 authorities have used this advice. Of course housing problems are not solely defined in physical terms. Within each area, again perhaps relying initially on census data, it is important to establish the distribution of socio-economic groups across the product groups. This may indicate problems of segregation, within public as well as private sectors, and perhaps hint at the problem of access of particular socio-economic groups to existing product groups. More problematically, it is essential to establish the burden of housing costs that particular groups encounter in each product group. This pattern, and the associated pattern of housing subsidies cannot be established easily from existing data. There is not presently a single study which reveals such patterns within a British city (though the Rowntree Foundation's research programme is now examining six areas in this way). It is a condemnation of the British approach to housing policy that, despite vast public expenditure on housing capital and current subsidies, the local impact on housing conditions of subsidy distribution remains uncharted.

An identification of the static structure of the housing system is a useful starting point for housing planning and it helps to establish the nature of housing system outcomes, some of which may be viewed as being problematic. However housing problems may arise not only from patterns of outcomes but also because of difficulties encountered in the processes of funding and building housing. Housing planning therefore has to be involved in establishing how housing processes operate and the reaction of residents to outcomes.

So far, in examining comprehensive housing planning different tenures have not been emphasised. In the following sections monitoring of public and private systems is discussed separately for a number of reasons. First, since the allocation processes are different, the signals generated will be different in nature (queues, etc in the public sector, prices in the private sector). Secondly, in the public sector the authority is provider and manager as well as planner.

Monitoring in the public sector
Even without formal forecasting or the simple extrapolation of present circumstances into the future, housing planning would be advanced by undertaking monitoring of existing housing systems. Most housing authorities possesses a great deal of potentially useable data which arises from their day to day activities. Whilst knowledge may create planning benefits, data is costly to collect and to process. But what is outlined below is based upon data, most of which is already collected but which remains unused for research and management purposes. With proper organisation of this data (often collected for statutory purposes), authorities could monitor the key aspects of public housing

for around £3 per dwelling per annum and, in the private sector, for around £2.

Until the mid-1970s government advice to local authorities was often concerned with problems of development and financing of public housing. It was only really with the advent of HIPs that advice on monitoring was provided. Although the quality of advice from central to local governments on monitoring has varied over regions and time, guidance on public sector monitoring has generally been better than adequate. For instance, the Scottish Development Department's Scottish Housing Needs Assessment Handbook (SDD 1977), based on trial applications to the city of Dundee, provided a monitoring methodology which did not, at that time, lag behind academic perspectives on how to analyse the public sector. This method provides useful insights on the nature of housing conditions and problems within a local public sector. However, it is not clear how the information generated guides investment decisions, either within or across authorities. Relatively few authorities, even in Scotland, have adopted the systematic approach indicated in the handbook. The outline of important monitoring for the public sector presented here, therefore, merely generalises and expands upon known public sector monitoring techniques.

Public housing as a local system
From an applied (economic) research standpoint public housing systems may be characterised in the following way. A local authority offers a variety of housing product groups to selected client groups. In general these houses are offered at below market rents. As a result the demand for public housing, or at least for some product groups, exceeds the available supply. In consequence the main allocation device within the system is not rent but allocation by eligible queues. That is, queue formation and management is a critical task of the authority and the process will generate quantity rather than price signals to managers and planners. In addition, the authority as landlord has statutory obligations to collect rents, repair dwellings and have regard to the condition of its stock.

The dual functions of queue and property management create points of contact between customers, dwellings and managers. If these points of contact are extensive and repetitive, then a record of the nature of the interaction can form a consistent signal between the various parties. Some economic commentators argue that only price signals can guide economic action, but in many instances (even in the private sector) quantity indicators may be equally important. The broad outline suggested here is presented with the belief that many authorities underestimate what a review of their own actions can tell them. Further, new information technologies, with which future housing authorities must develop a familiarity, will ease this process. Many area offices, and housing associations, now use micro-computers for word processing and remain unaware that the same machines could be used for data storage or connection to a central, mainframe database.

Entry queue screening

The most important single set of signals for a housing authority stem from its waiting list — that is its process of queue formation. The use of this indicator has had supporters and detractors (Murie and Malpass 1986). The limitations of the list approach for local monitoring purposes can be subdivided into criticisms of the accuracy of the list and, second, the relevance of the data even if accurate.

Clearly where a list consists of applicants 'stacked-up' over a number of years, then its limitations are serious. As many as one third of the names on the list may become redundant but unremoved during a five year period (for instance), as households split or form, or as they find some preferred alternative, or as household circumstances alter. There is no reason, in a decentralised housing system with suitable information technology at the local scale, why such lists could not be revised every six months. Indeed a recent study (Maclennan et al 1989) indicates that most English authorities update the waiting list at least every two years. If the potential redundancy of information on the list is reduced then its usefulness will depend largely on the questions asked in the list screening/formation process.

From a national housing planning standpoint it is a great pity that a standard application form or a core set of questions is not applied nationwide. Such a standard application form for council housing could contain four main sections. First, it should record accurately the size and structure of the household, and any likely changes therein in the six months ahead. Second, it should establish in detail, for existing households, the nature of their current accommodation, including its tenure, condition, rent or mortgage payment etc. Third, it should establish in detail the economic status of the household, including its income and major assets. Such data would inform advice on tenure choice, the monitoring of the relative economic status of new applicants and the income mix in areas to which residents are to be allocated. Fourth, and also as part of the advisory process, authorities should examine the other alternatives that potential entrants may be searching for, and the intensity of search. It is also regrettable that within a planning area the waiting lists of the council are not co-ordinated with those of local housing associations. The accuracy of combined waiting lists would be enhanced if the housing corporation were to encourage the compilation of regional waiting lists from association data.

The authorities, at this stage, also have to establish the preferences of households. This is a difficult area in which to establish useful information (Maclennan 1977). However, as non-shelter dimensions of housing, such as the quality of neighbourhoods, become more important the monitoring and allocation task of authorities become more difficult. Household shelter and space requirements may be relatively easy for a third party to assess, but locational and environmental preferences are problematic. Studies of housing search in the private market, which also indicate that households with quite similar socio-economic status may have quite different neighbourhood preferences, indicate that households usually have two or three preferred neighbourhoods in which search is likely to be feasible. Within the public sector allocation process, neighbourhood preferences should be elicited. Moreover, since the entry price now has a large component defined in waiting time, the authority, if using already available desktop computer technology, could advise the prospective entrant of whether they qualify for a particular neighbourhood quality class and, given the length of eligible queues, how long they may have to wait (probabilistically) for a vacancy. Further, if the waiting time seems unduly lengthy, then other quality, rent level and delay options may be offered. Such information, aside from informing tenants, would allow the authority to monitor how different socio-economic groups react to rent and price rationing as well as indicating potential gaps in supply. In particular, authorities would do well to investigate why systematically last searched areas appear.

The above procedures assist public sector planning insofar as they identify those on the margin of council housing choice and also indicate areas of problems and preferences within the stock. But they also have their limitations — an authority, for instance, will be concerned about low income households who avoid the sector. Indeed, their decision making could be more informed by examining the reasons why some groups do not pursue council options. For instance, the recent debate on the 'residualisation' of council housing would have been much clarified by such information. Since 1989 housing associations in England and Wales (1990 in Scotland) have participated in the CORE system which systematically records information on association lettings. There is no reason why local authorities do not adopt a similar uniform system and, arguably, private landlords receiving public subsidies should be asked to provide such information too.

Thus a continuing updating of waiting lists, a thorough screening of entrants and an analysis of the rejection and acceptance of offers would allow councils and other landlords to develop a clearer conception of their customers and their own role, neither of which can now be taken for granted. Landlords must also have regard to their existing tenants. Requests to transfer can be handled in much the same way as new applications. But other forms of monitoring can also be carried out. An authority will know, even from rent accounting files, how households of particular types move through its stock. Are there well defined 'careers' in council housing? Can they be extrapolated to indicate changing house size and location requirements? What about the households who leave the public sector; do authorities, supposedly concerned with residualisation, ever ask who is leaving and why and where they are going? Authorities systematically ignore this issue at the neighbourhood, as well as the sectoral, scale. If they did examine such issues, would there now be so many low quality estates dominated exclusively by low income households?

An encouraging and recent trend in local authority service provision has been the commissioning of surveys of resident views on services, but fewer than five per cent of councils and associations had undertaken such measures by 1988. It is remarkable that British social landlords are often only pushed into remedial action either by specific complaints or by political protest within small areas. Why don't more landlords ask their tenants what they think of them in relation to service provision and whether or not they prefer the common coincidence of low rents and bad services to higher rent and better provision? If the public sector is to compete with private housing provision then such questions and policy decisions are now urgently needed. Service quality and rent levels are now (in most authorities and associations) a local trade-off and one which is often meeting a landlord response similar to rent controlled private landlords in the 1950s. In bad service provision and low rent levels lies the route to long run sector decline and residualisation. Is this negative strategy based upon ignorance of what consumers want?

Whilst establishing the nature of the clientele and probing reaction to service provision may be novel concerns, have landlords had a keener appreciation of the condition of their stock? The reality (see Maclennan et al. 1989) is rather discouraging. Some authorities have no readily available data on the detailed nature of their stock, and relatively few have computerised property record files. Such databases can be invaluable. They may form the basis of comparability rent schemes and planned maintenance systems, or help in explaining estate popularity or vacancy rates. Further, when they are linked to a computerised repair scheme they can indicate patterns of persistent disrepair for certain classes of dwelling.

Research during the last decade indicates the potential insights to be gained from linking tenant surveys, repair records and property record files. It reveals, fairly systematically, how repairs services work (absorbing one third of current budgets) takes place. But in the authorities without computerised property records and where repair requests are stored in old shoe boxes, just what is known about managing response repairs adequately, let alone designing efficient cyclic systems! In our experience linking property, repairs and consumer records costs about £1 for a year's activity per dwelling.

Even starting from an adequate property database and with maintenance monitoring an authority may lose track of property condition. Not all tenants perceive or report all important (especially structural) repairs. For housing planning purposes landlords would do well to emulate the few who have undertaken local house condition surveys. Such surveys (usually of 5 to 10 per cent representative samples from within an authority) generate technical and socio-economic information on disrepair problems which can assist in prioritising areas or property types for modernisation. What guides modernisation spending in British authorities at present — arbitrary criteria, local politics, age of scheme or neighbourhood collapse? None of these are clear criteria for efficient use of scarce funds. Again with reducing real resources and emerging large scale stock condition problems, councils will in the future have to be prepared to evaluate and prioritise modernisation programmes. If property condition surveys are to be repeated, say quinquennially, for the same sample of dwellings, then the evaluation of modernisation and rehabilitation programmes could move onto a new informed level. The uptake of various forms of grant-aid could be associated with particular socio-economic groups (indicating the required mix of public–private action), the impact of past spending on future condition could be assessed and, after say a decade, the factors which contribute to property obsolescence and disrepair firmly established.

If house condition surveys are undertaken quinquennially they would have an average direct cost of around £2.50 per dwelling per annum. Allowing for other data collection processing and analysis tasks, then for a maximum of £10 per tenant a moderate-to-large scale housing authority could convert its presently collected but noisy and unsorted signals into a coherent set of information to define its role and set its priorities. The Northern Ireland Housing Executive, perhaps because of the peculiar political pressures which forced it to be seen to be explicit or fair, or perhaps because it is a large multi-divisional housing authority, comes closest to the model outlined above, but it still has some way to go.

Monitoring in the private sector
This section, whilst intended to be complementary to the above, has a marked contrast in style. Government advice to authorities on how to monitor the private housing sector is appalling. In this sector the much lauded Scottish Housing Handbook merely notes that monitoring is 'difficult'. An examination of Scottish housing plans, and similar submissions for the large English cities and Northern Ireland produces a similar depressing picture. Crude, out-of-date and misleading national figures on price changes and tenure change are often used as a preamble to a guesstimate of future private provision. It is hardly surprising that in such a context arguments ranging from council housing's role through to the demand for green belt land remain unsettled and uninformed. But appropriate monitoring methods can be developed.

Whereas housing in the public sector is predominantly, but not exclusively, allocated by quantity rationing, price rationing dominates within the market system. Where price signals are monitored they can, regardless of the myriad of causes in shifting the relative balance of supply and demand, provide information regarding changes within the system. These signals are by no means perfect as they contain random noisy components and they are moderated by non-price adjustments. Nor do they always promote a speedy private sector response.

Short, and even long, run supply inelasticity is a major reason why housing authorities ought to monitor the local housing market. Relatively few builders undertake market research and there is some evidence that, in consequence, building is oriented to less risky, or more obvious or certain sectors of the market. For instance, in the Scottish context demographic trends have boosted the demand for lower income owner-occupied housing units, and this is reflected in the price distribution, since 1971. However, it was 1978 before a serious supply response was forthcoming. Housing authorities could facilitate the smoother operation of local housing markets by systematic monitoring.

There are other reasons for the involvement of housing authorities as market monitors. Since the 1960s they have, via land planning, advice and local authority mortgages, had an important role in the housing market, especially at 'the cheaper end'. This role has grown greatly in variety, if not excessively in substance, since the 1979 Conservative administration advocated their package of new, 'low cost' home-ownership initiatives. Joint private and local authority initiatives require authorities to have a clear view of where they will fit into the local market system. Similar remarks are pertinent to the private sector improvement and repair schemes which have formed an increased share of housing policy spending since the 1970s.

The needs of the public and private sector need to know about the operation of the housing market may be obvious, but the means to monitoring are not. Academic research on the British housing market, or at least particular cities, has been hamstrung by lack of finance and expertise. Research has been based upon small samples and has been in one-off, cross-sectional studies. How can this approach be changed? To a large extent database preparation for the private sector is similar to the process required in the public sector — the co-ordination and analysis of existing records. In this case, however, authorities would have to develop a co-operative approach with builders and building societies. Before indicating the dimensions of such co-operation it is useful to set out what exists within public records at present.

In Scotland, as in the rest of Britain, the individual importance of property transactions is such that the details of transactions are legally recorded. The difference, in Scotland, is that the deeds, recorded in the Register of Sasines, are already a public record. The keepers of the English Land Registry are now to pursue a similar liberated policy. And authorities could purchase the geo-coded price series produced by major building societies. Since 1974 the University of Glasgow has prepared and stored a computerised database for the City of Glasgow's private housing market. For each transaction, details of sale date, price, sources of finance and amount of loan are recorded. They are then coded and address referenced (unique grid reference) in a fashion which allows analysis for single houses or streets or large or small grid squares or political wards. In addition, data from household surveys, the census and the valuation roll can be made compatible with the price data base (see Maclennan, Wood and Munro 1987).

This database may serve the local authority in a number of ways. Is there a long tail of low price properties concealed in aggregate figures? Are there areas of sustained market depression or resilience? Are there gaps in the lending patterns of societies? Even wider insights may be gained by examining the temporal evolution of the system (see Hancock and Maclennan 1990).

House price data has its limitations and survey data may be required to indicate underlying processes in the market, particularly if it is intended to provide the empirical base for a local housing forecasting model. If titles in general, rather than stock turnover, were to be generated on computer then the local authority would have at its disposal a system of records which would be indispensable in giving housing advice, both by indicating patterns of small area price change and turnover, but also in reducing conveyancing search requirements. Such a system, which could be self-financing for an authority, costs about £1 per transaction to extract and store.

The real value of the price database developed for the City of Glasgow is only now coming to the fore and because significant additions have been made to it. In recent years data for the period since 1974 has been added for housing association investment, improvement grants, repair grants, statutory grants, environmental improvement, etc. The system, with more on-line data storage at the city council, could provide a way of managing grant applications and progress. Detailed mappings of grant aid for different periods can be produced, and patterns of incidence examined. When linked to the price database and turnover record the price effects of rehabilitation spending, the effect of grant aid on turnover, and the influence of categories of grant aid on resale prices, can be analysed. A well planned private sector policy, on the part of the local authority, requires insights into such questions. For the City of Glasgow, nine years of data have been processed for less than £50,000! For a year in which grant spending in the city totalled £70 mn the monitoring costs were £25,000.

Leaving aside analysis and related computing costs we are arguing that in a city the size of Glasgow, with nearly 700,000 inhabitants, sustained monitoring is feasible from existing data records. Their coding and co-ordination would require a total expenditure of £1 mn per annum in the public sector and £50,000 in the private sector.

There is a strong case for British local authorities to scrutinise their systems of collecting management information in order to establish what is actually happening in the housing system. The benefits may be extensive and the costs minimal. Once authorities have a well developed information system they may be in a position to link with other agencies. Why does the Building Societies Association not ensure that their members give loan application forms a common core — both common to societies and to the socio-economic content advocated for waiting list forms? Analysis of local tenure choice and preference would then be a more straightforward matter. And if builders are so interested in the demand for new housing, why don't they collect standard brief details on the economic status and origins of new purchasers? This could help make their decisions better informed, less speculative.

Almost all industries in Britain undertake research and development of some form, often amounting to ten per cent of industry costs. But what about the British housing industry? In the construction and rehabilitation sectors the captains of industry rely on central and local government technical advice, such as from the Building Research Establishment. In the area of market research, private builders and authorities do little research and even less product development. Ironically it is only the non-profit seeking financial institutions who have innovated extensively in the British housing system in the last decade, both in devising capital market instruments and in investment patterns. Lyndon Johnston once remarked, of the USA, that it was astounding that a nation which could put men on the moon couldn't improve the efficiency of housing investment. The British housing system is not only earthbound but hidebound!

Forecasting forward
A vital characteristic of the thinking authority is that it recognises not only the need for a strategy but that, given its objectives, it seeks some best strategy at least in the sense of developing the best first move. Since housing investment decisions create a long-lasting framework it is arguable that they be made with some view of costs and benefits discounted back from far into the future. However, it would be rare, and perhaps unwise, for a British housing authority to look forward more than five years — at least in any formal written statement. At present statutory obligations extend over three years. As central government only provides three year forward estimates of public expenditure on housing (and only in money terms) it makes little sense for authorities to plan beyond that horizon.

Even with a five year period of forward thinking in mind, an authority is faced with a particularly difficult forecasting task. For even if the external environment were not to change an existing housing system embodies its own dynamic. In such a period some dwelling stock will decay and may become obsolescent, existing households may grow or decline in size and there will be constant pressures to restructure the housing stock. However, these endogenous dynamic forces will usually be outweighed by changes in the external environment. And it is not as if housing demand were only principally influenced by a few simple variables or that such changes manifested themselves in changes in consumption or a specific housing service. Demand side changes are caused by a variety of factors and they manifest themselves in a plethora of ways. Their links into local social and economic systems are complex. Changes in the overall level and structure of housing demand arise from three main sources of change — economic, socio-demographic and technological. Economic changes will alter the level of employment (and hence unemployment as well as net migration) and the level and structure of the income distribution. Clearly net employment change influences the number of household units. In an economic analysis of the impacts of oil development on the Aberdeen housing market, Maclennan and Jones (1990) have indicated that job and household totals increased by more than ten per cent in five years. The failure to forecast this change led, at least in part, to a 73 per cent increase in dwelling prices within on year. And, although on a less spectacular scale, public and private supply erred on the side of caution for almost three years after rapid growth started. In that case rising housing and land prices and rising wage rates were the main costs of failure to generate adequate quantitative estimates of economic development. The Aberdeen context is clearly an extreme example in recent British economic history but most metropolitan housing markets, and more than a few rural authorities, have contained areas of localised growth.

In West Central Scotland, for example, the development of the microelectronics sector has selected new locations and generated new housing demands from those which already existed in the region. At present, for instance, there is a clear shortage of high value executive housing in such reception areas for inward investment. However, not one of the district housing plans (for 11 local authorities) in the area affected discusses electronics growth and its (industry specific) housing requirements.

Some industries may have a workforce which accords closely with existing labour skills and locations, but some may generate net migration of particular groups into particular peripheral locations. This implies that housing demand analysis has to pay much closer attention to the sectoral and spatial patterns of gross job gains and losses within their area. In many instances job losses will result in unemployment. Employed or unemployed status are now, and increasingly, an important determinant of housing tenure as ownership initiatives are pushing home-ownership further down the income spectrum. They will critically influence tenure and locational demands for housing within an area.

This is not to suggest that regional economic modelling is easy or indeed practiced widely. Previous research has emphasised the problems of small area forecasting, but employment projection models for metropolitan areas and their major constituent parts (core, periphery etc.) have been developed. Spatial, sectoral projects for larger area units and broader industrial groupings are feasible and have become more commonplace in British regions as recession has prompted a growing interest in local economic development. Of course, where the metropolitan economy is balkanised by a number of district housing authorities, then a supra-district integration of housing and economic planning may be required. Economic planning and private housing planning will often require a metropolitan-wide approach.

Although it is seldom dealt with explicitly most authorities do seem to be aware that job changes do influence household numbers. However, few housing plans consider the implications of local migration or income growth.

Small area forecasting of migration within a region is difficult if origin and destination regions are defined to be very small, say a neighbourhood. However, research suggests that projection of the rate and structure of intrametropolitan migration can be predicted relatively accurately. Of course, turnover and locational adjustment would be explained as outputs from a well developed model of a local housing system. Migration and turnover rates are rarely mentioned in British housing plans. Further, it is income which almost all housing research reports as the key influence on tenure choice, dwelling size and type, improvement and location choice. Income is fundamental to the dynamics of housing consumption, indeed the relationship between house prices and income in most regions of Britain has displayed a remarkable long term stability — but this important observation was not noted or used in any of the 25 housing plans read for the preparation of this paper.

Taking these comments on job change, unemployment and income growth together, British housing plans generate their estimates independently of any view on local, regional or national economic change. They also ignore the likely future path of inflation and interest rates. The housing system is treated as if it were disconnected from the local economy. This is a bizarre procedure in a country increasingly reliant upon private housing provision. Similarly, on the supply side of the system, the financial or labour market contexts for the industry may alter, new cost and technology conditions may arise and the balance between rehabilitation and new construction may alter. They are also generally disregarded.

Further, supply decisions in the local housing sector can have important short term effects on the buoyancy of the local economy. First, the volume of housing investment will influence jobs, and this is not unaffected by the split between new construction and rehabilitation. Second, at the localised neighbourhood scale, construction activity may have a particularly marked effect. In a number of countries, particularly Scandinavia, the employment effects of housing investment are regarded as being critical in formulating policy; in other countries they only matter in pre-election years. British housing authorities in defining their capital allocations are now beginning to consider this issue; a few have made guesstimates, even fewer have made precise calculations.

The main source of forecasts about housing demands, or at least needs, in most British housing plans comes from the changing local demography. This feature rings out from the Housing Plans of Glasgow or Belfast or Birmingham, and from city and rural authorities. Is it because Censuses and official population figures make such exercises possible? The combination of cohorts of population and well established headship rates appears irresistible and to yield firm estimates. But inevitably, and at a local scale for particularly important groups, they generate inaccurate forecasts. Indeed a number of recent studies of housing planning have stressed the need to refine this art.

The demographic approach is less than convincing. The conceptual approaches advocated by Ermisch (1990) deserve wider practical application. The use of headship rates can be criticised for three major reasons. First, headship rates are extrapolated on a purely mechanical basis from a limited number of historical points and this is particularly hazardous for new socio-demographic groups. Second, cross section explanations of spatial variations in headship rates have had a limited explanatory success. Finally, and most important, they dismiss the headship concept as being arbitrary and of decreasing relevance with growing household fission.

The alternative concept of minimal household units is analytically more appealing as is the attempt to explain socio-economic determinants of household formation — rather than taking headship rates as fixed, historically determined numbers. The decision to form a household is influenced by changing social attitudes and preferences as well as the constraints of incomes and the availability and cost of housing.

Clearly housing systems and policies can alter household formation rates and decisions about increasing family size, etc. At present, and into the foreseeable future, two demographic groups, young single persons and the elderly, are displaying household formation and housing behaviour not previously accounted for by historical averages. This not only alters the number of housing units but also their size structure. Indeed at present, in the plans examined, quantitatively unpredicted rises in single person household formation are the major cause of growing housing waiting lists. So new demographic forecasting approaches, linked to economic and housing sector changes will be of particular importance. Social and demographic change are more predictable and more easily identified than most housing planners care to consider. However, the demographic sector of planning models needs to be closely linked to the economic and housing systems. Disregard for these linkages may have been reasonable when public funds for housing investment were in elastic supply — demographic needs estimates led investment. In a demand oriented approach to housing strategy new approaches are required.

Pervasive technological change, which may have a dramatic impact within a decade on patterns of working and living, are also going to form the context in which housing is provided in the 1990s. Within a decade the new poor in Britain may be the informational poor. Should local authorities in the near future be installing microcomputers in their dwellings to assist in controlling domestic heating, lighting, security systems? Could such links also be used to key in repair requests, requests for listings of points scores and vacant dwellings? If residents are increasingly going to work at home, when will a work space become a necessity rather than a luxury? Should private builders be already developing such models?

Progressing the action plan
The previous section stressed, at some length, the ways in which authorities could improve upon the presently inadequate approach to data monitoring and forecasting. However once this action plan is prepared the planning function does not terminate.

Staff within the organisation have to be fully appraised of its contents. There has to be liaison and co-operation with other housing investors. Recent reports on 'working together' for Scotland and England indicate that there is limited strategic planning co-operation between authorities and associations. And how many local authorities have a formal annual meeting with builders and building societies operating in their areas? Do some authorities have a political preference not to undertake such co-operation? If so, how are they likely to liaise with new private landlords or new social landlords whom they regard as predatory? Strategic planning may be a matter of political preference as well as officer competence.

Last, and by no means least, how are councils to involve residents, especially tenants, in the planning process? It is relatively easy to involve tenants in the planning of neighbourhood rehabilitation and even new social housing construction. But these actions follow the basic plan formation. Can tenants become involved in the process at an earlier stage, even where the authority establishes views by market research?

When the action plan is agreed and implementation initiated the authority has to continue monitoring and to adapt its plans. Whilst the authority's own investment strategy may be implemented or revised in a relatively straightforward fashion, what of the sectors for which the authority acts as enabler? Have authority actions, controls and incentives created the desired response by private investors and other social agencies? If not, why not? Could it be because the authority lacks effective enabling powers and finances?

The last question poses key issues about new legislative proposals, namely are there tensions or patterns of power which now prevent an enabling role? Before moving to the penultimate section of this chapter, it has to be concluded that until now most British housing authorities have not pursued their planning role with competence or conviction. Central government has been misguided in its initial assumption, thereby revealing its own ignorance of how housing is planned, that there are good grounds for seeing municipalities as strategic housing planners.

The new context and conflicts of interest

In planning future housing strategies British authorities are now confronted with a changing perception of the role of housing policy as well as a shift in the approved agencies for investment. Recent policy statements, especially in Scotland, have stressed the importance of remaking social housing neighbourhoods. That is, housing strategies, as well as management policies, are to have a more localised dimension within local authority areas. Housing is no longer to be planned as a quantitative target for a particular tenure, but its case has to be argued upon a wider range of localised impacts.

The promotion of 'neighbourhood' to a central concern in housing policy will place severe planning demands upon authorities. For not only will authorities require a more detailed view of how local systems operate but also how they have developed and are now changing. Moreover at such a scale, inter-sectoral links between housing investment, environmental upgrading, community development, policing, education and community economic initiatives will be of increasing concern. The day of 'housing only' planning is truly finished. Unfortunately there is little in the way of academic understanding of social neighbourhood change or appropriate data to guide strategy formulation.

Remaking neighbourhoods, unlike the grand development phase, is also unlikely to be successful if it does involve the interests and energies of local communities. Residents must be involved in the social area redevelopment planning process. This shift in perspective is to be welcomed but it may prove difficult, though not impossible, to reconcile with the new emphasis given to mixed or private financing of these schemes. Private finance requires an acceptable rate of return. Clearly defined strategy and assessment of risk must be handmaidens of private investment in any remaking strategy. The shift of social housing to decentralised or smaller independent units will also erode the scope for pooling of estate costs and revenues and this also implies a more thorough risk conscious appraisal strategy than historically operated by authorities.

If authorities now face a more demanding financial and planning framework they may also, due to legislative developments, be confronted with fewer controls over other investors as well as a new, basic, conflict of interest between their roles as planner and provider.

Authorities must, if they are to survive, let alone thrive, develop a clear organisational strategy for council housing provision. Authorities may choose to react co-operatively with new providers, and as many as half of English authorities have signalled this possibility. Others may react negatively. Co-operation and competition are both possible, even desirable, reactions to takeover proposals.

Where authorities adopt a co-operative 'puppy-dog' strategy, this may reflect a willing acceptance of pluralism. It would be interesting to know how many local authorities in Northern Ireland would like a return of local housing control which passed to the Housing Executive in the early 1970s. Others may believe that the scale of remaking required is beyond their competence. Glasgow's decision to transfer one quarter of its stock to co-operatives may, for instance, be difficult for smaller authorities to follow. Many authorities may feel more comfortable when they recognise that the costs of rehabilitation in conjunction with extremely low resident incomes will, in the main, preclude privately rather than socially financed alternative landlords. Pluralism and privatisation should not be confused.

However at least some large scale landlords are likely to react competitively. If councils really are monopolists then this implies that they have considerable scope to adjust costs and outputs and remain in business. Where centralised local authorities react, strategically signalling market protection intentions, by decentralising services, raising tenant participation and sorting out rent schemes and maintenance systems, then consumers would benefit from potential market contestability of the new proposals. If, however, advertising and scare campaigns reduce interest in the tenants' charter then potential competition will not necessarily bring customer benefits. Such conduct, in the general product market, could provoke referral to the Monopolies Commission. Whilst such referrals have protected the British consumers' interest in air flights, condoms and whisky consumption, they have never been used in relation to exploited tenants.

Local authorities could also adopt powerful strategies to threaten or dissuade potential investors. New landlords could be refused planning permission or have improvement grants strictly rationed. In one British city there is already a campaign of 'Chinese whispers' with officials and councillors hinting to architects and developers that their flow of municipal work will dry up if they co-operate with a large 'alternative' landlord. And councils could fail to target environmental works, policing and community projects to estates being remade by private or unwelcome alternative landlords. Even allocation policies could be used to threaten new investors, say by concentrating anti-social tenants next to developments by alternative landlords. Even the threat of such action can dissuade or make more risky privately financed schemes for rent or owner-occupation. Who is to monitor, judge and penalise such action, which is clearly not in the public interest?

Central government has considerable capacity to penalise non-co-operative landlords. Most crudely, capital allocations could be adjusted, though it is arguable that with housing revenue accounts ring-fenced authorities should be free to choose their own desired levels of capital expenditure. That is, there may be a case for allowing authorities to make their own investment strategies. And through the Housing Action Trust's (HAT) legislation, central government could create enclaves of Whitehall sovereignty within estates. However, imposed HATs will fail for lack of community support and HAT territories cannot be properly replanned and reintegrated into the local economy and society if they are isolated from other local actions. In Scotland, where HATs have not been introduced, central government will use the incentive of additional resources, provided through alternative landlords supported by Scottish Homes, to induce co-operation. If an authority excludes Scottish Homes there will be many other areas prepared to welcome additional resources. A council which does this over a sustained period may well suffer adverse electoral consequences.

Where competition is to be real, or where a mixed competitive and co-operative strategy is to prevail, can the local authority be left as the strategic authority? Whose strategy is to prevail, the local authorities', the housing corporation's, the regional controller's or, in Scotland, Scottish Homes'? Planning powers in relation to land use and other essential service provision may still lie with the authority, but they have no controls over the approval of alternative landlords and, critically, they will not have financial control (even if the 1989 Local Government Bill does allow authorities to assist alternative landlords from local tax revenues). They also have no nomination rights to enable the fulfillment of strategic tasks such as helping the homeless.

European experience, most notably in the run-down French grand ensembles indicates that where there is a plurality of social landlords co-ordination of management processes as well as investment decision is essential. European solutions to this problem differ from country to country. In France, the Regional Prefect (a central government official) scrutinises municipality and social housing proposals and approves finance. That is, regionally located central government officials (such as the Department of the Environment's regional controllers, or the regional controllers of the NIHE and Scottish Homes regional 'supremos'), make the strategic decisions. In Sweden, municipalities have financial powers to assist municipal housing companies (of which two to three operate in the average municipality) and can control company decisions. In the Netherlands a strong Housing Inspectorate polices the adequacy of strategies largely implemented by municipalities and financed by central government block grants. But in none of these systems, which all give more strategic power to non-municipal agencies than in Great Britain, does the strategy involve removing properties from unwilling municipalities.

In Scotland, Wales and Northern Ireland where non-municipal strategic agents are powerful, the issues of strategy domination will be obvious and, in Scotland and Wales, require resolution in the near future. The issues will be less obvious, if no less important, in England. However the question does arise whether the centralised bureaucracies of DoE and the Housing Corporation would not be better decentralised, to existing regional offices, to form a series of powerful housing agencies. If the new pluralistic approach is to succeed, 'London Homes', 'Northern Homes' etc. may eventually be required. If proposals to radically alter civil service organisation by converting departments into agencies, are implemented, this proposal may become a possibility. Would the able but peripatetic senior civil servants who run housing divisions in Marsham Street not be better used in more committed housing careers nearer both to problems and to opportunities? The Swedish Minister for Housing runs a more than adequate housing policy with a headquarters staff of 20 or so senior officials.

Conclusions

This chapter has ranged widely around the issues surrounding housing planning in the UK. For the existing system, as James Thurber would say, 'The fat is in the fire, the cat is out of the bag, the jig is up and the goose is cooked'. We have to hope for a new housing planning system.

This process would start by reiterating the spirit of 1977 when housing plans and HIPs were introduced. Plans have to cover all tenures and investors and to do so with credible information and techniques. Central government, large agencies, municipalities and individual investors all need to be committed to the process of strategy development. Local authorities have only a short period — say five years — in which they can begin to undertake this function effectively. And this may be difficult if they are 'disabled' and hostile to the new pluralism. They cannot presume that everywhere and always they will be regarded as the natural strategic enablers for housing provision in Britain.

References

Ansoff I (1987) *Corporate Strategy* Harmondsworth: Penguin Books.

Audit Commission (1986) *Managing the Crisis in Council Housing* London: HMSO.

Brook R (1990) *Managing the Enabling Authority* London: Longman.

Ermisch J (1990) *Fewer Babies, Better Lives* York: Rowntree Foundation.

The Grieve Report (1987) Glasgow District Council.

Hancock K and Maclennan D (1990) *A House Price Monitoring System: Tayside Region* Scottish Office, Edinburgh.

Inquiry into British Housing (1985) National Federation of Housing Associations.

Maclennan D (1977) *Information, Space and Housing Preferences* Scottish Journal of Political Economy **24.**

Maclennan D (1982) *Housing Economics* London: Longmans.

Maclennan D (1987) *Housing Demand* Central Research Unit Discussion Paper, Scottish Office.

Maclennan D et al (1989) *The Nature and Effectiveness of Housing Management in England* London: HMSO.

Maclennan D and Jones C A (1990) *Economic Change and the Local Housing* Market Environment and Planning (Series A), forthcoming.

Maclennan D, Wood G A and Munro M (1987) Housing choices and the structure of housing markets in Turner B et al (eds) *Between State and Market: Housing in the Post Industrial Era* Stockholm: Almquist and Wicksell.

Massie A (1986) *Augustus: A Novel* Oxford: Bodley Head.

Murie and Malpass (1986).

Rao N (1990) *The Changing Role of Local Housing Authorities* Policy Studies Institute, London.

Schelling T C (1960) *The Strategy of Conflict* Cambridge: Harvard University Press.

Scottish Development Department (1977).

Chapter 13
Joining the professionals? The future of housing staff and their work

Introduction

Much of the debate about the future of the public housing services is conducted at the strategic level with a focus on national programmes and policies and their relative effectiveness in meeting objectives such as fair allocations and value for money. While such debate is entirely legitimate it was a preoccupation which until recently overshadowed equally important issues such as what the consumer actually wanted or how housing services should be organised and delivered. In reality, and as we now know, whatever the policies agreed nationally it is in local areas that they become real for the consumer, and they do so via the different housing organisations involved in delivering housing services to owners and tenants.

The issue of service delivery and more particularly the direction, shape and structure of the organisation involved, and the quality and quantity of their staff, has been much neglected by governments, practitioners and academics. Indeed within the now considerable literature devoted to housing there is still a remarkably small amount devoted to the question of the staffing and organisation of housing work. In seeking to correct this omission, at least in a partial and preliminary way, this chapter considers a number of interrelated issues surrounding the development of housing work, training and education, and the emergence of a housing profession. Following this introduction we undertake a brief historical review of housing work and housing education. We then move on to explore the interconnections between the issues confronting the housing service and the developing moves towards ensuring well trained and professional staff. We conclude by speculating on the future of public housing services and whether it is too late to achieve the changes needed.

Housing Work

The quality of the housing service delivered to consumers rests heavily on the capacities of staff who work within housing organisations. It is a sad reality that attempts to improve the service given, by training and educating staff, have had weak support, and that housing remains one of the areas of public service where training has been particularly inadequate. The problems created by this situation are magnified today by the complex issues being faced such as reduced funding, new technologies and management practices, rising consumer demands and expectations, unemployment and poverty. While housing work is certainly more complex now than in the past, the failure to recognise the complexity of outwardly simple and mundane daily practices such as rent collection or dwelling allocations allowed many individuals and organisations to ignore the need for training, or indeed for any careful and sustained education which might expose the underlying complexities of these practices.

Moreover, this failure to train and educate has been used by others as yet another indication of the supposed lack of ability of housing staff. It is commonplace to lay the blame for the current problems besetting the public housing services at the door of the staff who run it. In reality their actual performance has probably been no worse than other so called professionalised groups, e.g. planners or social workers, yet because their professional image is weaker it has been easy to condemn housing staff and the housing services they operate. Equally, because of the low priority given to education and training, it has appeared that there is nothing to housing work beyond doing it — at best all it requires is practitioners to codify their work and for staff to learn communication skills. Analysis and assessment, commonplace to the world of education, has been neglected and this was reflected in a housing eduction system which up to the 1980s was, in many ways, simply a modest external representation of internal job needs and most notably it lacked educational logic and structure.

The poor status and organisation of housing alongside its weakly delivered education and training thus tended to sustain a view of housing that all changes which came about were externally driven, i.e. that housing and housing staff are so uncritical (and incapable) that change must be imposed. Recently the emergence of a better trained and educated staff and a growing professionalisation has substantially enhanced the possibility of change from within and the development of more creative and adaptive housing services. Indeed, as we have suggested from the outset, staff have to be involved, as do consumers, in the changing future of housing services.

The charges of lack of professionalism and inadequate skills have some basis in reality but they are not unique to housing nor do they provide in themselves a sufficient explanation of the current difficulties. The history of housing service in many local authorities is one of continuing rearguard action by other professional groupings and departments to frustrate the emergence of any unified housing service which might get closer to tackling the housing problems which abound. This resistance has reflected an ignorance about housing, blatant power politics, and a continuing paternalistic view of council housing. Moreover, the slow progress towards the establishment of such a structure both sustains and reflects the relatively weak professionalism of housing work (and by extension inflates the status of the other areas of work). Local authorities have in some respects been made less capable by the stranglehold of professional bodies and 'disciplinary departments'. The fragmented housing service would seem to be an excellent example of the negative consequences of these processes. Equally, the fact that housing is a district rather than a county responsibility has confined it to the lowest and least professionalised tier of local government. One consequence of this is that the 'prestige' departments are few and far between — mainly in metropolitan areas.

Historical development of the housing service

A brief historical review of the housing service reveals its slow development. While a number of local authorities had by the late 1880s begun to establish a rudimentary direct housing function the service was almost always provided via existing central departments such as valuers, engineers, borough treasurers and public health, with each picking up individual elements, but taking no overall responsibility for housing. This fragmentation frustrated such a development and sustained a dominant focus on the property rather than the occupants. The housing service was ancillary and therefore had to be run with the minimum of frills (and certainly not on the lines proposed by Miss Octavia Hill which involve all manner of social services!).

The London County Council appointed its first housing manager in 1912 though even then the function was spread between departments. In Bristol, housing was initially the responsibility of the engineers and treasurer's departments, and although a housing manager was appointed in 1920, to the town clerk's department, the rent collectors were part of the medical officer of health's inspectorate. It was not until 1930 that a separate department was created. By 1935 only 13 per cent of local authorities in Britain had appointed a housing manager (though there were by this time estates managers, often female, in a number of authorities). Progress continued to be slow. The Central Housing Advisory Committee (CHAC) Report of 1959 indicated that in the 54 authorities surveyed 46 (85 per cent) had officers called 'housing managers' though in only 20 per cent of the authorities were they in charge of a separate department (and even then repairs were typically the responsibility of the Engineer's Department).

The call to establish comprehensive housing departments has been made throughout the now one hundred years history of public housing, and it has been made by government committees, professional bodies, academics, and many others. Yet in 1985, the Audit Commission found that there were still 12 housing authorities with no separate housing department and that in 108 authorities the treasurer was responsible for rent collection, arrears and housing benefit. Substantially less than half of all housing authorities had what might be called a 'comprehensive' housing department and many were still joint with the environmental health or social services department (the former notably in Wales). Comprehensive departments are still being created but this trend is also offset by both the closure of small departments and continuing mergers with other functions (e.g. environmental health, social services). The unions and the profession have opposed such closures but typically to no avail — reflecting continuing uncertainties and rivalries about housing functions at a local level. Housing associations perhaps came closest to the ideal, having a single focus on housing and with all staff working to that end, though even here there is ample evidence of departmentalism.

The housing service has grown and changed. It has direct responsibility for over 5 million dwellings and the homes of over 12 million people. It provides a range of services including aid and advice, benefit, repair and maintenance, agency services, mortgages, grants, partnership schemes, sales, research and strategy, direct labour, management and design, such that its coverage probably reaches out to double that number of households. As the departments have changed, so housing work is no longer just rent collection but a sophisticated and complex bundle of activities which range from close and caring contact with individual consumers, advocacy and participation schemes, through to advanced financial management, the application of new technology and the development of organisations and interdepartmental working. With the rapid emergence of housing associations as a powerful and important housing provider, a further set of dimensions has been created.

Despite the financial and political pressures upon the housing service it continues to expand in terms of opportunities. Taking the UK as a whole there are over 73,000 people employed in local authority housing functions and 30,000 in housing associations giving a grand total of at least 103,000. Employment has continued to grow partly through central government initiatives which have required further staffing (e.g. right-to-buy, housing benefit) but also due to decentralisation, new technology and organisational change. White collar work is expanding at the cost of blue collar work — a process likely to strengthen with the concern to establish local offices staffed by generic rather than specialist officers. The Audit Commission has suggested that staffing levels in local authorities in England and Wales could be reduced by 8000 if all organisations were structured and operated as efficiently as the 'best'. Such a figure may underestimate the variation between authorities in terms of their problems and priorities. For the present, at least, there is little suggestion that employment will fall and if external demands continue to increase then it may continue to rise. However it is hard to predict the consequences of the new financial regimes. For individual local authorities and especially those facing reduced subsidy entitlement, or significant rent increases, under ring-fencing there will be pressures to reduce staff. For associations uncertainties regarding funding may curb tendencies to recruit more staff. In addition, concerns with performance and value for money will increasingly exercise a downward momentum on staff numbers.

The professionalisation of housing work

The weak departmental development of the housing service has significantly influenced both the process of professionalisation and related housing education and training. As we have noted, from its beginning there has been a tendency to view the housing service as a purely administrative function of allocating dwellings and collecting rents.

In part this was because of the existing division of labour within local authorities which meant that the architect's department designed them, the engineers department built and maintained the dwellings, the town clerk's department administered them and the treasurer's department financed them. Professional judgment was thus exercised in the upper echelons of these departments rather than in any housing section, a pattern which has continued until today in some small authorities.

As authorities began to operate estates, a small number recruited women members of organisations such as the Association of Women House Property Managers to act as estates officers. These women brought with them a clear sense of the training necessary to do the job, and by 1932 the different women's groups had formed a Society of Women Housing Estate Officers with a quarterly bulletin and training scheme. The predominantly male Institute of Housing, which was essentially concerned only with public housing, was registered in 1938 and began its own programme of instruction and examination in that year. Thus by the end of the 1930s there was clear evidence of a desire to professionalise, train and educate on behalf of people working in housing. Progress was slow and there were significant differences in attitude and class origins between the two bodies.

The Society took the view that intensive management was the correct way to operate the service and their training programme reflected this covering surveying, economics, government, social welfare and construction *plus* a period of supervised training in a range of organisations. The Institute, by contrast, sought to separate the rent and repairs functions from the social welfare element and argued that these should be in different departments. Their approach favoured a more extensive approach to housing management with contact with tenants being limited to contractual obligations. The Institute's examinations reflected this, giving considerable weight to technical skills. There was no supervised training element. That the two bodies differed in their approach was unsurprising given that the Society's members were largely middle class graduates working in trusts, associations and the private sector, while the Institute drew its membership from local government (where departments ruled), and from a broader social and educational spectrum.

The Central Housing Advisory Committee in 1938 (CHAC 1938) took evidence from both organisations with respect to the best training to give to housing managers. The committee were unable to recommend the approach of either organisation in its entirety and suggested that the two key issues were personality and a training which covered 'sociological' subjects and, where relevant, 'technical' subjects. They suggested that all managers in control of large estates should hold a degree. What their report suggests is that there was early recognition of the need to train and educate housing staff. However, because housing was the responsibility of so many departments and so many established professional interests, there was little likelihood of such recommendations being taken up in any major way. Moreover, it did not correct the inherent bias to more technocratic and economic approaches to management. In a situation where housing was controlled by the main-line technical departments in a local authority there was little prospect of new social work-type posts being approved, or indeed a social ethos developing. Little wonder there remained a dominant concern with managing the property.

Although the two traditions of housing management and training were established early on it was not until the late 1970s that this seems to have generated any substantial debate. Under pressure from central government and local politicians to decentralise and improve performance, local authorities have paid renewed attention to the way they organise their services in relation to the housing consumer. Until the mid 1960s training and education programmes devised by the two professional bodies were organised and delivered by these bodies themselves (and indeed few other organisations took a sustained interest in training at all). They did not involve the higher and further education system in any substantial way, instead relying heavily on experienced housing staff 'teaching' the less experienced. Thus the education system remained largely unused with courses being delivered in a scattering of colleges but as yet no housing degrees or diplomas being established (nor any departments of housing studies). In contrast planning, surveying and architecture all benefitted considerably with a large number of departments, often staffed by former practitioners, opening up in tertiary institutions. Such a process gave a substantial lift to the professionalisation of those areas of work and it gave further grounds for viewing housing work as a poor relation.

In 1965 the Society and the Institute merged but the combined resources of the two organisations remained small and certainly insufficient to promote housing work, education and training to a high level. Progress was made with the annual conference, journal, and various publications but it was slow compared to other areas of local authority activity. A number of reports including the Cullingworth report (1969) and the City University study of 1981 (City University 1981) indicated a need to enhance training and education in housing a view echoed in the work of the Housing Services Advisory Group on training (HSAG 1978).

By the beginning of the 1980s the pace of change had begun to increase. Degree courses had opened up in some seven institutions and the Institute of Housing recognised the need to pursue this further, along with a developed training programme. Its own qualification was revamped, with practical experience making a return to the qualification process. By the 1990s the Institute had embraced an expansionist education and training programme likely to substantially increase opportunities for staff at all levels and to generate a significant upgrading in professional image and capacity. The Royal Institution of Chartered Surveyors had also given some indications of renewed interest by reviving its General Practice Division (Housing Option) and beginning to explore housing ideas and housing education questions.

The question now is whether these changes and improvements have come soon enough to secure a future for publicly provided services? Elsewhere in this volume suggestions have been made as to what may happen. Here we would wish to focus on aspects of professionalisation, education and training. The commitment of the Department of the Environment, the Scottish Office and the Welsh Office to provide postgraduate bursaries for housing students is an important development and one which has given major momentum to the Institute of Housing's programme of restructuring. Although a review of the funding of English postgraduate courses has recently been undertaken by the Cabinet Office it is believed it does not recommend cessation of this support. The planned introduction of continuing professional development for its members (via, for example, the weekly publication *Inside Housing*) mean housing staff are more likely to be better equipped to face both current and future demands.

Many who are quick to condemn the housing service overlook its relatively short history and the fight that has been made against established interests, political sea changes and a chaotic financial system. Only a minority of those working in housing wish to restrict entry to housing work (by making specific qualifications mandatory) but most agree with the need for standards to rise. Indeed, by coming late to the development of training and education, housing may have an excellent opportunity to learn from the mistakes of other areas of work and professional development and to build its programmes carefully, though inevitably the cutbacks in education expenditure do limit what can be achieved. The question remains, however, whether change in the external environment may overtake this creative phase as the previous chapter makes clear.

Current perspectives

Publicly provided housing services have now reached a watershed in their development and this in turn has raised issues about the future of housing management and the housing profession. There are a number of reasons for the heightened debate about the nature of the housing service as it is delivered. First, there has been a slowing down, and in most cases a complete stop, in the development of new local authority housing. Instead of building housing and focusing attention on questions of aggregate need, the central problem has become the management of the housing service, and the repair and maintenance of existing properties (which have in some cases turned out to have been seriously flawed in their design and construction). Coping with the urgent demands of residents on these estates, or the chargepayers nearby them, has demanded special and particularly 'housing' (as opposed to solely engineering or architectural) skills, including dealing with, for example, the issues of arrears, racial harassment, crime prevention, and 'unlettability'. Finally, the increase in homelessness which has been evident in the late 1980s, both in urban and rural areas, has created an additional and major demand on the housing service.

Second, the old consensus that the expanded provision of council housing in particular was a laudible all–party goal which had dominated policy until the yearly 1970s seems to have been replaced by a new consensus which is opposed to municipal housing. The 'right-to-buy' is one of the main planks of the Conservative manifesto (and 'rents-into-mortgages' is likely to follow) and is held to represent the new reliance on self sufficiency, pride in ownership and a 'rolling back of the state', in this case local government. Individual purchase is one mechanism but a second strand of policy has been to diminish the local authority's role as a major landlord as explicitly set out in the Housing Act 1988 through 'tenant's choice'. Through this, and the voluntary transfer schemes initiated by authorities themselves and the Housing Action Trusts promoted by Government, mass transfer becomes a possibility — though the overall impact of these different initiatives has been limited to date. The Parliamentary Labour Party's proposals while being less opposed to public accommodation as such, have the goal of consumer sovereignty over the choice of which tenure to occupy (and greater consumer control over all tenures) as a main focus in contrast to the 'municipal provision' ideals of earlier decades. Moreover severe political divisions have encroached into the administration of the local authority housing service itself. In a number of cases, authorities have explicitly evaluated the political attitudes of officers in making senior appointments; indeed there is some discussion of whether straightforwardly political appointments, or fixed term appointments might become a feature of the service. In addition, the type of staff attracted to the service recently have tended to be much more aware of wider political aspects of housing, particularly when carrying out politically motivated policies. An explicit commitment to specific housing policies could influence the shape and pace of change though not necessarily enhance the professionalism of housing work. Some organisations regard qualifications as elitist and would regard commitment as more important.

Third, in addition to these shifts, the attitudes of consumers as tenants towards their housing and its administration have changed. There is an increased demand for a better and more responsive service, and for greater control over that service. No longer are council tenants the compliant and obedient recipients of municipal munificence. The many failures of the service now provoke loud complaints, and demands for improvement to be supplied, if possible, without the penalty of rent increases. The response to these demands requires a much more informed and competent approach to housing issues than was previously evident. The client, the tenant, rightly expects that housing officers will have some skill and specialist knowledge in dealing with the difficulties and problems brought to them. In fact in many cases this knowledge and these skills are only now being established, but the demand for them is one which must be met by developing them as quickly and systematically as possible.

Fourth, one practical consequence of these changes in attitude has been a variety of practical experiments and restructurings. These have included decentralisation programmes of various types, sometimes involving other departments as well as housing, the priority estates programmes, the decanting and sale of whole blocks or estates as well as tenant cooperative schemes, and the privatisation of estates services such as caretaking and cleaning. The opportunities for more radical changes in management arrangements have been extended and given further impetus through the recent legislation.

Fifth, a key technical development which has influenced the pace of change has been the availability of computerised technology to administer the housing service. This has allowed many of the moves towards decentralisation, by permitting remote access to essential information, as well as opening the opportunity for devolution of control. This accessibility of information may also lead to a much greater awareness amongst staff generally of the details of the authority's administration and stock. Further, it is leading to a much greater degree of standardisation and consistency of administration as authorities share packages, specifications, and advice in devising their own individual systems. This technical exchange has lead to both the need to think about the system, and a greater desire to look at other authorities' practices. This standardisation process is also reflected in the growing recruitment of qualified staff, i.e. people who have themselves received a specified package of 'housing education'.

Sixth, as educational standards and political awareness have risen along with a desire for further training, and access to detailed information has increased, there has been increased questioning of traditional attitudes and practices in authorities, a process which has developed as staff progress through the organisation or go from authority to authority. They may also bring with them a more militant attitude to labour relations, where practices are seen as not only defective but also leading to poor working methods and conditions. Furthermore it would seem that housing staff, when confronted with problems of working practice have sought to resolve the matter via union negotiation, without the added consideration of professional practice and training. One example is in the response to client violence in some housing departments, often involving industrial action to insist on the immediate provision of security screens, arranged via the union. Equally, the introduction of decentralisation or new technology into departments has quite rightly led to detailed negotiations with union representatives over changed working conditions, but often without a concurrent exploration of the professional implications of the changes. Finally we should not ignore the impact of moves towards creating a performance culture and giving assurance regarding the quality of the services provided. Given a concern with higher standards authorities will be under pressure to meet and exceed them. This will in turn lead to a more structured approach to management.

Professionalising practice

Paralleling these developments within the housing service itself, there has been a considerable upsurge in the 1980s in the appearance of reports and studies, mainly but not exclusively from non-local authority sources, dealing with the methods of management. These come from bodies as diverse as the Audit Commission, the National Association for the Care and Resettlement of Offenders, and the City University, as well as from housing organisations such as the Institute of Housing or National Federation of Housing Associations. The emergence of this growing body of hard research and informed discussion of the issues in public housing management is of critical importance for the development of the housing profession, and for the development of housing education and training.

These various reports have two major features in common which make them important, and which demarcate the emergence of housing administration as a proper subject of study and debate. First, they base their conclusions on defined empirical evidence, open to debate on its methodological adequacy and relevance, as well as its accuracy. Second, they are organised directly around questions of housing administration and the quality of the housing service. This recognition of the need for the development of autonomous terms of reference for the debate about housing administration as opposed to debate in terms provided by other disciplines, emphasises the need to directly address housing management issues. Previous housing management texts have tended to be the reflections and advice of respected practitioners (Macey and Baker 1978, Smith 1988, Derby and Smith 1982), based partly on the legal and administrative framework, and partly from the distilled experience of many years of practice. Assertions were seldom systematically justified in any detail, which would have been inappropriate given the nature of the writing.

These new, more empirical studies form the nucleus of material which attempts to combine research and objective standards with practitioner perspectives. They often deal with a variety of locations and local authority areas and make comparisons and conclusions that are argued for empirically and have general application. They therefore go beyond the experience of one authority or practitioner, and attempt to set up objective means to monitor and improve housing management performance.

The impact of this widening of the debate on what constitutes good practice, along with the increasing willingness to investigate the basis of that practice in a systematic way, will have an immediate effect on staff training. Its impact on housing services may take longer to filter through although the pressure is building up for a much more rapid change. As we have indicated earlier, much of the training traditionally given in housing was derived from other related professions, e.g. architecture, engineering, building technology, law, and public administration (partly because officers with these qualifications had been carrying out many of the housing functions in authorities). The new emphasis on housing skills and knowledge does not repudiate the need to have an awareness of the basics of these related disciplines, but it re-emphasises the unique housing aspects and approach in a number of ways which can usefully be summarised here.

The administration of housing is increasingly seen as an activity primarily on behalf of the client, that is the tenant or consumer, rather than on behalf of the authority itself, the chargepayer, the architect or anyone else. While still needing to take account of these other interests (and to train staff regarding interdepartmental professional working) this shift of focus is an important one. Previously the housing department was seen as enabling the architect or the engineer to get on with their jobs by 'dealing with' the tricky business of moving the tenants or residents so that important problems could be dealt with elsewhere in the authority. In such circumstances the administration of housing was more on behalf of the architect or in line with engineering priorities and timetables than it was directed at the needs and aspirations of the residents themselves. This change is readily apparent in the desire to examine and control the central charges levied by other sections of the organisation on housing budgets.

Equally the social work aspects of housing administration tended in some cases to deal with the property as the main issue and to have been directed at ensuring that the tenant treated it with due respect. This concern with respect for property was felt to lead to a better moral well-being and an altogether healthier general attitude, and this for many was the key aim of tenant management. The notion that the tenants had the right to use, improve, alter and utilise the property as best suited them is a development which has taken a very long time to mature. So too has the idea that the aim of housing welfare work was in normal circumstances to assist tenants with their difficulties in coping with the accommodation by tackling these difficulties, rather than to insist that the tenant accommodate to the property and neighbourhood, and develop suitable habits and behaviour (and if they were unable or unwilling to change, to evict them as problem tenants).

In addition to this new approach to basic housing management, there is a clear move to the 'comprehensive' approach to housing, an approach which recognises that local authorities' responsibilities include the homeless, and the owner-occupier (particularly, for example, the elderly owner-occupier) not just the municipal tenant; and in taking on these responsibilities the administration of housing becomes much more than just building houses and collecting the rent. The introduction of homelessness legislation, area improvement and grants legislation, the housing benefit legislation and the right-to-buy all in different ways emphasise the role of local authorities and housing associations in providing for the needs of the whole community, not just those whom it chose to cater for. Equally the disasters of some post-war estates established that the analysis that emphasised that growth and more tower blocks were the answer to Britain's housing problems (and never mind the management) was shown to be spectacularly wrong (Dunleavy 1981). This was not so much because the design and construction were defective (although their many faults are evident) but because of the failure to consider in any detail and with any seriousness the issues and problems of the management of that sector, or the alternatives to it. More recently, the stress in the new housing legislation on the 'strategic and enabling' role of authorities, though sadly at the expense of their landlord function, increases the impetus to take a wider view.

We have argued here that housing problems have a unique character of their own and, while similar to problems in architecture, social work or planning, cannot be reduced to problems in these other disciplinary areas. Housing skills, therefore relate to particular and detailed housing problems: e.g. What are effective means to ensure physical security of a block which will also be supported by residents? What is an effective means of counselling tenants in arrears? What is the most cost efficient means of assisting elderly owners in dilapidated properties? How best can people coming out of care be assisted in becoming independent householders? Which allocation practices avoid racial discrimination and which encourage it? How can voids be minimised? How can mobility be encouraged? What can be done for the single homeless? All of these questions start from the perspective of the consumer's housing demands and requirements, rather than the authority's own requirements, and while drawing in technical and social services skills and information, they can in no way be reduced to problems in those other fields.

A future for housing workers

Public housing in the future will be very different from the old pattern of monolithic departments dominated by central management — particularly in view of the current political commitment to break up the public housing service and the public stock in a variety of ways. Additional developments of the service stem both from current trends in decentralisation or 'local control' and the already proceeding privatisation of management and ownership through trusts, co-ops and 'special initiatives' of various kinds. Does this mean that there will be no role for housing managers or housing administrators in the future, and that the housing profession is waking up to its failures just at the time that it is to be disbanded? This is not the case for two main reasons.

First, management issues remain, as do the need for qualified professional managers even if the blocks, estates, or properties are hived off from local authority control or ownership. This can be seen in part in the growth of housing associations which take a much more progressive view of staff training and conditions than many authorities. There may well, however, be a tendency for some to prefer estate management qualified staff, particularly in the more desirable privatised blocks, just as the clients in self management blocks could decide as a matter of principle that the attitudes of a traditional local authority trained officer were the last thing they needed. Other residents may, however, recognise that the failures in the past have stemmed from organisational structures rather than the agents and from an emphasis on the property at the expense of the residents, and thus opt to employ staff with a strong housing management background. Either way there would probably be a growth in short term contracts, agency arrangements and consultancies.

Second, the role of the central core of the local authority housing departments will become more clearly defined. They will have a clearer role in assessing local needs and strategic planning, co-ordinating housing aid, discharging central statutory duties such as the prevention of homelessness, co-ordination of the control of disrepair and improvement strategy, investment planning, central budgeting, monitoring the provision of specialist accommodation, and ensuring equitable allocation and management of the stock within their control. The monitoring role should extend to trusts or co–ops in their area, ensuring that proper standards of management are being maintained and financial monitoring is adequate. The creation of a unified waiting list ought also to be on the agenda. There are, indeed many unanswered questions here about relationships with privatised management. The main issues concern allocations, rent levels, capital investment and major repairs, enforcement of tenancy conditions, the avoidance of discrimination, the equality of treatment of all applicants and tenants, financial probity and the subsequent disposal of the stock. Where many of the functions of the public landlord are being provided by secondary bodies and agents, the central role of co-ordination and 'policing' would become all the more important. In addition the authority itself would almost certainly retain a stock of dwellings directly in its own management, to deal with urgent homelessness if nothing else. The more strategic role of the central core would itself involve the housing administrators in the corporate management of the authority in a way that would reinforce their claim to be treated as an autonomous professional group.

Conclusion

In conclusion, there is undoubtedly a continuing role for both public housing services and 'housing professionals'. What this role will be, however, depends on how quickly they sort out that 'profession' in responding to the many new and pressing demands. The stock has been found to have severe repair and management problems, and it is likely there will continue to be severely limited resources to deal with these problems. There is a pressing need to establish objectively proven and comprehensively detailed standards of management, and management objectives. These standards must be based on an awareness of the centrality of client satisfaction and involvement rather than the convenience of the authority. The task of developing these standards and attitudes has, however, only just begun. Equally important to develop in parallel is the proper training and involvement of the staff, especially front-line service delivery staff. The history of housing training reveals a slow development, overshadowed by the dominance of the other related professions, and an absence of clear direction and a comprehensive approach to training. Moves have already been made to improve this, but there is still a very long way to travel before the framework of an adequate training system is fully established, or, even more importantly, fully accepted by the majority of public housing service providers.

The housing service now faces the challenges of change. Change is both necessary and inevitable and it will arise not simply because of government policy but also through the changing expectations, demands and needs of the customers it serves. The challenges will arise on every front — the structure of the organisations, the attitudes underpinning them, the qualities and qualifications of staff, the roles to be undertaken, and even the types of organisation in which they work and people to whom they are responsible.

In suggesting dramatic changes will come about we are far from pessimistic as to the future of housing work and housing workers. There are real opportunities emerging which will carry many staff towards the goals they had always felt were desirable but were often unachievable. The market for housing services is changing and a period of adaptation and development has come. Housing management skills will certainly be needed in the future though it cannot be said with any clear guarantee that local authorities will exercise them except in a strategic and enabling way. Direct management may well pass in its entirety to associations, co-ops, and local authority nominees. For some staff then the future may be working outside of local authorities in organisations where control is more directly by the consumers. For those who do remain their duties may change form actual property and tenant management towards a monitoring and supervising role, assessing needs, regulating provision and standards, and drawing all resources together from whatever sector or market to meet all local needs and demands.

Given these possibilities, the challenge for the housing worker is not only to adapt to change but to exercise some control over it. This might be via a number of routes — the work place, the union, the professional structures and Institute, or through training. Essential in this process will be a much clearer and sustained definition of the tasks to be undertaken and the skills required. Now is the time for housing professionals to persuade others of the complex tasks undertaken and the need for precise knowledge and skills. In essence this suggests rapid professionalisation set within a framework of service to the community. Professionalisation does not have to lead to exclusivity and unresponsiveness to consumer needs and demands. It can be brought about by doing a job well. The reality of housing, indeed one of its strengths, is that it is a broad and open area of work where a variety of backgrounds and skills come together. In such a setting professional monopolies are unlikely as well as undesirable. However that does not mean high levels of housing education and training are not necessary. As we have sought to show they are absolutely essential to the relevant and responsive professionalism now taking root in housing.

References

Anchor (1986) *Anchor's Older People: What do they think?*
Audit Commission (1984) *Bringing Council Tenants' Rent Under Control* London: HMSO
Audit Commission (1986) *Managing the Crisis in Council Housing* London: HMSO
CHAC (1938) *The Management of Municipal Housing Estates* London: HMSO
City University Housing Research Group (1981) *Could Local Authorities be Better Landlords?* London: The City University
Commission for Racial Equality (1984) *Hackney Housing Investigated*
Cullingworth Report (1969) Council Housing; Purposes, Procedures and Priorities, London: HMSO
Derby C. and Smith G (eds) (1982) *Best Practice in Housing* London: LGC
Dunleavy P. (1981) *The Politics of Mass Housing in Britain 1945–1975* London: Clarendon
Institute of Housing (1985) *New Technology* London: Institute of Housing
Institute of Housing (1986) Public Sector Housing: Future Use, Control and Management, North London IOH
Macey J and Baker C (1978) *Housing Management* 3rd Edition London: Estates Gazette
Metropolitan Boroughs Association (1963) *General Review of Housing Management* London: MBA
NACRO (1985) *After Entryphones* London: NACRO
National Federation of Housing Associations (1987) *Standards for Housing Management* London: NFHA
Power A (1987) *Property Before People* London: Allen and Unwin
Smith M (1988) *A Guide to Housing* London: Housing Centre Trust
Somerville P (1986) 'Nero Fiddles, While Rome Burns' Housing, May 17–20
Welsh Office (1989) *The Relative Effectiveness of Different Forms of Housing Management in Wales* Welsh Office
Williams P (1987) 'A Curriculum for Housing Work' in Garnett D and Williams P eds The Future of Housing Education; A Symposium, Working Paper 65, School for Advanced Urban Studies, Bristol.

Chapter 14
A service for people

Introduction

This book ranges too widely to be concluded with a neat summary of its main arguments. Instead, we draw it to a close with some reflections on the housing service of the future. Since we were writing primarily for those who work in this service or have some personal interest in it, we focus mainly on the local scale of action. But we shall also have something to say about the national framework which goes far to determine what the service is capable of doing.

We start by asking what the service is for, and what its main aims should be. Then we look briefly at the policy environment in which it has to operate. Next we turn to the service itself in two sections dealing, first, with central government, and then with local government. Having looked at the service from the top down, we pose some of the same questions from the bottom up in a section discussing the special needs it has to meet. Finally, we draw a few general conclusions.

Problems and principles

The quality of our housing is far better than it used to be, and is still improving. More and more people own their own homes. Rents have risen, but only at roughly the same rate as the cost of living; and in the public and private sectors alike housing costs take a smaller proportion of average incomes than they do in many neighbouring countries. So do we need a public housing service at all? For many years after the first Housing Acts were passed, a lot of people believed that government intervention in this field would be no more than a temporary necessity which could be abandoned before long. Some say that the time has now come to do this.

The most compelling arguments for public action start from preventable human suffering — pain for short. So what kinds of pain are we talking about in the field of housing? We are talking about the couple with two young children living in a damp, windswept caravan never intended for winter use, worrying about where they will go when they get turned out to make room for the high-paying summer visitors. (They are on the council's waiting list, but few people move off it these days; and, as newcomers to the district, they have little hope of getting rehoused.)

We are talking about the elderly widow with her own roomy but decaying home with no-one to help fix the leaking roof and no way of paying for urgently needed repairs. (The council abandoned its repairs grant scheme when it was rate-capped.)

Then there's the young woman who was placed, with her baby, in a desolate council estate when she sought refuge from a violent husband. She is now terrorised by the even more violent thieves and drug pushers who rule the neighbourhood (so she shuts herself in all day in the bare flat which she cannot furnish because the social fund's drastically reduced 'single payments' no longer run to that).

The needs of these people are vividly obvious to anyone who meets them: the stuff of which television programmes are made. But there are less obvious cases of pain that can be equally harrowing.

Take the elderly man, once aggressively fit but now confined to a wheel chair, who has not been out for the past two years because he cannot get down the stairs. (The council had to sell to its tenants most of the more popular street-level houses which he had hoped to transfer to.)

Or take the young couple who bought a house in London because it was the only way they could get a home, and they thought that by postponing having a family — perhaps forever — they could just manage mortgage payments totalling half their joint incomes (until interest rates rose still higher and they found they could cope no longer).

Or the middle aged man who sits all day in his overcoat in an unheated flat, knowing and seeing no-one because he has spent the last thirty years in a hospital for mentally handicapped people. (Social workers, now run off their feet visiting children thought to be at risk of sexual abuse, have no time to call on him. And they are in any case reluctant to visit this neighbourhood where they have to move in pairs lest they get attacked.)

Or the unemployed man who had to leave his family in a perfectly good house in Tyneside in order to take a job in the south where he hasn't a hope of finding a home he can afford. (Now he must either go home to live on the dole and watch the mould gather in the rooms he can no longer afford to heat, or stay down south in lodgings while his marriage breaks up. Meanwhile the regional policies which used to bring some jobs to Tyneside, and the housing policies which built new towns for people moving to the south have both been abolished.)

This is a bleak picture, and things don't go as badly as this everywhere. But these cases are real and we could add many more like them. They serve to show what we are talking about. Housing problems form an interlocking pattern of pain, poverty, powerlessness and stigma which box people in — sometimes literally imprisoning them in bleak and dreary homes. Hopelessness is the experience which all these people share. Their pain is largely caused by poverty. Their poverty could be relieved or prevented if they were not powerless: so powerless, indeed, that the Government can with impunity abolish the very programmes which used to help them. Their pain, their poverty and their powerlessness are reinforced by public neglect — hostility even — towards them and the neighbourhoods in which they live.

Note the diversity of these people and their problems. The mass of working class families, huddled many years ago in the smokey terraces that belonged to private landlords, were eventually able to mobilise nationwide movements for better housing, backed by the trade unions their men belonged to. But the poor today seldom come into contact with each other. Many of them are unable to work and therefore do not belong to trade unions, or to any other movement which could speak for them. The policies required to help them are equally diverse; and impossible, therefore, to summarise in simple slogans.

Housing provides classic examples of the fact that pain, poverty, powerlessness and stigma tend to go together. They are different aspects of the same fundamental problem. To tackle this problem successfully we must give its victim more skills and earning power, more opportunities to make choices, more freedom from anxiety, a more confident conviction that they are citizens with rights, supported by a greater sense of fellowship within a more equal society. That cannot be achieved by action confined to housing alone.

Some of the cases quoted reflect difficulties which originate elsewhere, and emerge later in the guise of housing problems. Because bad housing is often so visible, the service responsible for it often takes the blame for failures in other services such as the abandonment of regional planning, the cruder decisions of the hospital service, the withdrawal of social security payments for furniture, and the scarcity of social workers; also the economic policies which rein in growing prosperity and halt the decline in unemployment, long before their benefits reach the poorest neighbourhoods.

At the same time, we have reasons for hope. Although housing conditions at the bottom of an increasingly unequal society are bad, they were transformed during the generation after the second world war. Similar achievements can be seen throughout Europe — largely thanks to collective action in which the state played a central part. We can resume that progress towards better things. But new strategies will be needed for this purpose. How can we set about doing that? First we need a clearer understanding of the world we have to deal with.

The policy environment

Whatever Government we have, there are some features of the world in which the makers of housing policy have to operate that can be forecast with confidence.

The incomes of people in secure, full-time jobs have risen and are likely to go on rising, although probably not so rapidly as in recent years. But large groups of people have been excluded from this growth in prosperity. Whether that increase in inequality sets in as a long-term trend or proves to be a more temporary divergence from the previously equalising tendencies of capitalism, is still unclear. It seems likely, however, to continue for some years more. 1992 and the restructuring of industries which will follow from the creation of a genuinely common European market will exacerbate the divisions between those in the prosperous core of this continent's economy and those left on its impoverished margins. A rising tide does *not* lift all boats. The economy we have created and our procedures for managing its development ensure that large numbers of people will not share in the prosperity it offers to the more fortunate.

Nevertheless, more and more people are buying houses. (For most of them that's the only way of getting a decent home. Whereas surveys of the British used to show that more of them wanted to buy than expected to do so, the latest show that marginally more expect to buy than want to do so.) The drive towards home ownership, backed by Governments which have made this one of the principal symbols of their success, is unlikely to be reversed.

Two things follow directly from these trends for those concerned with housing policies. The persistence of poverty among low paid workers, lone parents, the older pensioners, youngsters living on their own, and the unemployed whose huge numbers are unlikely to decline rapidly means that there will always be a lot of people who have no hope of buying a house. So the right to rent a decent home at a price which they can afford must be a central commitment of Governments if they are to eliminate squalor and avoid scandal.

Both groups, the tenants and the buyers, will need subsidies of some sort if they are to be properly housed: the tenants for long periods, because so many have low incomes; and the buyers for parts of their lives — particularly when they are starting out, sometimes if they become widowed or separated from the main earner in their families, and for some, finally, when they and their houses grow old.

We conceal these realities by a self-serving trick of language which describes the (now dwindling) support provided for tenants as 'subsidies', while the rapidly growing payments made to home buyers are called 'tax reliefs'. It would be more sensible to think of both groups as tenants (half the buyers' homes belong to a building society or some other lender who, in effect, rents them to the householders) and to recognise that both are heavily subsidised in different ways. That would remind us that we should try equally hard to make all these payments as fair and as efficient for their purposes as possible. At the moment we target what are conventionally called subsidies towards the poorest while dishing out tax reliefs to anyone who can borrow money on a house for any purpose — to buy a new car or a time-share in Spain perhaps. The richer the buyers are, the more they get. (Adrian Kearns and Duncan Maclennan say much more about these problems in Chapter 2 of this book.)

How the large quantity of decent rented housing we shall need should be provided is an open question. But some of the basic principles of the answer to that question are clear. Monopolies of all kinds are dangerous, and particularly dangerous when the people who depend upon them are vulnerable and powerless. Competing alternatives will be needed. Meanwhile things should be organised so as to ensure that the people who manage the houses are accountable first and foremost to their customers. (David Clapham and Keith Kintrea discuss the implications of these requirements in Chapters 3 and 4.)

It is also clear that the old fashioned private landlord will not re-enter the mass market to provide good rented housing for working families. Anyone from whom he could make an unsubsidised profit does better to buy their own (generously subsidised) home. Private landlords will retain a foothold in specialist corners of the market, serving people who are not housed by other providers — foreign visitors and students, for example, and people needing a temporary home while they prepare to buy one. Private sector institutions, funded by building societies and their like, will provide some new rented housing, but they will depend heavily on housing benefit to support their poorer customers. (Peter Kemp, in Chapter 5, discusses the problems of administering this benefit.)

But before getting too deeply immersed in housing itself we should recall that, in a world where the great majority of people have decent homes, the houses are no longer the crucial issue. It is often the place in which the house stands that matters most, for that determines whether the house provides a safe, clean, attractive setting for family life and gives all members of the household opportunities for work, education, shopping, recreation and the other things they need. The value of similar houses ranges from the astronomical to the unsaleable and unlettable, depending on the reputation of the neighbourhood, the quality of the surrounding environment and the opportunities within reach.

So urban policy is even more important than housing policy. If we create towns and neighbourhoods in which no-one with any choice in the matter would live, we shall find that, no matter how good their houses are, the poor, the powerless and the stigmatised end up there. They will then be neglected by investors and power holders in the public and private sectors alike, and housing problems will follow. Effective civic leadership and the capacity to create and defend places which everyone can be proud of are essential foundations for housing policy.

A housing policy, therefore, will have to take account of the changing character of the population to be housed, the growth and distribution of incomes, taxation and subsidies, strategies for regional and urban development, and many other things besides the building, repair and management of houses. (Duncan Maclennan, in Chapter 12, shows the demands these requirements make of a local housing service.)

Central responsibilities

This book is mainly about local services. But before getting to them we should reflect briefly on the part played by central governments.

A healthy rate of economic development, leading us back towards full employment and spreading to all social classes and all parts of the country — these are an essential foundation for a successful housing policy. They will not be achieved by central economic management alone. They call for effective local civic leadership, backed by central resources, which focuses efforts to renew and regenerate the cities and regions contending with the worst economic troubles.

Jobs are not all we need: many people in these places cannot work. For them, social security programmes which provide adequate pensions, unemployment, sickness and disability benefits, income support and child benefits will be more important. A generous housing benefit scheme will be needed to ensure that people can pay for the housing they should be entitled to. But how generous that has to be will depend on the basic levels of income provided by wages and other social benefits.

In the housing field itself the central government's crucial tasks should be to create a supportive system of taxation and subsidies, and more generally to lead and co-ordinate the nation's efforts to improve its housing. Tax reliefs for house buyers should not be abolished: they should be focused on those who most need this help — the first-time buyers (for a few years only) and poorer people buying, modernizing or repairing cheaper houses. (The Japanese, those guiding lights of capitalism, have done this pretty well.) The new council should be related to incomes, becoming more like a local income tax (of the sort that many other countries have). Private developers and builders are entitled to make their profits — but by building what a democratic government wants, in the places and for the people whose needs are judged to be greatest (as in Sweden): not by underpaying lump labour and bullying planning authorities to change their policies for land use.

Among local authorities, those responsible for the more prosperous and stable places, with no need for large building and modernisation programmes, should be prepared to contribute from the surpluses they make on their housing revenue and capital accounts to funds which go back into housing in the places where more needs to be done. Laggard authorities should be pressed to improve the worst houses, to prevent abuses and harassment, to keep their own houses in decent repair, to charge rents high enough to make that possible, and to fulfil their duties to the homeless. (Rob McNaughton, in Chapter 6, shows how repairs and maintenance should be organised. In Chapter 11, Maclennan and Alison More discuss the rent policies which will help to pay for responsible housing management).

This is contentious work. To gain the credibility with local civic leaders which enables them to keep things moving forward in these ways. Governments, and particularly their housing Ministers, must convincingly place themselves at the head of a nationwide movement for better housing. Whatever their party, that used to be generally recognised as the Minister's main job. But Britain's present Government has abandoned all that. For years it had a tenure policy, designed to boost owner-occupation at the expense of renting, and a taxation policy, designed to reduce income tax by cutting public expenditure. Public housing was the main victim of both: those responsible for it no longer had a spokesman in Parliament.

Now an even more determined attempt is being made to break up the public sector and transfer its housing to other owners, to destroy civic leadership and reduce local authorities' powers in all fields. Meanwhile the rent paying capacity of many of the poorest people is being reduced by the introduction of new local taxes, by the imposition of new rent and local tax burdens on people living on social assistance payments and by the withdrawal of grants which used to help the homeless to acquire basic furniture when they were rehoused. Not surprisingly, rent arrears, the numbers on the waiting lists for housing and the numbers who are homeless are all rising. Meanwhile in the private sector, where more and more people have felt compelled to buy, there are signs of stress too: mortgage arrears and repossessions are rising.

What should local authorities do about all this? Do we *need* local housing authorities any more?

The local housing service

The first task of those who lead the local housing service is to know their own towns and districts and keep track of what's going on there: who's moving in or out and why, what kinds of houses are going up, coming down, or being used in new ways — everything which throws light on the constantly changing housing market. For that they will need systematic information gathered by their officials who should seek help from local solicitors, building societies, estate agents and developers in assembling it. But there can be no substitute for tramping the streets, knocking on doors and talking with the people. Councillors, if they do their job, will usually know more than anyone else about their wards.

The housing committee, through its director and senior staff, is responsible for developing a local housing strategy. They will encourage investment by private developers and voluntary agencies which will meet the more urgent needs of their areas, find and prepare sites for these developments, and ensure there is a choice of house types and tenures in the right places to support opportunities developing elsewhere in the local economy. That is a complex planning task which only the bigger authorities are equipped to tackle. We may need regional authorities, like Scottish Homes and the Northern Ireland Housing executive, to help local councils prepare such strategies and to support the efforts of those who follow their lead — authorities capable of looking further ahead than the next election.

Chapter 12 explores these requirements. In human terms, they mean that every place should offer its people mutually sustaining 'ladders of opportunity' in different sectors of its economy, so that youngsters who do well in school are not compelled to leave town for lack of a suitable job, and people who do well in their jobs are not compelled to leave in search of a suitable house. If that means selling council houses in neighbourhoods where there are masses of them and too few available to buy, so be it. Likewise, if it means buying houses so that they can be let in areas where there are few good rented homes, that, too, must be done. It is up to the housing strategists to keep their sector of the local economy humanely in tune with other sectors, raising minimum standards, but, beyond that, meeting changing demands before they become urgent 'special needs'. They should clear their minds of ideological preferences for (or against) rented (or owner-occupied) housing.

Owner-occupiers living on reduced incomes may need help in repairing and improving their homes — or just in hanging onto them. The housing service which arranged, willingly or unwillingly, for many of them to buy their homes must not turn its back on them if they get into difficulties.

There must be sufficient rented housing for people who cannot buy or do not wish to. That housing is likely to be better managed if it is provided by competing suppliers, each doing their best to win their tenants' loyalty. Some, at least, of this housing should be cooperatively owned by the residents, and much of that belonging to other owners should be managed co-operatively by tenants for themselves. But there is no magic about housing associations and co-operatives. If they had to operate on the large scale of the local authorities and at their lower management costs, they would do no better than the councils. Whoever owns it, all rented housing should be managed from offices readily accessible to the customers by people who have a compelling loyalty to them — not by officials shut away in town halls and distant offices.

A traditional housing department which is encouraging developments of this kind will wish to avoid two dangers. If it hands over its houses to housing associations and co-operatives, it may find itself unable to meet its obligations to the homeless and other vulnerable people. Social rented housing may be 'balkanised' into many unco-ordinated, competing units, among which ghettos emerge — possibly in the dwindling public sector — to which the poor and the powerless are consigned. (Chapter 4 warns of these dangers.)

The local authority must therefore make contracts with each landlord (various possibilities are available) which ensure that they all play their part in meeting needs, while the public housing service monitors their performance and keeps them up to the mark. That will usually mean that the service must retain, and build, houses of its own. But whether, at the end of the day, the local authority does this, or whether it operates entirely through other accountable agencies will depend on local needs, resources and preferences. Municipal housing is not the only instrument for meeting needs: in most of Europe the local authorities rely mainly — in what was Western Germany entirely — on other bodies to build and manage subsidised, rented housing.

I have said that housing management, whoever does it, should be decentralised to bring staff as close as possible to their customers. (Tim Mason in Chapter 7, Robina Goodlad in Chapter 8 and Ian Cole and his colleagues in Chapter 10, explore and develop the whole theme of making bureaucracies accountable to their customers.) But the customers' needs are not confined to housing. They may want to get the park tidied up, the refuse cleared, or the vandals chased away by the police. They may want advice about their welfare rights — not only to housing benefit but also to pensions, free school meals or bus passes. They may want a home help for their aged mother or a social worker for their errant son. It will be better to bring as many as possible of these services under the same roof. That will provide a more responsive and efficient organisation, and save a lot of telephoning and tramping about in the rain for staff and customers alike.

In the real disaster areas which are a disgrace to central and local departments of the state, where people and their houses are left to rot, it will be essential to bring these and other services together in special initiatives to put things right. We are not short of brave examples of such initiatives. The Government's plan for housing action trusts, which seems primarily designed to dismember public housing and hand it over to other owners, is a pretty tawdry response to these problems — so provocative that it has roused against it even the worst treated tenants in the most neglected housing estates.

These areas need responsible, healing civic leadership, not bovver boys sent in by central government to bust things up. They need a programme, extending well beyond housing, to create jobs in collaboration with local people. Every investment in improving these estates should be used as an opportunity to train local people and to generate local enterprises which will help deprived communities fight their way back into their cities' economies. The private sector too must play its part in renewing these neighbourhoods. Every firm — indeed, every university and hospital too — has a stake in the reputation of the city in which it operates. Experience shows that private investment will be forthcoming, but only when the public sector has demonstrated by heavy expenditure, sustained over some years, its determination to transform such areas.

'Special' needs

Thus far we have dealt mainly with neighbourhoods and communities — large groups and large areas. But some of the most extreme housing needs, such as those described at the start of this chapter, afflict scattered, isolated people, not visibly concentrated in particular places: the needs of black minorities, for example, or those of battered wives, the physically handicapped, travelling people and the single home-less. These are sometimes called 'special needs' in the jargon of the housing trade. But that is a misleading phrase, suggesting that there is something abnormal about them, calling for a special response at the point where problems demand attention. Too often such responses then build into our arrangements procedures which per-petuate the problem and reinforce the victimisation of the people concerned.

Take the example of the single homeless: to describe them as hav-ing special needs too easily leads to the erection of hostels built spe-cially for them by people who never took the trouble to discover that most of the homeless hate hostels and prefer to live in ordinary hous-es. If we start, instead, by recognising that any of us could become homeless and then consult them about their needs, that may help to ensure that more rented housing is made available for single people, that they get enough points in the allocation procedures to qualify for it, that they are offered help, if they need it, in acquiring some furni-ture, and that advice about shopping, cooking and housekeeping will be offered to those who want it. Most of them then manage pretty well in mainstream housing and cease to be regarded as 'special'. The few who do need further help from social workers or medical staff would have needed it anyway, but they are much more likely to benefit from it if they first get a secure home and all the social security payments to which they are entitled.

Likewise to describe the disabled as having special needs encourages landlords to instal, after long delay, rather expensive modifications to their homes. Many of these would not have been necessary if archi-tects had been reminded that all of us who live to our full span are like-ly to become at least partly disabled. Since every house is likely to accommodate a disabled person at some point in its life, all should be designed to make life easy for them.

Every supposedly special need demands careful thought leading to a different strategy. But these strategies have common features - in particular, a determination to consult the people who experience the need in question and to listen to what they have to say; a willingness to go back to the beginning and redesign systems, structures and procedures to meet demands before they emerge as special needs; a capacity to draw in resources from other services, instead of seeking solutions only within the armoury of housing powers; and a capacity to monitor what happens, so as to reveal patterns of discrimination and hardship and put them right without compelling people to create an uproar of some sort before anyone will listen to them. (Hamish Allan and Joseph Evaskitas discuss these issues in Chapter 9.)

These strategies also depend for their success on a large stock of rented housing in the hands of a local authority or some other publicly accountable collective owner. Left to itself, private enterprise cannot tackle these problems. Indeed, by excluding the vulnerable and the smaller minorities, it creates them.

Conclusion

To what general conclusions do these arguments lead? They should reinforce our respect for civic leadership and the capacity of good local government to create cities and neighbourhoods of which people can be proud. That means giving more choices, more freedom, more rights, to people who will otherwise get imprisoned in appalling situations.

This chapter is also a call for new forms of government which will be less hierarchical, less tied to the concerns of a particular service or profession, focusing instead upon issues and problems in an open, community-based and economically oriented fashion. (Bert Provan and Peter Williams discuss, in Chapter 13, the demands this new kind of professionalism will make on housing managers).

To create such a regime we must struggle to free ourselves from the knee-jerk responses inculcated by the cruder spokesmen of the Right and Left alike: the unquestioning, ideological commitment to tenancy (or owner-occupation), to public enterprise (or privatisation). The decay of once-humane, Left wing ideals into a mere imperialism of the public sector alienated those whom socialists originally set out to serve. That opened the way for a counter attack upon an edifice which had fewer and fewer enthusiastic defenders. It is not institutions but people who should be our main concern.

Bibliography

Alexander D (1982) *Council House Allocations in Scotland* Shelter (Scotland).

Annual Housing Plan (1986) Glasgow Housing Publications.

Ansoff H I (1987) *Corporate Strategy* Harmondsworth: Penguin.

Armstrong D (ed.) *Miles Better, Miles to Go* Glasgow: Housetalk.

Association of Metropolitan Authorities (1985) *Housing and Race: Policy and Practice of Local Authorities* London: AMA.

Archbishop of Canterbury's Commission (1985) *Faith in the City. A Case for Action by Church and Nation* The Report of the Archbishop of Canterbury's Commission on Urban Priority Areas. Church House Publishing.

Atkinson A, Hills J and Le Grand J (1987) The welfare state in Layard R. and Dornbusch R (eds) *The Performance of the British Economy* Oxford: Clarendon Press.

Audit Commision (1984) *Bringing Council Tenants' Rent Arears under Control* London: HMSO.

Audit Commission (1986) *Making a Reality of Community Care* London: HMSO.

Audit Commission (1986) *Managing the Crisis in Council Housing* London: HMSO.

Audit Commission for Local Authorities in England and Wales (1986) *Improving Council House Maintenance* pp. 12–17 London: HMSO.

Audit Commission for Local Authorities in England and Wales (1986) Improving Council House Maintenance p. 6 London: HMSO.

Audit Commission (1989) *Survey of Local Authority Housing Rent Arrears* Information Paper No. 1, London: HMSO.

Barclay P (1982) *Social Workers — Their Role and Task* London: Bedford Square Press.

Berthoud R (1989) Social security and the economics of housing in Dilnot A and Walker I (eds) *The Economics of Social Security* Oxford: Oxford University Press.

Birchall J (1988) *Building Communities: The Co-operative Way* London: Routledge & Kegan Paul.

Blunkett D and Green G (1983) *Building from the Bottom: The Sheffield Experience* Fabian Tract, No. 491.

Boaden N, Goldsmith M, Hampton W and Stringer P (1982) *Public Participation in Local Services* London: Longman.

Bradshaw J (1972) A taxonomy of social need, pp. 71–82 in Maclachlan G (ed.) *Problems and Progress in Medical Care* 7th Series, London: Oxford University Press.

Brailey M (1981) The needs of particular groups in Centre for Urban and Regional Research *Allocation and Transfer of Council Houses* Discussion Paper No. 40, Centre for Urban and Regional Research, University of Glasgow.

Building Use Studies (1987) *Monitoring the Cost of Local Housing Management* Royal Institute of Public Administration.

Burns T and Stalker G M (1961) *The Management of Innovation* London: Tavistock.

Cairncross L, Clapham D and Goodlad R (1990) *Tenant Participation in Housing Management* Coventry Salford: Institute of Housing/Tenant Participation Advisory Service (England).

Cairncross L, Clapham D and Goodlad R (1990) *The Pattern of Tenant Participation in Housing Management* Discussion Paper Number 31, Glasgow: Centre for Housing Research, University of Glasgow.

Cantle E (1986) The deterioration of public sector housing, pp. 57–86 in Malpass P (ed.) *The Housing Crisis* Beckenham: Croom Helm.

Central Housing Advisory Committee (1938) *The Management of Municipal Housing Estates* London: HMSO.

Central Housing Advisory Committee (1959) *Councils and their Houses* London: HMSO.

Central Housing Advisory Committee (1969) *Council Housing: Purposes, Procedures and Priorities* London: HMSO.

Central Housing Advisory Committee Report (1939) *The Management of Municipal Housing Estates* London: HMSO.

Central Housing Advisory Committee (1959) *Councils and their Houses* London: HMSO.

Centre for Housing Research (1989) *The Nature and Effectiveness of Housing Management in England* London: HMSO.

City University Housing Research Group (1981) *Can Local Authorities be Better Landlords?* The City University.

Clapham D and Kintrea K (1984) Allocation systems and housing choice *Urban Studies* **21** pp. 26–9.

Clapham D and Kintrea K (1986) Rationing choice and constraint: the allocation of public sector housing in Glasgow, *Journal of Social Policy* **15** pp. 51–67.

Clapham D and Kintrea K (1986) The social consequences of the allocation process: evidence from Glasgow *Housing Review* 35 pp 83 -4.

Clapham D, Kintrea K and Munro M (1987) Tenure choice: an empirical investigation *Area* **19** pp 11–18.

Clinton A, Groves R and Williams P (1986) *Housing Information Research Project Final Report* Institute of Housing.

Cochrane L, Downie A, Gillespie B and Wilson S (eds) (1986) *But Will it Fly, Mr. Wright?* Community Development Housing Group, Glasgow: TPAS.

Cole I (1987) The delivery of housing services in Willmott P. (ed.) *Local Government Decentralisation and Community* Policy Studies Institute.

Cole I, Arnold P and Windle K (1988b) *Decentralisation — the Views of Elected Members* Housing Decentralisation Research Project Working Paper 4, School of Urban Studies, Sheffield City Polytechnic.

Cole I, Windle K and Arnold P (1988a) *The Impact of Decentralisation* Housing Decentralisation Research Project Working Paper 3, School of Urban Studies, Sheffield City Polytechnic.

Commission for Racial Equality (1984) *Hackney Housing Investigated* London: CRE.

Community Development Project (1976) *Whatever Happened to Council Housing?* Community Development Project.

Cook R (1983) in Brown G and Cook R (eds) *Housing and Deprivation in Scotland: The Real Divide* Mainstream Publishing.

Cooper P (1988) Access and the market *Housing* **24**(5) pp. 16–18.

Craddock J (1975) *Tenants' Participation in Housing Management* London: ALHE.

Craig P (1988) *Costs and Benefits: A Review of Recent Research on Take Up of Means Tested Benefits.*

Cullingworth Report (1969) *Council Housing: Purposes, Procedures, Priorities* London CHAC, HMSO.

Dalton M and Daghlian S (1989) *Housing Associations and Ethnic Minorities in Glasgow* London: Commission for Racial Equality.

Dawson D (1986) *Analysing Organisation* (London: Macmillan).

Deacon N (1984) Decentralisation: Panacea or Blind Alley *Local Government Policy-Making.*

Dearlove J (1979) *The Reorganisation of British Local Government,* Cambridge: Cambridge University Press.

DHSS (1977) *The Way Forward* London: HMSO.

DHSS (1980) *Care in the Community* London: HMSO.

DHSS (1985) *Reform of Social Security, Vol. 2: Programmes for Change* London: HMSO.

DoE (1975) *Report of the Working Party on Housing Co-operatives (The Campbell Report)* London: HMSO.

DoE (1977) *Housing Policy Review: Housing Management — A Tenants' Charter :A Consultation Paper* HPR /MAN (77), 2, London: DoE.

DoE (1978) *Tenants' Rights: Involvement in Management* London: DoE.

DoE (1979) *Legislation on Housing: Tenants' Charter Provision* London: DoE.

DoE (1983) *The Organisation of Housing Management in English Local Authorities* London: HMSO.

DoE (1983) *Housing for Mentally Ill and Mentally Handicapped People* London: HMSO.

DoE (1987) *Finance for Housing Associations: The Government's Proposals* London: DoE.

DoE (1988) *Capital Expenditure and Finance. A Consultation Paper* London: DoE.

DoE (1988) *New Financial Regime for Local Authority Housing in England and Wales. A Consultation Paper* London:DoE.

DoE (1988) *Improvement Grants. A Consultation Paper* London: DoE.

DoE (1989) *The Nature and Effectiveness of Housing Management in England* London: HMSO.

Donnison D (1979) Benefits of Simplicity *Roof.* London: Shelter.

Donnison D (1983) *Urban policies: a New Approach* Fabian Tract, 487 London: Fabian Society.

Donnison D and Ungerson C (1982) *Housing Policy* Harmondsworth: Penguin.

Drake M, O'Brien M and Biebuyck T (1981) *Single and Homeless* London: HMSO.

Duffy J (1985) *Rehousing Hostel Residents: The Experience in Glasgow* Glasgow Council for the Single Homeless.

Dunleavy P (1981) *The Politics of Mass Housing in Britain 1945–1975*, London: Clarendon Press.

du Parcq L (1987) Neighbourhood Services: The Islington Experience in Willmott P (ed) *Local Government Decentralisation and Community* Police Studies Institute.

English J (1982) Must council housing become welfare housing *Housing Review* **31**, 154–7, 212–3.

Ermisch J (1990) *Fewer Babies, Better Lives* York: Rowntree Foundation.

Fraser R and Platt S (1988) Breaking the link without breaking the bank *Roof* September and October, London: Shelter.

Forrest R and Murie A (1983) Residualisation and council housing: aspects of the changing social relations of housing tenure *Journal of Society Policy* **12** 453–68.

Gallagher P (1982) Ideology and housing management in English J (ed.) *The Future of Council Housing* London: Croom Helm.

Glasgow Council for the Single Homeless (1981) *Homeless Men Speak for Themselves.*

Glasgow Council for the Single Homeless (1983) *Homeless Women in Glasgow.*

Glasgow District Council (1984) *Annual Housing Review 1984.*

Glasgow District Council (1986) *Annual Housing Review 1985.*

Glasgow District Council (1987) *Review of Allocations Consultative Paper.*

Glasgow Housing Department (1986) *Priority Areas for Housing Provision for the Elderly.*

Glasgow Housing Department (1986) *Residential Respite Care for Mentally Handicapped People.*

Glasgow Housing Department (1987) *Accommodation for the Recovering Mentally Ill.*

Goodlad R (1986) *Telling the Tenants* Glasgow: Scottish Consumer Council.

Great Britain (1977) *Housing Policy — a Consultative Document* Cmnd 6851 London: HMSO.

Grey A, Hepworth N and Odling-Smee J (1981) *Housing Costs, Rents and Subsidies* (2nd edn) London: CIPFA.

Griffiths D and Holmes C (1985) *A New Housing Policy for Labour* Fabian Tract505 London: Fabian Society.

The Grieve Report (1987) Glasgow District Council.

Gyford J (1984) *Local Politics in Britain* London: Croom Helm.

Gyford J (1985) *The Politics of Local Socialism* London: Allen & Unwin.

Hancock K and Maclennan D (1990) *A House Price Monitoring System: Tayside Region* Scottish Office, Edinburgh.

Hambleton R (1978) *Policy Planning and Local Government* London: Hutchinson.

Handy C B (1987) *Understanding Organisations* Harmondsworth: Penguin.

Harloe M (1985) Landlord/tenant relations in Europe and America — the limits and functions of the legal framework *Urban Law and Policy* (7) 359–83.

Harrison P (1983) *Inside the Inner City* Harmondsworth: Penguin.

Haynes R (1980) *Organisation Theory and Local Government* London: George Allen & Unwin.

Heald D (1983) *Public Expenditure* Oxford: Martin Robertson.

Henderson J and Karn V (1984) Race, class and the allocation of public housing in Britain *Urban Studies* **21**, 115–28.

Henney A (1985) *Trust the Tenant: Developing Municipal Housing* Centre for Policy Studies.

Herzberg F (1968) *Work and the Nature of Man* London: Staples Press.

Hill O (1933) *Extracts from Octavia Hill's Letters to Fellow Workers, 1864–1911, Compiled by her Niece, Eleanor Southwood Ouvry* London: Adelphi Bookshop.

Hills J (1987) When is a grant not a grant? The current system of housing association finance *Welfare State Programmes Discussion Page Number 13* London: STICERD, London School of Economics.

Hills J (1988) Twenty-first century housing subsidies: durable rent fixing and subsidy arrangements for social housing *Welfare State Programme Discussion Paper Number 33* London: STICERD, London School of Economics.

Hoggett P (1987) Going beyond a rearrangement of the deckchairs: some practical hints for councillors and managers in Hoggett P and Hambleton R (eds) *Decentralisation and Democracy: Localising Public Services* Bristol: School for Advanced Urban Studies, University of Bristol.

Hood M (1990) Taking notice of the tenants *Housing Review* **39** No. 3 May - June.

Housing Act 1957.

Housing Act 1985.

Housing Act 1988.

Housing Benefit Review Team (1985) *Housing Benefit Review. Report of the Review Team* London: HMSO.

Housing Co-operatives Review Committee (1984) *Housing Co-operatives in Scotland* Co-operative Union, Glasgow: TPAS.

Housing Corporation (1988) *Setting Standards in Housing Management: Allocations* Edinburgh.

Housing and Local Government Act, 1990.

Housing (Homeless Persons) Act 1977.

Housing and Local Government, 1990.

Housing and Planning Research Unit (1985) *Housing Executive Staff Attitude Survey* Northern Ireland Housing Executive, March 1986, internal report.

Housing Research Group (1981) *Could Local Authorities be Better Landlords?* London: City University .

Housing (Scotland) Act 1986.

Housing (Scotland) Act 1987.

Housing (Scotland) Act 1988.

Housing Services Advisory Group (1977) *Tenancy Agreements* London: D o E.

Housing Services Advisory Group (1978) *Housing for People* London: D O E.

Housing Services Advisory Group (1978) *Organising a Comprehensive Housing Services* London: DoE.

Housing Trust (1988) *Rents and Incomes.*

Hunter D and Wyston G (1987) *Community Care in Britain: Variation on a Theme* London: King's Fund Centre.

Inquiry into British Housing (1985) National Federation of Housing Associations.

Institute of Housing (1986) *Public Sector Housing: Future Use, Control and Management* London: I O H.

Institute of Housing (1987) *Preparing for Change* London: I O H.

Jones G and Stewart J (1985) *The Case for Local Government* London: Allen & Unwin.

Karn V (1982) Private housing at all costs: some lessons from America in English J (ed.) *The Future of Council Housing* London: Croom Helm.

Kay A, Legg C and Foot J (undated) *The 1980 Tenants' Rights in Practice* London: City University.

Kearns A (1988) Affordable rents and flexible HAG. New finance for housing associations, *Centre for Housing Research Discussion Paper Number 17* Glasgow: University of Glasgow.

Kemp P A (1984) *The Cost of Chaos: A Survey of the Housing Benefit Scheme* London: SHAC.

Kemp P A (1984) McLennan D et al. (1989) *The Nature and Effectiveness of Housing Management in England* London: HMSO.

Kemp P A (1984) *Housing Benefit: The Way Forward* London: SHAC.

Kemp P A (1985) *The Housing Benefit Review: An Evaluation* University of Glasgow, Centre for Housing Research Discussion Paper.

Kemp P A (1987) The reform of housing benefit *Social Policy and Administration* **21**.

Kilcoyne D (1989) Central control and local discretion: the operation of the housing benefit scheme. Paper presented to a Department of Sociology Seminar, University of Salford, Salford.

Kileen D (1984) *Homeless Young People in Glasgow* Shelter (Scotland).

Kintrea K and Clapham D (1986) Housing choice and search strategies within an administered housing system *Environment and Planning A* **18** 1281–96.

Labour Co-ordinating Committee (1984) *Go Local to Survive* London.

Labour Party (1981) *A Future for Public Housing* London: The Labour Party.

Laffin M (1986) *Professionalism and Policy* Aldershot: Gower.

Leather P and Murie A (1986) The decline in public expenditure in Malpass P (ed.) *The Housing Crisis* London: Croom Helm.

Leeds City Council (1948) *Housing Annual Report 1947–48*. Leeds City Council.

London Borough of Islington (1987) *Going Local: Decentralisation in Practice* Islington Council Press.

Lowe S (1986) *Urban Social Movements* London: Macmillan.

McCafferty P and Riley D (1989) *A Study of Co-operative Housing* London: HMSO.

Maclennan D (1982) *Housing Economics* London: Longman.

Maclennan D (1987) *Housing Demand* Central Research Unit Discussion Paper, Scottish Office.

Maclennan D, Clapham D, Goodlad R, Kemp P, Malcolm J, Satsangi M and Whitefield L (1989) *The Nature and Effectiveness of Housing Management in England* London: HMSO.

Maclennan D and Gibb A (1988) From No Mean City to Miles Better *Centre for Housing Research Discussion Paper Number 18* Glasgow: University of Glasgow.

Maclennan D and Jones C A (forthcoming) *Economic Change and the Local Housing Market* Environment and Planning (Series A).

Maclennan D, Wood G A and Munro M (1987) Housing choices and the structure of housing markets in Turner B et al. (eds) *Between*

State and Market: Housing in the Post Industrial Era Stockholm: Almquist and Wicksell.

Macey J and Baker C (1978) *Housing Management* (3rd ed) Estates Gazette.

Mainwaring R (1988) *The Walsall Experience* London: HMSO.

Malpass P (1982) Octavia Hill *New Society* 4 November reprinted in Barker P (ed.) *Founders of the Welfare State* Heinemann 1984 and Spicker P Legacy of Octavia Hill *Housing* June 1985 39–40.

Malpass P (1983) Residualisation and the restructuring of housing tenure *Housing Review* **32** 44–5.

Maslow A (1943) A theory of human motivation *Psychological Review* **50** 370– 96.

Maslow A (1954) *Motivation and Personality* New York: Harper and Row.

Massie A (1986) *Augustus: The Memoirs of the Emperor* London: Bodley Head.

Merrett S (1985) The right to rent: a feasibility study *GLC Housing Research and Policy Report* 2 London: Greater London Council.

Metropolitan Boroughs Association (1963) *General Review of Housing Management* London: M.B.A.

Mori (1987) *Council Tenants' Attitudes Towards Housing* Richmond upon Thames, Surrey.

Morphet J (1987) Local authority decentralisation —Tower Hamlets *Policy and Politics* **15** No. 2.

Moseley R (1984) Liberating the public sector *Rights to a Home*. Labour Housing Group, Nottingham: Spokesman.

Murie A (1983) *Housing Inequality and Deprivation* London: Heinemann.

NACRO (1985) *After Entryphones* London: NACRO.

National Association of Citizens Advice Bureaux (1989) *System overload: The Housing Benefit System in Crisis* London: NACAB.

National Audit Office (1989) Department of Social Security: Housing Benefit London: HMSO.

National Consumer Council (1976) *Tenancy Agreements* London: NCC.

National Federation of Housing Association (1987) *Standards for Housing Management* London: N.F.H.A.

National Federation of Housing Associations (1988) *Census of New Tenants.*

New Islington and Hackney Housing Association (1988) *Talking Back.*

Niner P and Karn V *Housing Association Allocations: Advancing Racial Equality* London: Runnymede Trust.

Nugent M (1985) *Allocation, Policies and Lettings Procedures of the Twenty-three Community Based Housing Associations in Glasgow: A Survey Jan/Feb* Glasgow: Shelter.

National Federation of Housing Associations (1987) *Standards for Housing Management* London: N F H A.

Phillips D (1986) *What Price Equality* GLC Housing Research and Policy Report No 9 London: G L C.

Platt S, Piepe R and Smyth J (1987) *Heard or Ignored?* London: National Federation of Housing Associations.

Power A (1976) *Tenant Management Co-operatives in the U.S.: Report for the North Islington Housing Rights Project* The Priority Estates Project.

Power A (1982) Priority Estates Project 1982. *Improving Council Estates: A Summary of Aims and Progress* London: DoE.

Power A (1987) *The Priority Estates Project Guide to Local Housing Management* (Part 2, section 9) The Priority Estates Project, London: the Department of the Environment.

Power A (1987) *Property Before People: The Management of Twentieth Century Council Housing* London: Allen & Unwin.

Prescott-Clarke P (1983) *Decentralisation of Council Services in Hackney: A Survey of Residents* London: Social Community Planning and Research.

Purkis A and Hodson P (1982) *Housing and Community Care* London: Bedford Square Press.

Rao N (1990) *The Changing Role of Local Housing Authorities* Policy Studies Institute, London.

Raynsford N (1984) Allocating public housing, pp. 121–129 in Labour Housing Group *Right to a Home* Nottingham: Spokesman.

Richardson A (1977) *Tenant Participation in Council House Management* Housing Development Directorate, Occasional Paper 2/77 London: DoE.

Richardson A (1983) *Participation* London: Routledge & Kegan Paul.

Safe Neighbourhoods Unit (1987) *Your Views for a Change* Reading Borough Council.

Satsangi M and Clapham D (1990) *The Management and Effectiveness of Housing Co-operatives* London: HMSO.

Satsangi M and Clapham D (1990) *Management Performance In Housing Co-operatives* London: HMSO.

Schelling T C (1960) *The Strategy of Conflict* Cambridge: Harvard University Press.

Scottish Council for the Single Homeless (1981) *Think Single: An Assessment of the Accommodation Experiences, Needs and Preferences of Single People* Edinburgh: SCSH.

Scottish Council for the Single Homeless (1984) *Opening Doors: A Report on Allocating Housing to Single People* Edinburgh: SCSH.

Scottish Development Department (1985) *Scotland's Travelling People: Site Provision — District Pitch Targets* Circular No. 13.

Scottish Development Department (1987) *Scottish Homes: A New Agency for Housing in Scotland.*

Scottish Federation of Housing Associations (1988) *Who Do We House* Glasgow: SFHA.

Scottish Home and Health Department (1984) *Mental Health in Focus* Edinburgh: HMSO.

Scottish Housing Advisory Committee (1988) *The Allocation and Transfer of Council Houses* Edinburgh: HMSO.

Seabrook J (1984) *The Idea of Neighbourhood: What Local Politics Should be All About* London: Pluto.

Secretary of State's Advisory Committee (1982) *Third Report 1979–1982,* Secretary of State's Advisory Committee on Scotland's Travelling People, Edinburgh: HMSO.

Shelter (Scotland) (1982) *Council House Allocation in Scotland* Edinburgh: Shelter.

Shields R and Webber J (1986) Hackney lurches local *Community Development Journal* **21** No. 2.

Somerville P (1986) 'Nero Fiddles, While Rome Burns', *Housing* May 17–20.

Spicker P (1983) *The Allocation of Council Housing* London: Shelter.

Stanforth J, Malcolm J and Maclennan D (1986) *The Delivery of Repair Services in Public Sector Housing in Scotland* Scottish Office. Department of the Environment (1989) *The Nature and Effectiveness of Housing Management in England,* p 78 London: HMSO.

Stearn J (1988) Who do they house? *Housing* **24**(5) 21–4.

Stewart J (1971) *Management in Local Government* London: Charles Knight.

Stewart J (1988) *The New Management of Housing Departments* Luton: Local Government Training Board.

Tenants' Rights etc. (Scotland Act 1980.

Tomlinson M (1986) *Decentralisation — Learning the Lessons? The Radical Failure of Decentralisation in Hackney 1981–83.* PCL Planning Study 18, Polytechnic of Central London.

Townsend P and Davidson N (1982) *Inequalities in Health — The Black Report* Harmondsworth: Penguin Books.

Walker R (1985) *Housing Benefit: The Experience of Implementation* Housing Centre Trusts, London.

Walker R (1986) Aspects of administration in Kemp P A (ed) *The Future of Housing Benefits* Studies in Housing No. 1, University of Glasgow, Centre for Housing Research.

Ward M and Zebedee J (1990) *Guide to Housing Benefit and Community Charge Benefit: 1990–91* (4th ed) London: SHAC/Institute of Housing.

Welsh Office (1989) *The Relative Effectiveness of Different Forms of Housing Management in Wales,* Welsh Office.

Windle K, Cole I and Arnold P (1988) *Decentralisation of Housing: Structure and Process* Housing Decentralisation Project Working Paper 2, School of Urban Studies, Sheffield City Polytechnic.

Williams P (1987) 'A Curriculum for Housing Work' in Garnett D and Williams P (eds.) *The Future of Housing Education: A Symposium,* Working Paper 65 School for Advanced Urban Studies, Bristol.

Young R (1977) *The Search for Democracy* Paisley: Heatherbank Press.

Index